STRESS, TRAUMA, AND DECISION-MAKING
FOR SOCIAL WORKERS

Stress, Trauma, and Decision-Making for Social Workers

Cheryl Regehr

Columbia University Press *New York*

Columbia University Press
Publishers Since 1893
New York   Chichester, West Sussex
cup.columbia.edu
Copyright © 2018 Columbia University Press

Library of Congress Cataloging-in-Publication Data
Names: Regehr, Cheryl, author.
Title: Stress, trauma, and decision-making for social workers / Cheryl Regehr.
Description: New York : Columbia University Press, [2018] | Includes bibliographical
    references and index.
Identifiers: LCCN 2018007438 (print) | LCCN 2018011492 (e-book) | ISBN 9780231542371
    (e-book) | ISBN 9780231180122 (hardcover) | ISBN 9780231180139 (pbk.)
Subjects: LCSH: Social workers—Job stress. | Social service—Decision making
Classification: LCC HV40.35 (e-book) | LCC HV40.35 .R44 2018 (print) |
    DDC 361.301/9—dc23
LC record available at https://lccn.loc.gov/2018007438

Columbia University Press books are printed on permanent and durable acid-free paper.
Printed in the United States of America
Cover design: Lisa Hamm

This book is dedicated to Graham, Kaitlyn, and Dylan, all scholars, who are the foundation of my life (and coauthors on various projects).

Contents

Acknowledgments

I began my work in the area of trauma and recovery as a social worker and social work manager in intensive care, emergency rooms, and sexual assault care centers. My early research focused on recovery in victims of sexual violence. Upon being given the opportunity to lead a crisis team at a major international airport, I became involved in training, interventions, and program development for emergency responders and airline personnel affected by trauma in the workplace. My subsequent research considered factors associated with trauma response in police, firefighters, paramedics, and child welfare social workers.

The high rates of trauma symptoms found in these groups were at first troubling but then led me to a question: if those serving the public are suffering from the impacts of stress and trauma exposure, does this place the public at risk? This presented the opportunity to integrate a parallel line of research I was conducting with colleagues on defining and measuring professional competence in social workers and social work students. The resulting combined program of research has considered the impact of stress and trauma on professional performance and decision-making in high-stakes situations.

Thus this book is founded on two decades of research conducted with colleagues. Key collaborators have been Professors Marion Bogo (University of Toronto), Vicki LeBlanc (University of Ottawa), and Glenn

Regehr (University of British Columbia). Others have included many multidisciplinary faculty colleagues, doctoral students (who are now faculty members elsewhere), community-based leaders in social work, and emergency service professionals. Their collective ideas, support, and challenges have shaped my thinking in important ways. I am most grateful to these friends and colleagues for their contributions.

Let me also thank Christina Borges, Kaitlyn McDonald, and Bradyn Ko, who conducted reviews of the literature for this book, and Savanna Jackson, who designed the artwork.

I wish to also acknowledge the Social Sciences Research Council of Canada and the Canadian Institute for Health Research, whose financial support made this research possible.

CHAPTER ONE

Introduction

On January 15, 2009, the lobby of the Marriott Hotel in New Orleans was a hive of activity familiar to all who were in attendance at the Society for Social Work Research annual meeting. Clusters of people were exchanging research ideas, catching up on news, and interviewing new scholars for faculty positions at their universities. Suddenly, the conversation and mood shifted as news spread that a plane had gone down in the Hudson River in New York City. Fears of a return to the days of 9/11 surfaced. Conference attendees huddled around television screens in the bar, stood watching the news alerts on the screens near the elevators, and checked their BlackBerry devices for messages. Those with New York–based colleagues who had not yet arrived in New Orleans anxiously tried to reach them. Mercifully it soon became clear that the plane had landed safely and everyone on board was unharmed. This near disaster became known as the *miracle on the Hudson.*

The minute-by-minute accounts of the events of that day do indeed seem miraculous. One hundred and fifty passengers boarded US Airways Flight 1549 at LaGuardia Airport and headed on a two-hour journey to Charlotte, North Carolina. It was a normal busy day, familiar to all who have been to LaGuardia. The weather in New York was clear but cold. The pilot, Captain Chesley "Sully" Sullenberger, had acquired nearly

FIGURE 1.1 The water landing of U.S. Airways Flight 1549 on the Hudson River
Source: Wikimedia Commons, Greg L.

twenty thousand hours of flying time over a forty-year career and was truly a veteran of the skies. The plane accelerated down the runway to begin its ascent at 3:24 P.M. (Smith, 2016).

At 3:27 P.M., as the plane reached an altitude of three thousand feet, one-third of the way to its ultimate flying altitude, a flock of Canada geese crossed its flight path, and some of the birds were sucked into both engines, causing them to immediately cease functioning. After unsuccessful attempts to restart the engines, Captain Sullenberger radioed air traffic control and announced that the plane would return to LaGuardia. One minute later, Sullenberger realized that with no thrust engines, and at such a low altitude, the plane would not make it to LaGuardia. Air traffic control offered the option of landing on Runway 1 of a small local airport called Teterboro, but Sullenberger decided this would not be possible. The conversation was recorded as follows:

> *Sullenberger*: We can't do it.
> *Air traffic control*: Okay, which runway would you like at
> Teterboro?
> *Sullenberger*: We're gonna be in the Hudson.
> *Air traffic control*: I'm sorry, say that again?

The plane cleared the George Washington Bridge with nine hundred feet to spare, and with no power left glided onto the Hudson River three and a half minutes after takeoff. All passengers and crew were evacuated onto the wings of the plane and were subsequently rescued by boats. This marked the fourth time in history that a commercial airliner intentionally landed on water (Smith, 2016).

Steven Johnson, in his book *Future Perfect: The Case for Progress in a Networked Age*, suggests that two narratives emerged out of the safe landing of US Airways 1549 on the Hudson River. The first was a *superhero narrative*. This account credited "Sully" Sullenberger for brilliantly navigating the plane and its inhabitants to safety under unthinkable pressure. The second narrative emerged from what Johnson called *quasi-magical rhetoric* resulting in the tagline *miracle on the Hudson*. "Those were the two options. That plane floating safely in the Hudson could only be explained by superheroes or miracles" (S. Johnson, 2012, xvi).

Johnson, however, suggested a third explanation. He asserted that Captain Sullenberger "was supported by a long history of decisions made by thousands of people over the preceding decades, all of which set up the conditions that made a perfect landing possible" (p. xvii). He pointed to the dense network of human intelligence that made a safe landing possible: research that tested the ability of jet engines to withstand impact with birds; technological innovation that allows cockpit guidance electronics to continue to work in the absence of engine power; and decades of decisions focused on improving airline safety in incremental ways.

Johnson was entirely correct; those factors were critical to the success of Sullenberger's landing. But Johnson's analysis missed some key elements. He did not refer to the training programs that prepare pilots to adapt to changing circumstances and respond in emergencies. He also did not refer to the years of experience that incrementally developed the expertise and decision-making capabilities of Captain Sullenberger. He did not note the characteristics and life experiences that allowed the captain to function at such an optimal level while under profound stress. While perhaps not a superhero narrative, this book is about those very aspects of expertise that influence professional decision-making in circumstances of extreme stress.

It is unusual perhaps to begin a book about stress, trauma, and social work decision-making with an example of decision-making by a commercial airline pilot. But all the elements involved in Captain Sullenberger's expertise and decision-making also apply to social workers. Social workers similarly make life-and-death decisions in situations of high stress.

- A client with a history of violence makes ominous statements regarding his partner. Are these credible threats, and should the social worker exercise the duty to warn and protect in this situation?
- A social worker responding to reports of child abuse visits the home of newly arrived refugees in an impoverished neighborhood. Is the child at risk of harm at the hands of her parents, and should she be removed from the home?
- A client with a long history of depression and substance use describes suicidal thoughts. Is the risk of self-harm more acute today than in the past, and should the client be assessed in a hospital?
- A fifteen-year-old girl seeking medical advice visits a drop-in center for street youth and reveals that her boyfriend arranges "dates" for her with older men. Should the social worker intervene?

Each of these decisions requires social workers to draw on their knowledge, sift through a vast amount of information, weigh the evidence, reflect on previous experiences, and select the best course of action. Over time, as social workers are regularly confronted with these types of decisions, they develop expertise. Although decision-making is at times still difficult, it becomes more intuitive as expertise develops and decisions are made with greater skill and less effort.

DEVELOPING EXPERTISE AND INTUITION

While definitions of expertise focus on individuals with authoritative knowledge or special skills in a particular area, research on expertise has examined the process of intuitive problem-solving and decision-making. In experts, intuition is the ability to capitalize on an extensive knowledge base and link together disparate pieces of information in a rapid and seemingly effortless manner (Dane & Pratt, 2007). The intuition of experts occurs outside the realm of conscious thought (Salas, Rosen, &

DiazGranados, 2009) and is often experienced as an affective feeling, colloquially referred to as a *gut feeling* (Gigerenzer & Goldstein, 1996). This intuition emerges from two sources: (1) education and experience, and (2) the way an individual approaches the world and its challenges.

Education and experience are processes through which individuals acquire information and learn rules in a given domain. Individuals are exposed to relevant information through reading, instruction, and observation of those who have already attained mastery in the area. With time, these individuals develop a conceptual understanding of the relationship between various pieces of information and an awareness of contextual factors in which the concepts or rules may or may not apply. Ultimately, individuals develop cognitive maps for making professional decisions. These cognitive maps become second nature; that is, they become unconscious and are experienced as intuitive (Dreyfus, 2005; Dreyfus & Dreyfus, 2005; Schmidt & Boshuizen, 1993).

To attain the intuition associated with expertise, an individual must sustain deliberate practice over a prolonged period (Chase & Simon, 1973). This practice must be characterized by a knowledge base that allows the individual to understand the nature of the issue and what needs to be accomplished; a learning environment that provides immediate corrective feedback on how the individual's performance or decision-making could be improved; reflection on what has been learned; and integration of the feedback in a manner that informs the next encounter (Ericsson, Krampe, & Tesch-Römer, 1993). Expertise is developed by working outside one's comfort zone (Zilbert, Murnaghan, Gallinger, Regehr, & Moulton, 2015) and resisting repetitive routines. Experts learn from each novel encounter, adding to their abilities in a dialectical manner (Scardamalia & Bereiter, 1991).

This ability to push oneself outside the comfort zone and integrate learning leads to the second set of key enabling factors that contribute to the development of expertise: the way an individual approaches the world and its challenges. One aspect of this is the enabling influence of motivation and determination (Ericsson, Krampe, & Tesch-Römer, 1993). More recently this has been described as *grit*, or the ability to maintain effort and interest despite setbacks (Duckworth, Peterson, Matthews, & Kelly, 2007). Another aspect is conceptual flexibility: the ability to adaptively respond to novel situations, rather than approaching them in a ritualized manner (G. Regehr, 1994). Experts continually refine and develop their understanding and approaches, are intrigued by challenge, and creatively build their skills. Finally, interpersonal capacities are critical, especially in social work, in which the ability to understand and engage others is central. Interpersonal capacities include the ability to understand the emotional world of others (E. Thorndike, 1920) and the ability to identify and draw on one's own feelings in guiding decisions and actions (Salovey & Mayer, 1990). Such qualities can be understood as meta-competencies (Bogo et al., 2006).

However, while personal characteristics may indeed be critical, it is important to note the centrality of opportunity structures and structural barriers that individuals encounter while trying to develop expertise. These include access to education, employment, and career development opportunities. Life experiences also lead to personal expectancies and worldviews that can have a significant impact on relations with others and can have a disruptive effect on performance and decision-making (Steele, 2011). Social workers enter the profession with preexisting experiences that influence their career choices, their sense of personal competence, and their views regarding the causes and consequences of challenges that their clients face. These personal life experiences are augmented by encounters in the workplace that further shape the framework in which professional decisions are made.

EXPOSURE TO TRAUMA

The nature of the profession exposes social workers to violence inflicted on individuals by physical and mental illness, social structures that exclude and limit opportunities, natural disasters that wreak havoc, and perhaps most disturbingly, violence inflicted by other humans. In addition, social workers are directly exposed to danger and violence against themselves. Social workers enter homes to determine whether a child is at risk of abuse, potentially threatening family bonds; they work with people suffering from psychosis or dementia who may at times strike out violently; they work with people who are guilty of violent crimes—all situations that research studies associate with a higher risk of violence against workers (Jayaratne, Croxton, & Mattison, 2004; Newhill, 1996).

Social workers report going alone into unsafe places where people were actively injecting drugs, working after hours alone, and exposing themselves to communicable diseases (Kosny & Eakin, 2008).

As a result, research conducted in various locations indicates that one-quarter to one-third of social workers report being assaulted at some time in their career, and approximately one-half to three-quarters have been threatened with physical harm (MacDonald & Sirotich, 2001, 2005; Newhill, 1996; C. Regehr, Leslie, Howe, & Chau, 2005; Rey, 1996). Social workers describe scenarios in which clients are verbally threatening or physically violent toward them, steal or destroy their property, and hurl racist verbal abuse at them (Kosny & Eakin, 2008).

COMMITMENT AND RESILIENCE

Despite exposure to trauma, social workers point to their sense of commitment and compassion. They often assert that exposure to violence is an acceptable risk when working with clients who have experienced multiple injustices in life, and they attribute client violence to systemic barriers, mental health challenges, or histories of previous abuse (Kosny & Eakin, 2008; Virkki, 2007). Some social work organizations have a culture that combines toughness and caring into what has been termed *white-knuckle caring*, as part of the excitement and challenge of the job (Baines & Cunningham, 2011). These types of reactions to direct harm, threat, and exposure to human suffering point to the resilience of social workers.

Resilience, the ability to bounce back or cope successfully despite significant adversity (Rutter, 1985), has been attributed to a number of personality factors. Such personality factors include a sense of personal worthiness, a sense of control over one's fate, a positive social orientation, social intelligence, openness to new experiences, and optimism (Earvolino-Ramirez, 2007; Grant & Kinman, 2012). Resilient individuals not only survive but also thrive and grow. That is, individuals can be positively transformed through their experience of adversity and trauma. Indeed, over 50 percent of individuals who experience life crises report some personal benefit, including enhanced social and personal resources and the development of new coping skills (Schaefer & Moos, 1998).

The process of developing new strengths, stronger relationships, expanded coping mechanisms, and psychological understandings that incorporate trauma experiences has been termed *posttraumatic growth* (Ben-porat, 2015; Joseph & Linley, 2005; Tedeschi, Park, & Calhoun, 1998). In social workers and other helping professionals, repeated exposure to traumatic material has been reported to create positive changes, such as increased sensitivity, compassion, and insight; an increased appreciation for the resilience of the human spirit; and an increased sense of the precious nature of life (Arnold, Calhoun, Tedeschi, & Cann, 2005). These experiences can expand the social worker's scope of understanding and range of possible approaches, positively impacting the development of expertise and improving decision-making.

TRAUMA REACTIONS

Nevertheless, exposure to violence and trauma in the workplace has been associated with a number of negative reactions such as acute stress, posttraumatic stress, and secondary traumatic stress, as well as longer-term reactions such as burnout, vicarious trauma, and allostatic load. Acute stress, posttraumatic stress, and secondary traumatic stress all involve three clusters of symptoms: *intrusion* of thoughts, nightmares, and intense psychological and/or physiological distress triggered by reminders of a traumatic event; *arousal* or biological activation resulting in sleep difficulties, emotional outbursts, difficulty concentrating, hypervigilance, and/or exaggerated startle response; and *avoidance* through numbing, detachment, loss of memory regarding a traumatic event, and/or efforts to avoid thoughts or stimuli that are reminiscent of the event. Studies of social workers in various settings suggest that between 15 and 22 percent report symptoms on scales at the level consistent with a diagnosis of posttraumatic stress disorder (Bride, 2007; C. Regehr, LeBlanc, Bogo, Paterson, & Birze, 2015; C. Regehr, LeBlanc, Shlonsky, & Bogo, 2010). Vicarious trauma refers to changes in cognitive schemas regarding self, others, or the safety of the world, as a result of repeated exposure to the suffering of others through providing therapy or other assistance to trauma survivors. These experiences have a profound impact on social workers. In addition however, there is a possibility that professional decision-making may be influenced by these symptoms.

ONGOING STRESSES

The nature of social work and the organizations in which social workers operate also expose them to chronic stress. These stresses may include excessive work demands caused by unwieldy caseloads, court appearances, and overwhelming paperwork; poor working conditions; negative public perceptions; and low salary (Collings & Murray, 1996; Guterman & Jayaratne, 1994; Vinokur-Kaplan, 1991). They may also include public scrutiny; legal or other reviews; and negative media attention when decisions result in negative outcomes, such as child death, suicide, or harm to another individual. One possible outcome of exposure to chronic stress is physiological depletion. *Allostatic load* is a model for understanding the physiological impact of adapting to environmental stressors that builds on Cannon's 1932 theory of homeostasis (Ganzel & Morris, 2011). That is, the chronic elevation of heart rate, blood pressure, respiration, and endocrine response (such as cortisol) in response to threat can result in physiological wear and tear and immune suppression (McEwen & Stellar, 1993).

Another possible outcome of chronic job stress is burnout (Maslach, Schaufeli, & Leiter, 2001). One of the most studied impacts of professional encounters on social workers, job burnout comprises a sense of emotional exhaustion, a sense of depersonalization, and a loss of personal accomplishment. Job burnout has been described as a dehumanizing process whereby clients are blamed for their problems and victimization as workers lose sympathy and respect for them. Burned-out workers become less flexible in their decision-making and interventions. They also blame other sources, such as the organization, society, or the clients themselves for difficult or unpopular decisions that they must make (Maslach, 1976). While the influence of these reactions on individual workers, their families, and their organizations is important, burnout and allostatic load may also affect the services that social workers provide to the public. That is, social workers' ability to make competent and consistent judgments may also be shaped by the symptomatology of chronic stress.

DECISION-MAKING THEORY

Theories of decision-making emerged from examination of how individuals make choices in the face of risk. Risk occurs when there are several possible outcomes of a decision, and the probability that each of these outcomes will occur is unknown (Mohr, Biele, & Heekeren, 2010). Three types of approaches have been suggested for understanding risk and making decisions in the face of risk: one involving logic, reason, and scientific deliberation; one involving fast, instinctive, intuitive reactions—a sort of feeling approach; and one involving politics and power dynamics that direct the definition and possible outcomes (Slovic, 1999; Slovic, Finucane, Peters, & MacGregor, 2004). The first of these approaches— logic, reason, and scientific deliberation—gave rise to *rational choice theory*. This theory emerged from the discipline of economics (Von Neumann & Morgenstern, 1947) but was subsequently applied to other situations in a manner that Benjamin Franklin called *moral* or *prudential algebra*. The rational choice model assumes that individuals will deliberately consider all the risks and benefits of the various decision alternatives available to them. Individuals will then weight each possible outcome of a decision according to the likelihood that it will occur and according to how much the outcome is desired. Finally, individuals will make a decision based on the weighted average they have calculated.

Despite the attractive simplicity of the rational choice model, research evidence in a variety of situations has repeatedly demonstrated that people rarely behave in the manner predicted by the model. Rather, people generally make decisions in much more efficient ways, based on partial information, and often unconsciously, using what appears to be intuition or instinct. These have been referred to as fast and frugal—or heuristic— approaches to problem solving that employ a practical method, not guaranteed to be optimal or perfect, but sufficient for the immediate goals (Gigerenzer & Gaissmaier, 2011). As discussed previously with respect to expertise, the basis on which people make quick decisions is often experienced as a gut feeling, appearing quickly in the consciousness, triggered automatically by external stimuli (Gigerenzer, 2007). Unlike "rational choice," gut feelings involve emotional responses. They are thus subject to biases based not only on information available but also on the context in which the decision occurs and emotions triggered by previous experiences.

The third approach to understanding decision-making involves politics, power, and organizations. This approach acknowledges that decisions are made within a context that limits the choices available and determines outcomes. A risk of the first two methods, rational choice and intuition, is that attributions of success or failure are often ascribed to the individual and not the larger situation. That is, individuals are viewed as free actors or masters of their own fate who are not subject to constraints. The political approach focuses on the constraints and context as primary influences of decisions and behavior.

PROFESSIONAL DECISION-MAKING

Research on clinical decision-making in situations of risk has suggested that there is great variability among professionals' decisions on any given case or situation, and great variability even among one professional's decisions at different times. In an effort to improve both the quality and consistency of professional decisions, tools to aid decision-making have been designed in a wide range of fields. Fast and frugal heuristics can be codified into simple decision trees that become part of the decision-makers' repertoire for addressing decisions. Such decision trees limit the information search and do not involve computation (Gigerenzer, 2007). While this is efficient and extremely useful for practitioners, such a method also carries a risk of bias. As noted above, one such bias is a fundamental attribution error whereby behaviors are attributed to some innate quality of the individual, rather than an environment that shapes behavior or offers few other options.

Actuarial tools parallel the rational decision method using statistical algorithms to predict specific risk outcomes such as child abuse, sexual violence, or suicide. They are developed by reviewing large data sets consisting of individuals who have committed the violent acts in question and identifying common variables among these individuals. Each variable is statistically weighted according to the strength of the relationship with the outcome and then summed in some manner to determine overall risk (Brown & Rakow, 2016; De Bortoli & Dolan, 2015). However, as many actuarial tools rely primarily on historic and static factors, they have been widely criticized for ignoring context. This may include social and political forces that increase "risk factors" in some individuals, such as previous history of arrests in communities in which police are more likely to press charges than in other communities. In a precedent-setting case in Canada, it was acknowledged that actuarial tools do not take into account structural factors leading to social distress in Indigenous Canadians (Gutierrez, Helmus, & Hanson, 2016; Hart, 2016). Further, the scales are based on predictive data acquired at the group level, which may not accurately reflect the characteristics of the client in question (C. Regehr, Stern, & Shlonsky, 2007). In this respect, tools assessing risk of sexual violence have been found to be accurate in predicting recidivism in Nordic and European offenders but not those of African or Asian descent (Långström, 2004).

As a result of drawbacks in both actuarial tools and clinical judgment alone, a newer approach to risk assessment has emerged that blends research evidence and clinical practice and incorporates concepts of risk management with risk assessment: the structured professional judgment (SPJ) approach. The SPJ approach focuses on the development of evidence-based guidelines or frameworks that encourage systemization and consistency but allow for flexibility in incorporating case-specific and contextual factors that influence risk (Doyle & Dolan, 2002).

Nevertheless, the studies that colleagues and I have conducted on social workers assessing risk of child abuse and suicide demonstrated considerable variation in not only overall clinical judgments but also scores on actuarial and structured professional judgment tools. Qualitative interviews that we conducted suggest that these social workers considered such factors as body language, relationships between the client and others, and the worker's own emotional reaction. Our research confirms that social workers are highly variable in their assessment of both future child abuse and suicide risk, with some workers viewing risk on a particular client to be high, and others viewing risk on the same client to be low. Thus there appear to be individual factors in the worker that are critical to clinical judgment regarding risk. A key element is the worker's previous and current experiences of stress and trauma on the job and his or her reactions to the stressors encountered.

EMOTIONS AND DECISION-MAKING

There is strong evidence that emotions have considerable influence over cognitive appraisals and ultimately behavior when individuals are making choices under conditions of risk and uncertainty (Mohr, Biele, & Heekeren, 2010; Vartanian & Mandel, 2011). Emotions, which in large part arise from positive and negative life experiences, serve as frames of reference and affect the manner in which information is gathered, stored, recalled, and used to make judgments (Nabi, 2003). People's interpretation of the world around them thus tends to reflect their current emotional state. In addition, emotions are linked to physiological responses and serve as "mental representations of physiological changes" (Dolan, 2002, p. 1193). Individuals then use the physiological and emotional state as evidence of the degree of risk. That is, the individual believes that physiological arousal and heightened anxiety are reliable indicators that there is a high risk of a negative outcome. This is known as the *affect heuristic* (Slovic et al., 2004). Thus gut feelings have affective and somatic components, both of which influence judgment.

Social workers and other professionals approach clinical decision-making with rich personal and professional histories that affect the manner in which they appraise situations and the decisions they make. On one hand, this history contributes to their expertise, providing the ability to draw on a knowledge base of similar situations while also recognizing the unique factors and context of the current situation. The feelings evoked can serve as useful guides and contribute to what appear to be highly developed intuitive skills. On the other hand, the feelings evoked may also carry risk, biasing judgments and restricting the ability to consider all factors relevant to the decision.

IMPACT OF STRESS AND TRAUMA ON DECISION-MAKING

Professional decision-making can be affected by both acute stress related to the current situation and traumatic stress responses to previous encounters. Individuals in acutely stressful situations may experience selective attention, focusing particularly on threat stimuli with limited ability to consider other factors. Acute stress impacts computational capacity, requiring individuals to rely more heavily on heuristics as deliberative cognitive processing and decision-making capacities are constricted. Acute stress also affects memory, including the ability to retrieve, store, consolidate, and manipulate information (LeBlanc, 2009). Despite this, acute stress can also enhance performance in some individuals. These individuals are able to make use of heightened physiological reactions to address challenges.

Posttraumatic stress is also associated with performance deficits in some situations. In particular, posttraumatic stress disorder (PTSD) affects the ability to focus attention, the speed of information processing, and both working memory and verbal memory (Brewin, Kleiner, Vasterling, & Field, 2007; Scott et al., 2015). In a series of five experimental design studies involving four high-stress occupational groups—police recruits, paramedics, police communicators, and social workers—my research team explored the association between stress, trauma, and decision-making. The results of this series of studies suggest that the relationship between stress, PTSD, and performance is complex. That is, we did not find evidence that PTSD has a direct impact on global performance on tasks for which emergency responders are highly trained. However, PTSD did impact assessment of risk in situations that required complex professional judgment. Specifically, and perhaps paradoxically, individuals suffering from PTSD symptoms perceived risk of child abuse and suicide to be lower. Further, we found that the combined effect of traumatic stress and acute stress was highly problematic. Individuals experiencing posttraumatic stress symptoms reported higher levels of acute stress when faced with stressful work situations. Acute stress in these studies was associated with performance deficits on complex cognitive tasks, verbal memory impairment, and heightened assessment of risk (C. Regehr & LeBlanc, 2017).

FACTORS THAT INFLUENCE STRESS
AND TRAUMA RESPONSES

If we are to mitigate the impact of stress and trauma on professional decision-making, we must first understand the factors that contribute to symptoms arising. While diagnostic categories for PTSD and acute stress disorder suggest that exposure to horrifying events will necessarily result in symptoms, research evidence does not support this assumption. Indeed, while most individuals may experience symptoms of intrusion, arousal, and reexperiencing in the days and weeks immediately following certain high-impact events, the degree and nature of exposures do not predict the severity of symptoms over the longer term. Rather, there is a complex interaction between the individual, the organization, and the societal environment.

At the individual level, vulnerabilities and resilience capacities include genetic predisposition and characteristic patterns of interacting with others, understanding the world, and approaching challenges. Preexisting strengths and vulnerabilities set the stage for peritraumatic responses—that is, responses that occur during and in the immediate aftermath of a traumatic event. Physiological reactions such as increased heart rate and cortisol secretion are linked to psychological response—that is, the degree of fear, panic, and helplessness the person encounters as the event unfolds. They are also linked to the individual's cognitive appraisal of the event, including perceived threat, the degree of control they believe they have over the event, and their behavioral response to it. This combination of cognitive appraisal at the time of the event and psychological and biological response predicts long-term symptom severity.

In the longer-term aftermath of a traumatic event, environmental factors contribute to resilience and lower PTSD symptom levels. For instance, the nature of the social work environment—including workload, organizational climate, peer support, and supervision—contributes to resilience (McFadden, Campbell, & Taylor, 2015). The recovery environment also includes the larger society, social policies that require investigations when terrible outcomes occur, such as the death of a child, and the media's tendency to reduce complex practice to heroes and villains.

Similarly, the large body of research literature addressing occupational stress has long focused on the important interaction between the work, the workplace, and the worker. Work factors include the balance between demands and the control afforded to the worker to manage these demands, and the degree of role ambiguity and role conflict inherent in the work. In social work this not only includes the unpredictability and needs of clients, but also societal demands in which deeply held beliefs are in conflict. Importantly, however, the manner in which individuals interact with their work is also a factor that can exacerbate or moderate stress. These factors include the degree and nature of empathic engagement, the approach to managing emotional labor, and coping styles.

MITIGATING THE IMPACT OF STRESS AND TRAUMA

The recognition that the work and the workplace environment are primary contributors to the experience of stress and trauma symptoms requires that organizations take responsibility for reducing exposure to the extent possible, for mitigating the impacts of stress and trauma exposure, and for providing services when individual social workers are suffering. First, organizations have an obligation to enhance the safety of social workers by creating a culture in which workers know that their safety is paramount; by establishing policies and procedures and designing environments that reduce risk; and by ensuring that workers have the training to assess and avoid risk (National Association of Social Workers, 2013). Organizations must also build cultures of support in which supervisors and managers assist and stand by social workers and in which peer support mechanisms are encouraged and facilitated. When adverse events occur, organizations must not only ensure that they address liability concerns of social workers and manage media and government concerns but also have proactive strategies in these areas.

While it should be made very clear that social workers cannot be blamed for manifesting symptoms of stress and trauma in environments that expose them to distressing situations and ongoing workload pressures, there are approaches that workers can take to protect themselves. One is advocating for safe working conditions and contributing to a supportive workplace environment. In addition, social workers can obtain training in evidence-based stress reduction techniques and understand approaches to empathic practice that both enhance effectiveness and reduce risk of trauma contagion. Finally, while practice within organizations is characterized by policies, procedures, and rules, social workers can identify the breadth of discretion available to them and bravely make decisions based on knowledge, expertise, and values, thereby affording them a sense of power and accomplishment.

Schools of social work also have key responsibilities for providing education that addresses issues of safety and resilience. Indeed, the Professional Capabilities Framework of the British Association of Social Workers explicitly states that prior to entering practicum, students must, among other things, describe and demonstrate the importance of professional behavior, the importance of personal and professional boundaries, and the importance of emotional resilience (British Association of Social Workers, 2017). In addition, leadership training opportunities must be enhanced so that social work supervisors and managers can perform vital functions related to safety, stress, and trauma in workers. The intensive relationship between schools of social work and social agencies through the field faculty liaison role also provides an opportunity for leadership training of social work staff members who supervise students.

IMPROVING DECISION-MAKING IN SITUATIONS OF RISK AND UNCERTAINTY

In the end, actuarial tools, standard professional judgment tools, and fast and frugal decision trees remain guides for professional decision-making. However, other individual worker factors appear to override these guides, directing professional judgment in one way or another. Regardless of the degree that we might wish to make professional decision-making "rational," people will continue to "misbehave" according to rules of rational decision theory. Understanding the factors that influence individual differences in professional decision-making raises the possibility that professionals will be able to design their own fast and frugal methods and modify structured professional judgment tools to take into account their own unique application of decision-making in situations of risk. This unique approach should involve invoking analysis derived from research evidence, deliberately applying expert knowledge, listening to gut feelings that inform experiential knowledge, and understanding the social and political context in which risky decisions are being made.

STRUCTURE OF THIS BOOK

Chapter 2 describes the nature of the exposure to stress and trauma that social workers encounter in the workplace and its impact on them.

Trauma exposure includes acute events that arise from dangerous working conditions, including direct threats and assaults against social workers. This can result in acute stress and posttraumatic stress. Trauma exposure also includes repeated indirect exposure: bearing witness to the physical impacts on clients who are victims of spousal violence, child abuse, sexual violence, torture, and other horrific life experiences. This exposure can result in compassion fatigue, secondary traumatic stress, and vicarious trauma. In addition, social workers encounter ongoing stressors both in the workplace (unwieldy caseloads, increased regulatory requirements, and frequent organizational change) and in the broader society, where they face public disapproval, negative media attention, and shifting public policy. All of these stressors can result in physiological symptoms as measured by allostatic load and psychological and emotional burnout.

However, while most individuals experience some symptoms in response to highly distressing exposure to trauma, the degree and nature of the exposure do not in and of themselves predict the severity of symptoms over the longer term. Building on research that demonstrates that the response to trauma exposure can be highly varied, chapter 3 discusses the multiplicity of factors that may contribute to trauma response in social workers. The research presented in this chapter demonstrates that individual factors, incident factors, organizational factors, and societal factors combine to predict posttraumatic stress in social workers. Of these factors, organizational and societal factors have the strongest association with distress. That is, ongoing organizational stressors related to workload, challenging clients, and caseload mix; media attention and public condemnation; and the nature of organizational supports have a profound impact on the individual's experience of traumatic events encountered in the workplace.

Chapter 4 reviews theories for understanding response to stress and empirical evidence supporting these theoretical models. Models explaining response to risk considered in this chapter fall into two broad categories: individuals' engagement with their work, including such factors as empathy, emotional labor, and coping style; and the nature of the work, including role conflicts and the relative balance of workplace demands and worker control as determined by organizational policies, resources, and government legislation. The chapter concludes with a model for an integrated understanding of stress response that includes the individual, the nature of the work, and the nature of the workplace.

The book then focuses on the nature and development of expertise and the nature and process of professional decision-making. Chapter 5 reviews the theoretical foundations of expertise and competence, models for understanding the development of expertise, the role of intuition and meta-competencies in expertise, factors influencing expertise in social work, and finally factors that interfere with the application of expertise. Chapter 6 reviews research literature on cognition and decision-making, including theoretical models of decision-making, and the literature on decision-making and risk in social work. As discussed above, understanding decision-making in situations of risk and uncertainty can focus on logical, reasoned scientific analysis; on instinctive, intuitive decisions; or on the political context, including who controls how risk is defined and the relative desirability of various outcomes. In most cases, social workers' decisions will include each of these elements. Indeed, even scientifically validated tools for assessing risk in social work are subject to systemic biases arising from the population and context in which they were developed and tested and the way they are applied by an individual social worker.

A major focus of neuroscience research on judgment decision-making is the impact of emotions on decisions involving risk and uncertainty. When faced with risk decisions, the brain's emotion centers are activated. Research in this area, largely focusing on laboratory-based experiments and brain imaging, are reviewed in chapter 7. The chapter then brings together the research on stress and trauma with the research on decision-making and discusses original research that colleagues and I have conducted on stress, trauma, and decision-making in social workers and emergency-response professionals. This will provide practice-based examples to illustrate neurological models for understanding the influence of stress and trauma on performance and decision-making.

When stress and trauma negatively impact professional decision-making, an obvious solution is to develop and implement approaches that reduce exposure to stress and trauma, mitigate responses to stress and trauma when exposed, and ameliorate symptoms. Chapter 8 discusses organizational approaches to addressing stress and trauma, including attending to safety issues; building a culture of support that includes managerial supports and peer supports; managing liability issues when adverse events occur; establishing strategies for dealing with media and government responses to adverse events; and celebrating successes. Individual approaches considered include stress reduction techniques, moderating empathy and emotional labor, and taking control and demonstrating courage. Also discussed are curricula for schools of social work designed to promote safety and resilience in students and leadership development training for practicing social workers.

Improving decision-making nevertheless requires more than simply addressing stress and trauma. Rather, it requires a multi-targeted approach. Chapter 9 presents an approach that begins with self-awareness, including assessing and understanding one's own level of competence and expertise, personal decision-making frameworks and schemas, and emotional responses that contribute to intuitive decision-making. Other elements of the model include familiarity with decision-making tools, approaches to novel situations that sit at the boundaries of social workers' expertise, evaluating the outcomes of social workers' decisions, and modifying practices and professional judgment models to optimize decision-making and maximize the probability of positive outcomes for clients.

Stress and Trauma in Social Work

This book is about social workers' high-impact decisions: determining that a child is at risk of abuse, that an individual may attempt suicide, or that someone with a history of violence may harm another person. However, the nature of social workers' jobs and the high-impact decisions they make can also have profound impacts on the workers themselves. This may include immediate reactions such as acute stress, posttraumatic stress, and secondary traumatic stress, or longer-term reactions such as burnout, vicarious trauma, and allostatic load. While the impact of these reactions on individual workers, their families, and their organizations is important, they may also affect the services that social workers provide to the public. That is, social workers' ability to make competent and consistent judgments may be shaped by symptoms arising from previous traumatic experiences and their perception of personal risk experienced in any clinical context. This chapter considers the nature of social workers' exposure to stress and trauma in the workplace and the influence of this exposure on them.

EXPOSURE TO VIOLENCE

When social workers tell others about the nature of their work and the populations they serve, the response often focuses on how hard it must be facing the suffering of others. However, few people are aware that social workers face direct exposure to violence and physical risk. Here are three chilling examples:

On Friday, August 7, 2015, social worker Lara Sobel, an employee for fourteen years with the Vermont Department for Children and Families, was shot to death with a .270-caliber hunting rifle as she left her office for the weekend. Her killer, forty-year-old Jody Herring, had recently lost custody of her nine-year-old daughter. Scott Williams, a Washington County state's attorney who witnessed the murder, made the following statement to the police "She was a pit bull of an advocate for kids. She did not hesitate to let judges and lawyers know what was best for kids. I respected the hell out of her."
(Despart, 2015)

On January 26, 2016, twenty-two-year-old Swedish social worker Alexandra Mezher bled to death after being stabbed in a frenzied attack by a resident of an asylum center for male refugee youth. With only four months on the job, Ms. Mezher was called in to work the night shift alone. While admission to the asylum was limited to those under the age of eighteen, it was later revealed that many, including her attacker, were considerably older. According to her mother, "Alexandra knows how to handle children including violent ones—but those she was working with were big powerful guys—she could see it in their eyes and their bodies."
(Andersson & Drury, 2016)

From 1996 to 2002, Shauna Bailey, a mental health social worker in London, England, was stalked by her client Richard Jan. He bombarded her with phone calls. He followed her car, smashed it up, and set it on fire. Twice he attacked her outside her home late at night, resulting in injuries requiring hospitalization. The ordeal ended when Ms. Bailey moved from her home, quit her job, and changed her name. Jan, dubbed "Britain's worst stalker" by Detective Chief Inspector David Poole, was convicted in 2004 on two counts of arson and causing a public nuisance.

(BBC, 2004; Mintowt-Czyz & Edwards, 2004)

Events such as these reverberate throughout the world, causing social workers and their organizations to reflect on the risks encountered in the workplace. And while these horrifying consequences of the work remain relatively rare, social workers do regularly face the risk of physical violence. Approximately one-quarter to one-third of social workers report being assaulted at some time in their careers, and approximately one-half to three-quarters have been threatened with physical harm (MacDonald & Sirotich, 2001, 2005; C. Newhill, 1996; C. Regehr, Leslie, Howe, & Chau, 2005; Rey, 1996). For instance, in a Canadian study, 171 social workers responded to a questionnaire mailed to three hundred randomly selected members of the Ontario Association of Social Workers (MacDonald & Sirotich, 2005). Respondents worked in a wide variety of fields, including hospitals (28.2 percent), family services (13.5 percent), child protection (12.4 percent), education, mental health, seniors' services, and corrections. The high rates of verbal harassment, physical assault, racial harassment, and sexual harassment they reported can be found in table 2.1. These finding closely reflect those of a study of 175 randomly selected social workers in Nevada, in which social workers reported verbal abuse (88.8 percent), threats (59.6 percent), having property stolen (47.3 percent), physical assaults (23.0 percent), and threats with a weapon (17.5 percent) (Rey, 1996). A study that colleagues and I conducted with 175 child welfare workers in a large urban agency in Toronto found that 24 percent of social work staff reported being victims of assault on the job, and 53 percent had received verbal threats at one time in their career (C. Regehr, Leslie, et al., 2005). A British study determined that 363 social workers reported verbal abuse (93 percent), threats (71 percent), physical assault (56 percent), sexual abuse (29 percent), and racial abuse (9 percent) (Harris & Leather, 2011). Social workers in Australia reported having experienced, within the previous year, verbal abuse (57 percent), threats (47 percent), assault (9 percent), and sexual harassment (15 percent) (Koritsas, Coles, & Boyle, 2010). Among 645 social workers in Israel, 79.5 percent reported verbal aggression, 77.3 percent reported threats, and

TABLE 2.1

Prevalence of client violence

Type of Violence	In Last 2 Years		Over Career	
	N	%	N	%
Personally verbally harassed	92	56.1	144	87.8
Threatened with physical harm	33	19.6	106	63.5
Sexually Harassed	16	9.6	49	29.3
Threatened that harm would be done to family or colleague(s)	15	9.0	38	22.8
Physically assaulted by not injured	10	6.0	48	28.6
Stalked	8	4.8	27	16.3
Threatened damage to personal property	7	4.2	30	18
Racially or ethically harassed	7	4.2	25	15.1
Physically assaulted and injured	1	0.6	13	7.8

Note: the numbers for each category of violence vary due to missing data.
(MacDonald & Sirotich, 2005)

21.1 percent reported property damage, but only 8.53 percent had experienced physical violence at some point during their careers (Enosh & Tzafrir, 2015). Thus while some regional variations exist, social workers throughout the world are at high risk of verbal and physical violence.

The practice settings in which social workers are most likely to report violence include child protection, mental health, substance abuse, and corrections (Jayaratne, Croxton, & Mattison, 2004; Newhill, 1996). Rates of physical assault appear to be highest among social workers in residential settings. An Australian study found that 64 percent of social workers in a residential children's center had experienced assault, and 56 percent had been assaulted more than once (Winstanley & Hales, 2008). Our study of child welfare workers revealed that 70 percent of those in child residential settings experienced assault. However, these workers were less likely to report being distressed about the assault than workers in other parts of the organization, such as child protection workers, presumably because the perpetrator was a child and not an adult, and the assault occurred in a setting in which others were present, unlike child protection workers assaulted when conducting home visits (C. Regehr, Leslie, et al., 2005). In reflecting on violence against child welfare workers, one agency supervisor said, "One of the major stressors that we take for granted is that we send our people out alone, nobody else does. And when you look at the fact that we are tampering with the mother/child bond as being sacred to all societies, well I'm surprised we don't have more violence than we do" (C. Regehr, Chau, Leslie, & Howe, 2002a). Other factors associated with risk of client violence against social workers include age (younger social workers are at higher risk of assault [Jayaratne et al., 2004; Koritsas et al., 2010]), gender (male social workers report higher rates of property damage, threats, and physical assaults [Enosh & Tzafrir, 2015; Jayaratne et al., 2004; Koritsas et al., 2010; Newhill, 1996]), and practice location (rural social workers report higher risk than urban social workers [Koritsas et al., 2010]).

Interestingly, social workers' perceptions regarding risk of encountering client violence remains relatively low despite high rates of reported threats and assault. For instance, MacDonald and Sirotich (2005) found that despite high rates of actual threats and violence, only one of 171 respondents reported feeling unsafe with clients, and thirty-two (18.7 percent) reported feeling sometimes unsafe with clients. Kosny and Eakin investigated this discrepancy between perceived and actual reported client violence further in an ethnographic study involving three social work sites that provided emergency shelter, drop-in, and addiction services in Toronto (Kosny & Eakin, 2008). In this study social workers described scenarios in which clients were verbally threatening or physically violent toward them and stole or destroyed their property. Despite this, social workers described their sense of commitment and compassion, suggesting that exposure to violence was an acceptable risk when working with clients who had experienced multiple injustices in life. Indeed, the authors noted, "In certain circumstances, it seemed that workers' belief in organizational missions and their commitment to clients compelled them to behave in ways which were deleterious to their health" (p. 158). This included going alone into unsafe places where people were actively injecting drugs, working alone after hours, and exposing them-selves to communicable diseases. Further, workers described tolerating verbal racial abuse, attributing the behavior to systemic barriers, mental health challenges, or clients' history of abuse. One social worker in Kosny and Eakin's study said, "I can have a client here and they can call me 'nig-ger' today, and tomorrow they'll say 'Hi, how are you doing?' I don't keep it as a thing. . . . You have to be able to let things go in order to be more fulfilled in this work, because if you keep things in, it just builds up over the years, over the years builds up, and you develop a resentment to the client" (Kosny & Eakin, 2008, p. 160). Virkki described similar attitudes among Finnish social workers. In qualitative interviews conducted by the researchers, social workers did not recognize client violence "as 'real' violence but as an excusable expression of the clients' distress, or as a justifiable reaction to the employees' conduct" (Virkki, 2008, p. 247). One social worker in this study reported, "It doesn't feel like real vio-lence. Sometimes you think it's, in quotes, justified. It's like 'I need this, I believe that I'm allowed to have this and then this hag tells me that you're not going to get it.' It is just about discharging feelings of disap-pointment." Another said, "They make every effort to cover up that they are desperate and that's why they call me a bitch; even if they really mean 'help me, I feel so bad'" (Virkki, 2007, p. 224). These social workers be-lieved that, if they created positive interpersonal relationships and earned their clients' trust, their clients would not behave violently. In this re-spect, client violence was seen as a professional failing (Virkki, 2008), and social workers feared that disclosing the occurrence of abuse would result in negative reactions from colleagues and superiors.

Like other researchers, Baines notes that social workers do not re-port client violence because they feel sorry for clients or fear being blamed. In addition, she notes a culture of bravado in which social work-ers reinforce their own brand of toughness and caring (Baines, 2006), a sort of "white knuckle caring" that adds to the excitement and challenge of the job (Baines & Cunningham, 2011). One social worker in her study reported, "We all act tough—we can take it. Nobody wants to admit that they feel sick or discouraged or freaked out." Another said, "I've been tar-geted three times, which is not bad in a year, twice with a chair and once recently, where he literally threw me off the filing cabinets. . . . I've been assaulted so often [she laughs] over the years. . . . It's always going to happen" (Baines & Cunningham, 2011, pp. 769, 770). This bravado is familiar to me. In an inpatient forensic unit in which I worked, a favorite story told to new employees involved a hostage taking at gunpoint. An inpatient who had been charged with murder smuggled a gun into the unit. He used it to take Jennie, one of our nurses, hostage. Jennie was forced to open the locked door, accompany him onto the elevator, and leave the building. The perpetrator then told her to get into a waiting car. Jennie refused, telling him she would rather be shot on the spot than accompany him. He hit her with the weapon and released her. The message of the story was clear: we are so tough on this unit that not even guns scare us.

To better understand perceptions of client violence and the tendency for social workers to underreport violence committed against them, Tzafrir, Enosh, and Gur (2013) conducted in-depth interviews with forty social workers in Israel. After examining the interviews, the researchers proposed a four-stage reflective process (figure 2.1) in which social workers engaged: (1) rationalization, minimization, and self-blame; (2) emotional reactions including hurt, anger, helplessness, and shame; (3) reevaluation of beliefs, attitudes, and values; and (4) behavioral transformation. In the first proposed stage, social workers focus on accepting the client, including understanding the client's hardships and limitations, rationalizing aggressive behavior, putting their own needs second, and trying to determine what they might have done to "provoke" violence against them. These views are reflected in the Toronto study described earlier. In the second stage, social workers may feel angry and humiliated about the assault or abuse. Workers in this stage may be unable to shake negative feelings about a specific event and may generalize anger and intolerance to other clients. In the third stage, social workers reevaluate values and norms and begin to set boundaries to safeguard themselves and the clients with whom they work. One participant articulated this as differentiating between their clients' social difficulties and hardships and their clients' decision to become abusive or violent. This leads to the fourth stage, behavioral change, in which the social workers still accept clients with empathy and compassion but do not tolerate violence or abuse.

While abuse and assault may seem to be regular occurrences and may be normalized in many different ways, victimization in the workplace has profound effects on workers and their organizations. Enosh and

RATIONALIZATION, MINIMIZATION AND SELF-BLAME

$\downarrow$

EMOTIONAL RESPONSE
(hurt, anger, helplessness, shame)

$\downarrow$

REEVALUATION OF BELIEFS, ATTITUDES AND VALUES

$\downarrow$

BEHAVIOURAL TRANSFORMATION

FIGURE 2.1 Social workers' responses to violence
Source: Adapted from Tzafrir, Enosh, & Gur, 2013.

Tzafrir (2015) summarize these impacts in table 2.2. Not included in their analysis is the possibility of developing acute stress disorder or posttraumatic stress disorder when violence that has been experienced or witnessed is severe and horrifying. The examples described at the onset of this chapter may lead to such outcomes.

A second form of violence exposure that social workers may experience relates to working with individuals who are victims of trauma or violence. Several quantitative studies point to elevated rates of trauma symptoms in social workers providing services to traumatized individuals (Arvay & Uhlemann, 1996; Bober & Regehr, 2006; Brady, Guy, Poels-

TABLE 2.2

Short- and long-term effects of violence on the individual and organization

Time Frame Level:	Short-Term Effect	Long-Term Effects
Individual Worker	• Fear • Feeling threatened • Insecurity • Stress • Paralysis • Humiliation • Fear of submitting a complaint • Loneliness • Low performance	• Emotional burnout • Fear of violence • Helplessness • Fatigue • Nightmares • Prolonged absenteeism
Organization	• Antagonism of workers toward clients • Abstaining from house visits • Desire to transfer treatment of aggressive client to another worker • Decrease in daily performance • Loss of time—investing time in group adaptation processes	• Decrease in ongoing departmental work • Turnover and desire to change job • Burnout • Frustration and loss of trust in the system • Organizational helplessness • Absenteeism

(Enosh & Tzafrir, 2015)

tra, & Brokaw, 1999; Gates & Gillespie, 2008; Ortlepp & Friedman, 2002; Schauben & Frazier, 1995). One aspect of this is the repeated exposure to stories of one individual's inhumane behavior toward another. Ted Bober and I conducted a survey study (Bober & Regehr, 2006) with 259 trauma therapists, 47.7 percent of whom were social workers. Participants answered a series of questions about the nature of their practices and completed an instrument that captures posttraumatic stress symptoms, the Impact of Event Scale (IES) (Zilberg, Weiss, & Horowitz, 1982). In this study, the number of hours per week counseling trauma victims was a significant predictor of all three categories of posttraumatic stress symptoms and in particular levels of intrusion symptoms (explained below). While counseling all categories of victims was highly associated with trauma symptoms in workers, counseling sexual assault victims was associated with the highest level of symptoms, followed in descending order by victims of child sexual abuse, victims of spousal violence, child abuse victims, and torture victims.

In reflecting on the impact on ourselves and colleagues during our years of working in sexual assault crisis services, my colleague Susan Cadell and I identified six common themes (C. Regehr & Cadell, 1999):

- *Checking the closets*, reflecting an undermining of one's personal sense of safety and a tendency to become hypervigilant regarding potential risks
- *I can't watch the news anymore*, reflecting avoidance of material related to trauma
- *This job is affecting my social life*, in that faith in others may be undermined and anger at injustice may be displaced onto friends and loved ones who appear insensitive to social justice issues
- *Old scars rubbed anew*, in which memories of past personal experiences are triggered by client stories
- *There was no bear in the breezeway*, when repeated graphic images of torture and abuse described by clients begin to intrude on the waking fantasies and dreams of workers, creating a set of false memories
- *What can I do to help anyway*, reflecting a sense of hopelessness and being overwhelmed with the magnitude of the issue

An additional aspect of working with distressed and traumatized individuals is losing them to death. For instance, in our study of 175 child welfare workers, 31 percent reported that a child in their care had died due to accident, and 25 percent indicated that a child had died due to abuse or neglect (Regehr, Hemsworth, Leslie, Howe, & Chau, 2004). Losing a patient to suicide is another experience many social workers share (Palmieri et al., 2008; Ting, Jacobson, & Sanders, 2008). Indeed, 33 percent of mental health social workers report having lost a patient to suicide (Sanders, Jacobson, & Ting, 2008). In a study I conducted with colleagues involving mental health social workers who work with suicidal clients, 53 percent reported having a client die from suicide (C. Regehr, LeBlanc, Bogo, Paterson, & Birze, 2015). This experience undermines a sense of professional competence, causes acute stress and grief reactions, and leads to burnout (Gaffney et al., 2009; Linke, Wojciak, & Day, 2002).

ACUTE STRESS AND POSTTRAUMATIC STRESS REACTIONS TO WORKPLACE EXPOSURES

The experience of trauma as a reaction to horrifying events dates back to the earliest of literature on the human condition. Descriptions of Achilles, a soldier in the Greek war against Troy, in Homer's *Iliad* are remarkably similar to the experiences of combat veterans who returned from the Vietnam War (Shay, 1994). Shakespeare's *Titus Andronicus* describes in gruesome detail the rape and mutilation of Lavinia and the impact of the attack not only on her, but also on those around her (K. Regehr & Regehr, 2012). Early medical texts also described the experience of trauma. *The Anatomy of Melancholy*, originally published in 1651, described the impact of "perturbations" as "a cruel torture of the soul, inexplicable grief, poisoned worm, consuming body and soul, and gnawing at the very heart, a perpetual executioner, perpetual night, heating worse than fire and a battle that has no end" (Burton, 1850). By the late 1800s and early 1900s, the impact of traumatic exposure was described as an interaction between the psyche and physical ailments. Herbert William Page, in his book *Injuries to the Spine and Spinal Cord Without Apparent Lesion and Nervous Shock: In Their Surgical and Medico-Legal Aspects*, observes that "the incidents indeed of almost every railway collision are quite sufficient—even if no bodily injury is inflicted—to produce a very serious effect upon the mind, and to be the means of bringing about a state of collapse from fright, and from fright only" (Page, 1883, p. 147). At the same time, references to combat-related traumatic responses include the development of syndromes such as "irritable heart" described by DaCosta in 1871 (Oppenheimer & Rothschild, 1918). In addition, "neurasthenia" was a prevalent neurological condition described as "an ensemble of phenomena which result from the non-adaptation [*sic*] of the individual to a continuous emotive cause and the struggle of the individual for this adaptation" (Mott, 1918, p. 127).

Mott reflects that this term not only rendered mental disorder acceptable, but allowed for compensation under the UK Employer's Liability Act (C. Regehr & Glancy, 2014), something we view to be a novel policy innovation in the past few years.

The fifth and most recent edition of the American Psychiatric Association's *Diagnostic and Statistical Manual (DSM-5)* (American Psychological Association, 2013) describes two conditions that arise from exposure to horrifying events: acute stress disorder (ASD) and posttraumatic stress disorder (PTSD). These two conditions have similar etiologies and symptom patterns, the major difference being that acute stress symptoms occur between three days and one month after a traumatic event, whereas in posttraumatic stress, symptoms must last for more than one month. For both acute stress and posttraumatic stress, an individual must be exposed to actual or threatened death, serious injury, or sexual violation either directly, by witnessing events as they occur to others, or by learning that these events occurred to a close friend or family member. In addition, however, the latest edition of *DSM* acknowledges that ASD and PTSD can occur when an individual has experienced "repeated or extreme exposure to adverse details of the traumatic event(s)," and the manual provides specific examples of first responders who collect human remains and police officers who are repeatedly exposed to details of child abuse. Thus, social workers may be vulnerable to posttraumatic stress either through direct exposure to traumatic events at work or through repeated exposure to the traumatic experiences of others.

The recognition that PTSD and ASD can occur as a result of workplace exposure is now enshrined in the law in several jurisdictions. The U.S. Congress enacted the Combat PTSD Act in 2011–12, which declared that in cases of PTSD, experiences of combat with the enemy would be presumed to be the cause. The act clarified the meaning of combat with the enemy as follows: "for the purposes of proof of service-connection for veteran's disability compensation, as service on active duty: (1) in a theater of combat operations during a period of war, or (2) in combat against a hostile force during a period of hostilities." In 2012, Alberta was the first Canadian province to legislate that police officers, sheriffs, and paramedics should receive compensation for PTSD without having to provide evidence that the condition was work-related. In January 2016, Manitoba extended presumptive coverage for PTSD to all workers, indicating that the Worker's Compensation Board "can presume the PTSD is caused by the worker's employment unless the contrary is proven" (Workers Compensation Board of Manitoba, 2017). Thus, social workers can be covered presumptively in that province. Four months later, Ontario passed legislation with presumptive coverage but limited it to police, firefighters, and paramedics. Given that this legislation has very recently been brought into force, the impact is not yet clear; nevertheless, this signifies a growing acceptance that events encountered in the workplace can lead to mental health disturbance.

Symptoms of both acute stress and posttraumatic stress fall into three familiar and characteristic clusters. *Intrusion symptoms* are reminders of the exposure and include recurrent thoughts, nightmares, and intense psychological and/or physiological distress at exposure to cues that retrigger memory of the event. *Arousal symptoms* can be understood to be the result of biological activation and include difficulty falling or staying asleep, emotional outbursts, difficulty concentrating, hypervigilance, and exaggerated startle response. Biological correlates of activation include increased heart rate, skin conductance, and blood pressure (Pole, 2007). *Avoidance symptoms* may be thought of as deactivation and include numbing, feelings of detachment, inability to recall important aspects of the event, restricted affect, and efforts to avoid thoughts or stimuli that are reminiscent of the event. Sherin and Nemeroff note that these reactions are self-limiting by definition and in general improve relatively rapidly. However, these reactions do persist for a significant minority of individuals, leading to a diagnosis of PTSD (Sherin & Nemeroff, 2011). Factors that influence the severity of these symptoms will be discussed in the next chapter.

We have long known that exposure to an event that elicits attributions of fear or danger results in neurophysiological changes that enhance the capability for fight or flight (van der Kolk, 1997; Yehuda, 1999). Failure to modulate the neurobiological stress response in the early stages after traumatic exposure (the period of peritraumatic distress) may contribute to the development of chronic symptoms. In individuals suffering from posttraumatic stress, several biological alterations remain including: an exaggerated startle response that does not diminish; increased activation of the amygdala, a part of the brain involved in

TABLE 2.3

Biological correlates of trauma response

Biological Element	Effect on Trauma Response
Neuroendocrine	
Hypothalamic-pituitary-adrenal	• Changed cortisone levels affects fear processing
Hypothalamic-pituitary-thyroid	• Abnormal thyroid levels increase anxiety
Neurochemical	
Catecholamines	• Increased dopamine interferes with fear conditioning • Increased norepinephrine results in increased arousal, blood pressure and startle reflex
Serotonin	• Decreased 5HT increases vigilance, startle and memory intrusions
Neuroanatomical	
Hippocampus	• Reduced volume alters stress response through memory processing deficits
Amygdala	• Increased activity promotes hypervigilance

(Adapted from Sherin and Nemeroff 2011, p. 265)

processing fear (Antai-Otong, 2007); abnormal secretion of cortisol from the adrenal glands affecting fear processing (Shea, Walsh, MacMillan, & Steiner, 2004; Yehuda, 2002); increased dopamine and decreased serotonin, which contribute to arousal and intrusion symptoms (Sherin & Nemeroff, 2011); and reduced size of the hippocampus, a part of the brain involved in learning and memory (Lindauer, Olff, van Meijel, Carlier, & Gersons, 2006; Morgan et al., 2001). Sherin and Nemeroff (2011) provide an outstanding summary of the neurobiological impact of trauma, some aspects of which can be found in table 2.3. The impact of these changes on decision-making will be discussed later in this book.

COMPASSION FATIGUE, SECONDARY TRAUMATIC STRESS, AND VICARIOUS TRAUMATIZATION

The term *posttraumatic stress disorder* was first enshrined in *DSM-III* in 1980—arising from an awareness of the experiences of Vietnam veterans, as well as the experiences of rape victims, famously described by Ann Burgess and Linda Holmstrom (Burgess & Holmstrom, 1974). Among the diagnostic criteria for PTSD was Criterion A, which required that "the person has experienced an event that is outside the range of usual human experience and would be markedly distressing to almost anyone." This was assumed to apply to those individuals directly involved in the traumatic event—that is, the immediate victims. As a result, beginning in the 1980s, three overlapping concepts were suggested for explaining the experience of working with highly distressed and traumatized individuals: compassion fatigue, secondary traumatic stress, and vicarious trauma.

Social work professor Charles Figley investigated the clinical observation that family and friends of victims of crime may also be affected in ways similar to the victims themselves (Figley, 1988). This was in stark contrast to earlier clinical literature, which focused on families either as victimizing systems or in terms of their role in recovery. Thus, Figley suggested that "the number 'victims' of violent crime, accidents, and other traumatic events are grossly underestimated because they count only those directly in harm's way" (Figley, 1999, p. 6). In 1994, *DSM-IV* revised Criterion A to more clearly specify that the event involves threatened death, actual or threatened serious injury, or a threat to the personal integrity of another person. But in addition it added that learning about events experienced by a family member or other close associate could also result in PTSD.

Subsequent research focused on traumatic stress reactions in emergency responders, therapists, and others working with highly traumatized individuals and led to the notion of secondary traumatic stress (STS). Secondary traumatic stress was defined as "the natural consequent behaviors and emotions resulting from knowing about a traumatizing event experienced by a significant other—the stress resulting from helping or wanting to help a traumatized person" (Figley, 1995, p. 10). The symptoms of STS, however, are completely analogous to those of PTSD with the exception of the nature of the stressor (Figley, 1999). Indeed most studies investigating trauma in emergency service populations and other helping professions (including my own studies) have used posttraumatic stress scales to measure symptom level. As such, changes to the criteria for PTSD in *DSM-5* to include "repeated or extreme exposure to adverse details of the traumatic event(s)" make secondary traumatic stress and posttraumatic stress disorder indistinguishable. Thus, the term *secondary traumatic stress* merely differentiates the cause of the symptoms, not the nature or severity of symptoms.

Several studies have attempted to investigate levels of traumatic stress in social workers. Bride surveyed 294 master's level social workers randomly selected from a Southern U.S. state using the Secondary Traumatic Stress Survey. Results demonstrated that 40.5 percent indicated that they experienced intrusive thoughts, 10.9 percent indicated that they avoided people, places, or things that served as reminders of traumatized clients, 22.3 percent reported detachment from others, and 25.9 percent reported emotional numbing. Overall, the author reported that 15.2 percent met the core criteria for PTSD (Bride, 2007). A study focused on decision-making that colleagues and I conducted with ninety-six child welfare workers, revealed that 32 percent of participants fell in the high or severe range on the Impact of Event Scale—Revised (IES-R), and 19 percent fell in the severe range, which is considered consistent with a diagnosis of PTSD (C. Regehr, LeBlanc, Shlonsky, & Bogo, 2010). A similarly designed study with seventy-one mental health social workers revealed that 35.2 percent fell in the high or severe range of the IES-R and 22.5 percent fell in the range consistent with a diagnosis of PTSD (C. Regehr, LeBlanc, et al., 2015). Thus, it is clear that traumatic stress, whether called *secondary traumatic stress* or *posttraumatic stress,* is a significant issue for social workers.

The term *compassion fatigue* is often used interchangeably with STS. Compassion fatigue arises out of compassion for another, where compassion is defined as "a deep sympathy and sorrow for another who is stricken by suffering or misfortune accompanied by a strong desire to alleviate the pain or remove its cause" (Figley, 1995, p. 15). As a result of bearing witness to the suffering of others, and by seeking to view the world from the perspective of an individual who is suffering, a worker becomes preoccupied with the traumatizing material and remains in a constant state of tension (Figley, 2002). This then leads to posttraumatic symptoms. In addition, compassion fatigue can have a negative impact on the individual's quality of life and ultimately health. The Compassion Fatigue Questionnaire developed by Figley contains two subscales: one subscale focused on secondary traumatization, which specifies PTSD-type symptoms, and a second subscale that contains burnout symptoms. This demonstrates that compassion fatigue includes both symptoms reactive to acute stressors and symptoms reactive to chronic stressors. Factors associated with the development of compassion fatigue can be found in chapter 4.

Cohen and colleagues studied social workers in medical centers in Tel Aviv and Haifa following a three-year period of incessant terrorist attacks against buses and public places in Israel. Each of the fifty-three participants in this study had attended on average 4.4 terror incidents in which victims were brought to their hospitals. As a result, 48.2 percent reported symptoms of posttraumatic stress in the high or extremely high range, while 30.2 percent scored in the extremely low range. The majority, 81.1 percent, scored in the extremely low range of burnout scores, and none fell in the high range of burnout (Cohen, Gagin, & Peled-Avram, 2006). Boscarino, Figley, and Adams similarly found that involvement in the aftermath of the 9/11 terror attacks was associated with high levels of traumatic stress symptoms on the Compassion Fatigue Questionnaire, but burnout scores were not significantly associated (Boscarino, Figley, & Adams, 2004). Thus, following significant trauma exposure, posttraumatic stress and burnout are not necessarily linked in social workers.

Vicarious traumatization (VT), a concept proposed by Lisa McCann and Laurie Anne Pearlman, arises from constructivist self-development theory and refers to the manner in which graphic and painful material presented by clients intersects with the therapist's own schemas related to self, other, and the environment (McCann & Pearlman, 1990b). Schemas can be understood to be cognitive structures that reflect beliefs, assumptions, and expectations that have evolved through life experiences. They are attempts by the individual to organize and summarize personal motivations, feelings, and behavior, as well as the motivations, feelings, and behavior of others. Schemas influence how an individual is likely to perceive a situation or interaction with another and how the individual is likely to react (Beck, Emery, & Greenberg, 1985; Muran & Segal, 1992). They allow individuals to enter familiar and novel situations with a theory about how these interactions are likely to unfold. Schemas are relatively stable constructs but are nonetheless responsive to the environment. They can change and be shaped in response to discrepant information.

When an individual encounters a traumatic event, sensory images are stored in active memory and repeatedly experienced (intrusion symptoms) leading to emotional arousal (arousal symptoms). To manage the repeated experiencing of adverse stimuli, traumatic events must be integrated into existing schema. Alternatively they may be avoided, denied, or dealt with through emotional numbing (Horowitz, 1991). McCann, Sakheim, and Abrahamson suggest that upon encountering traumatic situations, an individual attempts to cope with arousal in one of three ways: (1) by failing to be sensitive to the discrepant input; (2) by interpreting the meaning of input in a manner that is consistent with existing schemas; or (3) by altering existing schemas (McCann, Sakheim, & Abrahamson, 1988). In the discussion above regarding social workers experiencing violence on the job, each of these processes is evident. Social workers may minimize the violence; they may interpret the violence as their own fault or explain it as a client's legitimate response to frustration; or they may begin to generally distrust clients and view them negatively.

In their groundbreaking book *Psychological Trauma and the Adult Survivor,* McCann and Pearlman suggested that trauma disrupts schemas in five fundamental areas: safety, trust, self-esteem, power, and intimacy (McCann & Pearlman, 1990a). Safety and trust arise from the ability to develop and sustain mutually supportive relationships with others. Self-efficacy or self-esteem arises from previous experiences with coping and the resultant expectation that one can overcome adversity. Power refers to two elements: an individual's ability to accept that some things that are truly out of one's control, such as a traumatic injury; and a sense of power to control the negative effects and outcome of the traumatic experience. With respect to intimacy, McCann and Pearlman suggest that the traumatic loss of loved ones can result in the shattering of intimate bonds "resulting in an intense fear that allowing themselves to love again will only result in suffering" (p. 77). These schemas may enhance functioning when individuals encounter new traumatic experiences or alternatively schemas may undermine resilience. For instance, positive beliefs regarding safety and trust may result in the ability to

TABLE 2.4

Self-schema and trauma recovery

Element of Self-Schema	Factors that Enhance Resilience	Factors that Undermine Resilience
Safety, Trust	Ability to develop and sustain supportive relationships	Fear of others Lack of critical judgement of others
Esteem, Self-efficacy	Confidence in personal coping based on previous coping	Insufficient opportunities to learn coping skills Previous experiences of poor coping
Power, Control	Acceptance that some events can occur outside one's control Belief in ability to control outcome of current situation	Unrealistic belief in ability to control all outcome View of self as powerless victim

(C. Regehr, 1996)

establish a strong, supportive network that can assist in times of distress. Alternatively, negative beliefs regarding others may be reinforced and intensified, leaving the individual to feel more alone and distressed. Elements of self-schema that may enhance or undermine recovery from trauma can be found in table 2.4.

EXPOSURE TO CHRONIC STRESS

While chronic stress can be found in most areas of social work practice, child welfare provides a good example of a stressful field of practice characterized by excessive work demands caused by unwieldy caseloads, court appearances, and overwhelming paperwork; poor working conditions; negative public perceptions; and low salary (Bradley & Sutherland, 1990; Collings & Murray, 1996; Gutterman & Jayaratne, 1994; Vinokur-Kaplan,

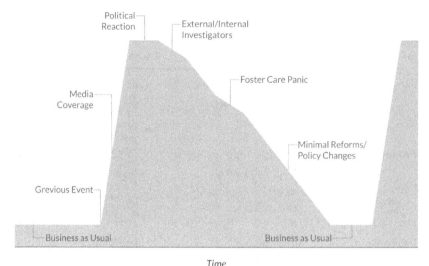

FIGURE 2.2 The vicious cycle of media and public response
Source: Chenot, 2011.

1991). Added to these administrative challenges are the difficulties associated with productively engaging involuntary clients and the awesome responsibility of protecting society's most vulnerable citizens (Munro, 1996; Lindsey & Regehr, 1993). Finally, child welfare practice is fraught with social and political pressures, including the conflicting pressures of the best interest of the child, concern for the parents, and shifting public policies (Gutterman & Jayaratne, 1994). Child welfare workers are charged with protecting children from abuse while maintaining the family as the bastion of liberty (Munro, 1996).

Public and media attention on child deaths due to neglect or maltreatment have been added to the list of stressors associated with child welfare. In both Europe and North America, much of this attention has been focused on the perceived failure of child welfare services to protect vulnerable children (Munroe, 1996; Sanders, Colton & Roberts, 1999). Chenot (2011) describes a "vicious cycle" (figure 2.2) in which media attention, public outrage, and political response result in changes to the decision-making process exemplified by a "foster care panic" in which more children are placed into care. Over time, as the media reports decrease and politicians move on to other vote-generating causes, the cycle reverts to business as usual.

In Ontario, Canada, several coroner's inquests were conducted within one year to survey the deaths of children who were known to children's aid societies. In addition to focusing considerable media and public attention on the issue of child maltreatment and murder, these inquests placed a greater burden on child welfare staff and management. More than four hundred recommendations emanated from the inquests, a subsequent Child Mortality Task Force Review, and an Accountability Review by the responsible ministry, resulting in an overhaul of the child welfare system in Ontario. Changes implemented included the introduction of a standardized risk assessment system, a new child welfare information system, a new funding formula, increased training, and accountability initiatives to increase service standardization. The impact of these changes was investigated in the study of 175 child welfare workers that colleagues and I conducted. The top-ranked stressors that participants identified included work quantity, documentation requirements, organizational change, and working with difficult or disruptive clients (table 2.5). New technology aimed at reducing workloads had actually added work time. Participants identified getting the same information by multiple means, such as e-mail, courier, and telephone, causing duplication of work as they sorted through priorities. As one participant stated, "It all impacts on the front line. It means that people don't have as much time to have direct contact with people. We are finding we are getting less and less clinical time and more and more reporting time" (C. Regehr et al., 2002b, p. 896).

Social work professionals also experience the day-to-day stresses of all those who have families. One respondent identified the apparent contradiction between leaving one's own sick children at home while attending to the needs of child clients. This person indicated that in the end, no decision—staying home or going to work—was guilt free (C. Regehr et al., 2002b).

BURNOUT

The term *job burnout* refers to a psychological syndrome that occurs in response to chronic stressors encountered in the workplace. The term

TABLE 2.5

Ongoing stressors in child welfare

Type of Stressor	Percentage Reporting
Amount of work	75.0
Documentation requirements	59.9
Difficult or disruptive clients	55.2
Organizational change	50.6
Conflicts with staff, supervisors, managers	39.5
Changing policies / standards	36.6
Risk of civil or legal liability	33.7
Court-related activities	33.1
Public or media scrutiny	32.2
Lack of community resources	31.6
Mandatory training	26.9
Travel	18.0
Conflict with community individuals	14.6

(C. Regehr et al., 2005)

itself evokes imagery of the smoldering embers of idealism and passion, replaced by fatigue. First proposed in 1976 by Christina Maslach in her paper "Burned-Out" (Maslach, 1976), job burnout is now one of the most frequently studied concepts in organizational and employment research in all occupations (Swider & Zimmerman, 2010), with hundreds of articles addressing burnout in social work. Maslach originally described burnout in human services as "the loss of concern for the people with whom one is working" (Maslach, 1976, p. 113). Encompassing a loss of sympathy or respect for clients arising from emotional exhaustion, job burnout results in a dehumanizing process whereby clients are blamed for their problems and victimization. Burned out workers become less flexible in their decision-making and interventions, and they blame organizational constraints to avoid the mental stress caused by making difficult or unpopular decisions (Maslach, 1976). The worker's inability to cope with chronic stress then results in low morale, impaired performance, absenteeism, and turnover (Maslach, 1978).

Although the concept of burnout has developed and evolved, three core elements have remained: emotional exhaustion, depersonalization, and personal accomplishment (Maslach & Jackson, 1981). In summarizing twenty-five years of research on burnout in 2001, Maslach and colleagues noted that the emotional exhaustion component has received the most research attention as it captures the stress dimension. As individuals attempt to cope with the experience of exhaustion, they begin to distance themselves emotionally and cognitively from their work and their clients. In doing so, workers "actively ignore the qualities that make [clients] unique and engaging individuals" (Maslach, Schaufeli, & Leiter, 2001, p. 403). This results in cynicism and negativity and ultimately poor quality service. Finally, the chronic and overwhelming demands undermine the individual's sense of effectiveness and accomplishment. In addition to the impacts of burnout on personal well-being, research evidence suggests that burnout is associated with employee disengagement in the organization, detachment from the work and clients, and lower levels of commitment to remain in the current place of employment (Dewa, Loong, Bonato, Thanh, & Jacobs, 2014; Jayaratne & Chess, 1984; Lizano & Barak, 2015; Travis, Lizano, & Barak, 2015).

Burnout has been identified in many human service professions. For instance, researchers report that as a result of regular exposure to stressors, physicians and medical students experience high rates of burnout and anxiety (Dyrbye et al., 2006; Quill & Williamson, 1990; Rutledge et al., 2009; N. Thomas, 2004; Zuardi, Ishara, & Bandeira, 2011). Overall, an estimated 25 percent to 60 percent of physicians suffer from burnout (Chambers & Belcher, 1994; Goehring, Gallacchi, Kunzi, & Bovier, 2005; Panagopoulou, Montgomery, & Benos, 2006; Renzi, Tabolli, Ianni, Di Pietro, & Puddu, 2005). Studies of nurses suggest rates of burnout ranging from 10 percent in surgical nurses (Ribeiro et al., 2014) to 86 percent in nurses in a tertiary case trauma facility (Mealer, Burnham, Goode, Rothbaum, & Moss, 2009), with an average across studies of 26 percent (Adriaenssens, De Gucht, & Maes, 2015). In other research comparing high-demand occupations, paramedics have the highest reported mean burnout score for any group of health professionals (Grigsby & McKnew, 1988).

However, a comparative analysis conducted by Johnson and colleagues revealed some stunning results. In comparing stress and satisfaction of over twenty-five thousand individuals in twenty-six occupations in England, "social services providing care" (social workers) scored first in terms of poor psychological well-being, third (after paramedics and teachers) in terms of poor physical health, and fifth in terms of poor job satisfaction (S. Johnson et al., 2005). A partial reporting of their results can be found in table 2.6, where a high rank indicates higher levels of distress. Johnson and colleagues attribute these troubling scores to the impact of emotional labor (discussed in chapter 3) arising from direct contact with distressed individuals.

Several studies have been conducted on burnout in social workers. An early study comparing social workers in family service, community mental health, and child welfare revealed high levels of job satisfaction and no significant differences in job satisfaction or emotional exhaustion

TABLE 2.6

Ranking professions for stress and burnout

Rank	Physical Health	Psychological Well-Being	Job Satisfaction
1	Ambulance	Social services providing care	Prison officer
2	Teachers	Teachers	Ambulance
3	Social services providing care	Fire brigade	Police
4	Customer services call centre	Ambulance	Customer services call centre
5	Bar staff	Vets	Social services providing care

(Johnson et al., 2005)

scores between the different groups of social workers (Jayaratne & Chess, 1984). A study of child welfare workers in Colorado revealed that only 7.7 percent were at high risk of burnout, while 48 percent were at high or very high risk of compassion fatigue (Conrad & Kellar-Guenther, 2006). In general, high levels of burnout have been found in mental health workers (Lasalvia et al., 2009; Pedrini et al., 2009). Among mental health workers, those working with clients with severe and persistent mental illness have been found to report higher levels of burnout and emotional exhaustion (G. M. Acker & Lawrence, 2009; Nelson, Johnson, & Bebbington, 2009).

Some studies suggest that rates of burnout appear to be similar among professions offering mental health and counseling services. Ben-Zur and Michael, for instance, found no significant differences in emotional exhaustion and accomplishment elements of burnout between social workers, psychologists, and nurses in Israel. In this study, high challenge and control in the job were related to lower levels of burnout (Ben-Zur & Michael, 2007). On the other hand, Evans and colleagues found that among mental health social workers in England and Wales, 47 percent indicated significant psychological distress on the General Health Questionnaire (GHQ-12). In this study, mental health social workers had higher mean emotional exhaustion and depersonalization scores than other mental health professionals, but they also had higher job satisfaction. Nevertheless, only 8 percent met the cut-off score for burnout (S. Evans et al., 2006), suggesting that burnout, while higher in social workers, was not high enough to be of concern. A study of gerontology social workers in the United States is an outlier in that approximately one-third of respondents reported low burnout, one-third moderate burnout, and one-third high burnout (Poulin & Walter, 1993).

Factors associated with burnout include job demands (Lizano & Barak, 2015; McFadden, Campbell, & Taylor, 2015), empathy (Vévodová, Vévoda, Vetešníková, Kisvetrová, & Chrastina, 2016), and work-family conflict, particularly in terms of time demands (Greenhaus & Beutell, 1985). Several authors have also examined the manner in which social location and experiences of discrimination may affect burnout. Salyers and Bond reported lower levels of burnout in African American social workers than in Caucasian social workers. However, small sample sizes ($N = 30$, $N = 37$) require caution (Salyers & Bond, 2001). Lent and Schwartz did not find differences in burnout with respect to race and gender in a sample of 304 professional counselors (Lent & Schwartz, 2012). However, this study found that racial incongruence—that is, a difference between the race of the counselor and that of the client population—was associated with greater burnout. They suggest that this may be related to the fact that racially congruent clients are more likely to keep appointments and less likely to use emergency mental health services, leading to better outcomes for both the client and the social worker. A meta-analysis of 183 studies conducted by Purvanova and Muros challenged commonly held beliefs that women were more susceptible to burnout. While women were slightly more emotionally exhausted, men reported higher levels of depersonalization, although in all cases effect sizes were small (Purvanova & Muros, 2010). In exploring differences in burnout between heterosexual and sexual minority workers, sexual minority men have been found to report higher levels of exhaustion, stress, and not feeling effective (Viehl & Dispenza, 2015). These findings reinforce a view that contributors to burnout are complex and that intersecting stressors must be considered.

ALLOSTATIC LOAD

To this point I have primarily discussed the psychological and emotional impact of managing stressful work environments. Allostatic load is a model for understanding the physiological impact of adapting to environmental stressors that builds on Cannon's 1932 theory of homeostasis (Ganzel & Morris, 2011). Homeostasis can be understood as a process by which the body restores physiological conditions to a state of balance or equilibrium once it has been disrupted by stress. However, as McEwen and Stellar add, return to homeostasis "does not adequately describe real life" (1993, p. 2094). Instead, mechanisms such as heart rate, endocrine output, and neural activity change in response to environmental challenges—ultimately resulting in a new steady state. They refer to this new state of normal as *allostasis* (McEwen & Stellar, 1993).

McEwen and Stellar suggest that while allostasis is a useful concept, it does not take into account the long-term effects of wear and tear caused by prolonged physiological stress response. That is, continued elevation of heart rate, endocrine response systems, and neural activity can ultimately predispose the individual to disease. Thus, they proposed a new

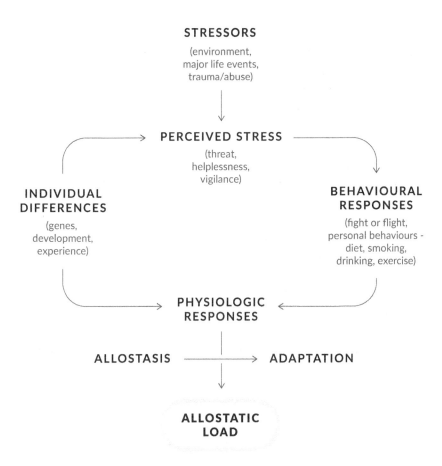

FIGURE 2.3 Allostatic load
Source: McEwen, 1998, p. 172.

term—*allostatic load*—to describe the effects of cumulative stress that eventually lead to compromised immune systems. McEwen and Steller also note that allostatic load is influenced not only by the environment, but also by the individual's psychological response and behavioral coping (for instance, use of alcohol). This concept is reflected in the study by Johnson and colleagues on stresses in various occupations in which physical health, psychological well-being, and job satisfaction were highly correlated (S. Johnson et al., 2005). It is also affected by an individual's preexisting biological makeup, including neurochemistry and the endocrine system (figure 2.3).

The amygdala, anterior cingulate cortex, hippocampus, and basal ganglia are identified as core emotional regions of the brain that are involved in allostatic accommodation (Ganzel & Morris, 2011). The amygdala is responsible for processing environmental stimuli; when it detects a stressor, it sends a signal to the hypothalamus, which in turn activates the sympathetic nervous system (SNS). The SNS then triggers the adrenal glands to release epinephrine into the blood stream. Subsequently heart rate, blood pressure, and respiration rate are increased, and blood sugar increases to provide energy. This allows the individual to adapt to the environment. If the stress abates and the individual can recover, the stress response will not contribute to allostatic load (von Thiele, Lindfors, & Lundberg, 2006). However, if the threat remains, the hypothalamus will trigger the hypothalamic-pituitary-adrenal (HPA) axis as a second line of defense. In this case, cortisol is released to maintain the fight-or-flight response. When chronic or repeated stress is encountered, physiological changes associated with allostatic load become engrained, and this level becomes the new homeostatis (i.e., allostasis) (Ganzel & Morris, 2011). Repeated stress negatively impacts neural functioning, particularly in relation to the hippocampus, which has high concentrations of cortisol receptors. As the hippocampus participates in verbal memory, impairment decreases the reliability and accuracy of contextual memories (Juster, McEwen, & Lupien, 2010; McEwen, 1998). Factors associated with high allostatic load include a low sense of control, high job demands, type A personality, increased age, career instability, and reward-effort imbalance (Juster et al., 2010).

RESILIENCE AND POSTTRAUMATIC GROWTH

Traumatic experiences and exposure to chronic stress can clearly have negative impacts on individuals in terms of psychological functioning, emotional health, social relations, and physical health. This book will explore how these exposures may influence decision-making in social workers. However, it is important not to depict social workers as victims. Focusing solely on the stressors and negative outcomes undermines the fact that the vast majority of social workers are high-functioning individuals who contribute to society, take pride in their work, and care about their clients.

Resilience is the ability to bounce back or cope successfully despite significant adversity (Rutter, 1985). Conceptual work and research on the concept originally began with observations of children, more than half of whom, despite "the most severe stressors and most glaring of adversities," appeared to be "invulnerable" to significant reactions (Rutter, 1985, p. 598). A variety of personality factors have been associated with resilience, including a sense of personal worthiness, a sense of control over one's fate, positive social orientation, social intelligence, and trust and hope for the future (Earvolino-Ramirez, 2007; Grant & Kinman, 2012). Resilient individuals are described as optimistic, zestful, energetic, and open to new experiences (Collins, 2007). Other related concepts include *hardiness*, or the ability to endure adversity (Earvolino-Ramirez, 2007), and more recently *grit*, defined as perseverance to achieve long-term goals and to maintain effort and interest despite failure and adversity (Duckworth, Peterson, Matthews, & Kelly, 2007).

Early work implied that resilience was related to early life factors including the attributes of the children themselves, attributes of their families, and characteristics of the social environment. Once established, resilience was thought to be a relatively stable attribute. More recently, however, it has been recognized that "positive adaptation despite exposure to adversity involves a developmental progression, such that new vulnerabilities and/or strengths often emerge with changing life circumstances" (Luthar, Cicchetti, & Becker, 2000, p. 3). This perspective links to the previous discussions in this chapter. That is, while stress and exposure to traumatized individuals can lead to such outcomes as vicarious trauma, burnout, and allostatic load, they also have the potential to build resilience.

In discussing resilience, Collins points to research revealing that despite the stressors, social workers report positive feelings about making a difference through their work with individuals and communities, building rewarding relationships with colleagues, and enjoying the challenge and variety of their job (Collins, 2007). Healthy, supportive work environments and clinical teams can further support and augment resilience and positive emotions, which in turn lead to the enhancement of individual physical, social, psychological, and intellectual resources—indeed, building further resilience. Collins then links these enhanced abilities to effective assessment and decision-making skills.

In a similar vein, others have focused on how life crises and trauma can lead to positive personal change. Caplan's Crisis Theory suggested that an individual facing a life challenge will experience a period of disorganization, followed by one of three outcomes: a return to the previous state of equilibrium; a new lower level of functioning; or a new higher level of functioning having been strengthened by adversity (Caplan, 1964). In 1946, Viktor Frankl described his experiences as a captive in Auschwitz: "In some ways suffering ceases to be suffering at the moment it finds a meaning, such as the meaning of a sacrifice" (Frankl, 1985). Schaefer and Moos suggested that individuals can be positively transformed through their experience of illness, bereavement, natural disasters, war, and combat. Indeed, over 50 percent of individuals who experience life crises report some personal benefit, including enhanced social and personal resources and the development of new coping skills (Schaefer & Moos, 1998). At the same time, Folkman expanded her well-known transactional model of coping to include the possibility of positive psychological outcomes (Folkman, 1997).

Tedeschi, Park, and Calhoun (1998) developed the concept of post-traumatic growth to denote the positive change experienced as a result of encountering life challenges, including bereavement, life-threatening illness, catastrophic injury, environmental disaster, and exposure to war trauma (Joseph & Linley, 2005). In the face of loss and confusion, some people are able to build new psychological constructs that prepare them to cope with future trauma, thereby developing new strength (Tedeschi, Park, & Calhoun, 1998). Posttraumatic growth is understood to have three elements: improved relationships that occur as a result of enhanced compassion and altruism; an improved sense of self that includes an acceptance of one's own vulnerabilities and limitations; and a new philosophy regarding the meaning of life and personal priorities (Ben-porat, 2015; Joseph & Linley, 2005). This growth can emerge from metacognition, or reflection on one's processing of the events. As noted earlier, traumatic events conflict with preexisting schemas regarding safety, one's power to control events, and one's sense of self. This dissonance results in intrusive and ruminative thoughts and imagery and emotional distress, which some individuals are able to use to create meaning and positive change. While individual differences are the best predictor of posttraumatic growth, gender differences have been noted, with women reporting higher levels of growth than men (Helgeson, Reynolds, &

Tomich, 2006; Linley & Joseph, 2004). In addition, members of racialized groups are more likely to report posttraumatic growth than members of majority populations (Helgeson et al., 2006).

Susan Cadell's doctoral research focused on posttraumatic growth in 174 individuals who cared for loved ones who died of AIDS. Factors considered in the analysis were levels of posttraumatic and depression symptoms, social supports, spirituality, and posttraumatic growth. As expected, spirituality and social support were both predictors of posttraumatic growth. Contrary to expectations, however, those with higher levels of posttraumatic stress and depression symptoms also reported higher levels of posttraumatic growth (Cadell, Regehr, & Hemsworth, 2003). Thus, the experience of challenge, hardship and even sorrow can be viewed by individuals as having positive outcomes related to personal development. It is important to note that growth and suffering are not necessarily mutually exclusive and that indeed individuals may continue to experience distress as well as growth (Tedeschi & Calhoun, 2004).

Like vicarious traumatization, vicarious posttraumatic growth (VPTG) has been identified in therapists. In a qualitative study of therapists, clinicians reported positive trait-oriented changes in themselves, such as increased sensitivity, compassion, and insight. Other benefits included increased appreciation for the resilience of the human spirit and

Posttraumatic Growth

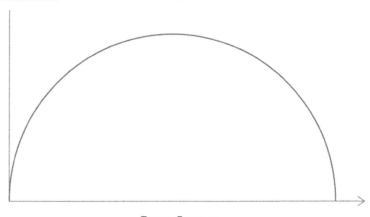

Trauma Exposure

FIGURE 2.4 Curvilinear relationship between exposure and outcome
Source: Author's own data.

increased sense of the precious nature of life (Arnold, Calhoun, Tedeschi, & Cann, 2005). A quantitative study of domestic violence therapists and social service department therapists in Israel revealed posttraumatic growth in both groups of therapists. However, there was a curvilinear relationship between VPTG and trauma exposure (Ben-porat, 2015). That is, those with low exposure and those with very high levels of exposure reported lower levels of growth. This is as predicted by stress theories. Thus, some stress or adversity is necessary to maximize performance, while excessive stress or adversity diminishes performance (figure 2.4).

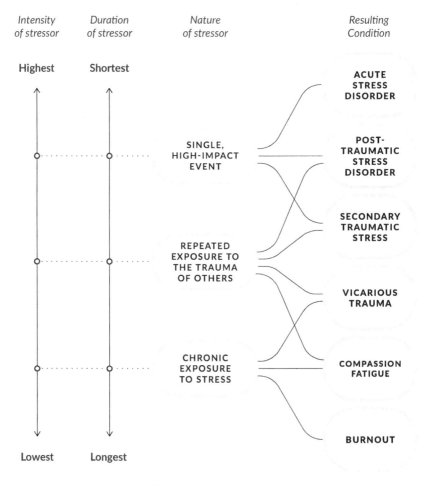

FIGURE 2.5 A continuum of responses to acute stress and trauma exposure
Source: Author's own data.

However, in the Ben-porate study social workers with more varied case-loads (in general social service practice) reported higher levels of growth than domestic violence workers who repeatedly and exclusively were exposed to accounts of intimate partner violence (Ben-porat, 2015). Thus, both degree and nature of exposure are important.

A CONTINUUM OF RESPONSES TO STRESS AND TRAUMA EXPOSURE

Social workers are regularly exposed to stressful and potentially traumatizing experiences. Psychological and physical reactions to these exposures can include a number of syndromes that vary according to the nature and source of stressful exposure and the nature, duration, and severity of symptoms (figure 2.5).

In chapter 3 I focus more directly on factors that contribute to the development of reactions to traumatic events, and in chapter 4 I focus on factors that contribute to the development of chronic stress reactions. This then sets the stage for understanding the impact that these experiences may have on the professional decision-making of social workers affected by stress and trauma response.

Factors Contributing to Trauma Response

The previous chapter considered the nature of stress and trauma reactions in social workers and others in high-stress occupations. Specifically, the focus was on two different but intersecting experiences: traumatic responses related to specific high-impact incidents, and chronic stress, allostatic load, and burnout related to ongoing stressors. Varied factors contribute to the development of each of these experiences. This chapter considers the many factors that contribute to the development of acute stress and posttraumatic stress reactions. As noted in the previous chapter, three other concepts have been proposed to explain the nature of trauma experienced by those who assist directly traumatized individuals: secondary traumatic stress, vicarious trauma, and compassion fatigue. Given that the most recent definitions of acute stress disorder (ASD) and posttraumatic stress disorder (PTSD) include reactions to exposure to trauma encountered by others, I will use the terms *acute stress* and *posttraumatic stress* in this chapter to also encompass secondary trauma, vicarious trauma, and compassion fatigue.

Traumatic stress reactions are by definition reactive to an event or series of events that are outside the normal experience. Indeed, the first criterion of *DSM5* (American Psychological Association, 2013) for posttraumatic stress disorder and acute stress disorder specifies that the person must have been exposed to actual or threatened death, serious injury, or sexual violence either directly, as a witness, or in the case of those in the helping professions, through repeated or extreme exposure to adverse details of the traumatic event. Often it is considered implicit in this definition that the intensity of the response covaries with the intensity of the exposure. Indeed, a body of literature supports the notion that in cases of extreme exposure there is a dose-effect relationship (Mollica, McInnes, Poole, & Tor, 1998). For instance, Cambodian refugees who escaped the genocide in their country in the late 1970s were found to have levels of traumatic stress proportional to their exposure to horrifying events (Mollica, Brooks, Tor, Lopes-Cardozo, & Silove, 2014). A systematic review and meta-analysis of studies of people in countries experiencing mass conflict and large numbers of displaced persons confirms the association between torture, exposure to other horrifying events, and levels of traumatic stress symptoms (Steel et al., 2009). Similarly, emergency responders (Bryant & Harvey, 1996) and war veterans (Orcutt, King, & King, 2003) who experienced higher levels of exposure also reported higher rates of PTSD, as did motor vehicle accident victims with greater numbers of injuries (Blanchard et al., 1995).

Nevertheless, when we move beyond extreme and prolonged trauma exposure, there is considerable evidence that individual response to distressing events is highly varied (C. Regehr & Glancy, 2014). Several studies have demonstrated that rates of trauma exposure over the life course is between 60 and 80 percent, but nevertheless, rates of PTSD are only 5 to 8 percent (Bonnano, Galea, Bucciarelli, & Vlahov, 2007; Kessler et al., 2005; Koenen, 2006; Ozer & Weiss, 2004). For instance, a nationally representative study of almost three thousand Canadians revealed that 75.9 percent reported lifetime exposure to one or more traumatic event, such as sexual assault or a life-threatening motor vehicle accident, but the lifetime prevalence rate for posttraumatic stress was only 9.2 percent (5.3 percent in men and 12.8 percent in women) and the current (point) prevalence rate was 2.4 percent (Van Ameringen, Mancini, Patterson, & Boyle, 2008). Populations who have been exposed to particular traumatizing events provide another viewpoint on the development of posttraumatic stress. For instance, 9.4 percent of Israelis who had been directly exposed to a terrorist attack (Bleich, Gelkopf, & Solomon, 2003) and 18 percent of Latinos in the United States who had experienced political violence in their homeland (Eisenman, Gelberg, Liu, & Shapiro, 2003) met the criteria for PTSD. Most interesting perhaps is a recent meta-analysis that compared PTSD prevalence in twenty-four countries, taking into account vulnerability factors in those countries based on the World Risk Report. This included such factors as health care, literacy, and political corruption (Dückers, Alisic, & Brewin, 2016). Perhaps paradoxically, this study reports that among those individuals exposed to trauma, rates of PTSD are highest in countries with the lowest levels of vulnerability. That is, individuals in countries with more resources and better health care have higher chances of developing PTSD (Dückers et al., 2016). On the basis of these types of findings, Shalev earlier suggested that "the term *traumatic events* should be replaced by *potentially traumatic events*" (2002, p. 533).

While some extreme situations, such as torture, are likely to lead to PTSD, there is no simple cause-effect or dose-effect relationship between posttraumatic stress reactions and exposure to potentially traumatizing events. Therefore, our model for understanding posttraumatic stress reactions related to workplace exposures needs to be more nuanced. Graham Glancy and I presented such a model in our book *Mental Health Social Work Practice in Canada* (C. Regehr & Glancy, 2014). This model considers the follow to contribute jointly to trauma response: event factors; social and environmental factors; and individual factors, including individual experiences and models of coping, peritraumatic reactions, and genetics (figure 3.1). In this chapter, I explore these concepts in more detail and provide research evidence regarding factors associated with posttraumatic reactions in the workplace.

INDIVIDUAL AND SOCIAL SUPPORT FACTORS

As discussed in chapter 2, *DSM-5* defines two types of reactions to traumatizing events: acute stress and posttraumatic stress. *Acute stress disorder* refers to the development of characteristic symptoms lasting from three days to one month following traumatic exposure. *Posttraumatic disorder* refers to the situation in which these symptoms persist for more than one month. This differentiation recognizes the repeated research finding that certain horrifying events will result in traumatic stress symptoms in the majority of individuals encountering the event, but that these symptoms remit within a reasonably short period of

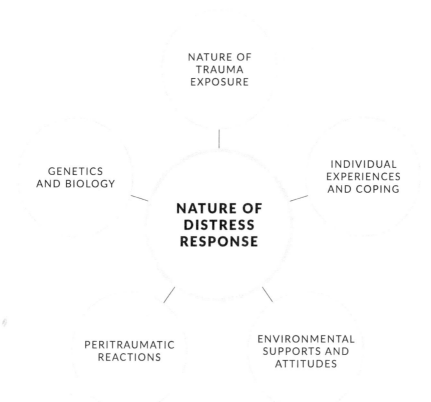

NATURE OF
TRAUMA
EXPOSURE

GENETICS
AND BIOLOGY

INDIVIDUAL
EXPERIENCES
AND COPING

**NATURE OF
DISTRESS
RESPONSE**

PERITRAUMATIC
REACTIONS

ENVIRONMENTAL
SUPPORTS AND
ATTITUDES

FIGURE 3.1 Model for understanding traumatic stress reactions
Source: Modified from C. Regehr & Glancy, 2014.

time. For instance, Rothbaum and colleagues demonstrated that while 94 percent of a sample of rape or attempted rape victims had symptoms consistent with PTSD in the first week following their assault, these diminished to 41 percent by week 9 (figures 3.2 and 3.3) and diminished sharply for all women in the first four weeks. Women who met the criteria for PTSD at three months post-assault showed no improvement after week 4. Women who did not meet the criteria at week 12 showed continuous improvement over time (Rothbaum, Foa, Riggs, Murdock, & Walsh, 1992).

Atkeson and colleagues used a similar methodology in assessing depression among women who were raped (figure 3.4). They similarly

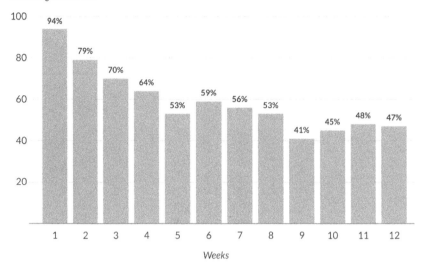

FIGURE 3.2 Percentage of victims with PTSD by week post-assault

Source: Rothbaum, Foa, Riggs, Murdock, & Walsh, 1992, p. 463.

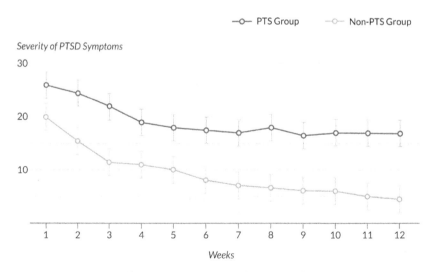

FIGURE 3.3 Severity of symptoms in victims who met the threshold of PTSD at one week post-assault and those who did not

Source: Rothbaum, Foa, Riggs, Murdock, & Walsh, 1992, p. 464.

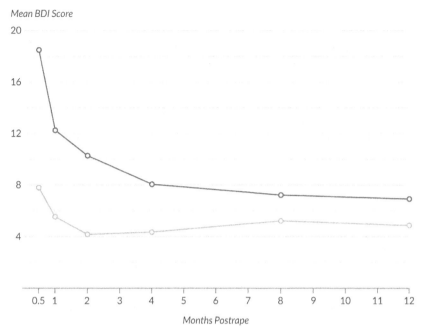

FIGURE 3.4 Mean scores on the Beck Depression Inventory for victims and controls at each assessment period

Source: Atkeson, Calhoun, Resick, & Ellis, 1982, p. 98.

found that initially, women who had been raped experienced significantly higher rates of depression than a control group of women, but at four months, rates of depression between the two groups were equivalent (Atkeson, Calhoun, Resick, & Ellis, 1982). More recently, a prospective longitudinal study of adolescents and young adults in Germany followed the course of PTSD in 125 individuals from baseline to thirty-four and fifty months. In 52 percent of the cases, PTSD remitted during the follow-up period, while 48 percent showed no remission. Those who did not remit were more likely to have avoidant symptoms and to report more help-seeking behaviors (Perkonigg et al., 2005).

These findings are consistent with a much earlier suggestion that while vulnerabilities and resilience capacity do not predict the occurrence of acute distress following exposure to a traumatic event, they are important in inhibiting its resolution or amelioration of symptoms

(Kardiner, 1941). Thus, while the severity of the stressor (or dosage) may be the primary determinant of acute trauma symptoms, individual factors such as prior life experiences, preexisting personality traits, the neurobiology of an individual's stress response, ability to tolerate fear, and capacity for self-modulation are presumed to be primary contributors to the development of chronic trauma symptomatology (McFarlane & Yehuda, 1996). Indeed, in two meta-analyses of predictors of PTSD, the strongest predictors were thought suppression (or avoidance symptoms), poor family functioning/low social support/social withdrawal, perceived life threat at the time of the event, and peritraumatic reactions. Each of these predictors had a larger effect than the trauma severity (Ozer, Best, Lipsey, & Weiss, 2003; Trickey, Siddaway, Meiser-Stedman, Serpell, & Field, 2012).

Let me begin the discussion of specific individual differences with a short discussion of the influence of biology. Yehuda and colleagues note that "for at least two decades after the diagnosis of PTSD was established in 1980, it would have been unheard of to propose that genes might be involved in the etiology or pathogenesis of this condition" (Yehuda, Koenen, Galea, & Flory, 2011, p. 67). Rather, the concept of PTSD was founded on the notion of *normal and expected* reactions to horrifying events. Nevertheless, the repeated observation that PTSD is not an inevitable outcome of traumatic exposure, combined with biological findings that were inconsistent with the theory, has led to the suggestion that PTSD might in fact be a failure to recover from exposure to potentially traumatizing events (Yehuda et al., 2011).

Twin studies have provided evidence for the contribution of genetic factors. Typically, these studies compare the incidence of certain events in monozygotic twins exposed to traumatic events versus dizygotic twins who have been similarly exposed. One of the sources of data for such studies is the Vietnam Era Twin (VET) Registry, which contains 4,774 sets of twins, 53.4 percent of whom are monozygotic. In an analysis of this database, True and colleagues determined that after adjusting for differences in combat exposure, genetic factors accounted for 13 to 30 percent of the variance in reexperiencing symptoms of PTSD, 30 to 34 percent of avoidance symptoms, and 28 to 32 percent of arousal symptoms. They found no evidence that a shared family environment contributed to the development of PTSD symptoms (True et al., 1993). Stein and colleagues recruited 406 twin pairs in the Vancouver, BC, area, 222 of whom were monozygotic (Stein, Jang, Taylor, Vernon, & Livesley, 2002). These researchers differentiated between trauma purposely inflicted by another person, which they termed *assaultive trauma* (hostage-taking and sexual assault) and *nonassaultive trauma* (such as motor vehicle accidents, fire, and natural disasters). Their research demonstrated that the development of PTSD symptoms after assaultive trauma was determined by a combination of genetic and environmental factors. On the contrary, symptoms following nonassaultive trauma were determined by environment alone. In a review of twin studies related to PTSD, Afifi and colleagues concluded that PTSD symptoms are moderately heritable (Afifi, Asmundson, Taylor, & Jang, 2010). Yet, while genetic predisposition appears to be a compelling factor, in reviewing evidence related to genetic expression and PTSD susceptibility Yehuda and colleagues concluded that the interaction between genetic factors and the environment in predicting PTSD symptom persistence is further moderated by the individual's personality (Yehuda et al., 2011).

Another avenue of biological research related to trauma has been the examination of the influence of peritraumatic distress, which refers to the panic-like state experienced during or immediately after a traumatic event that arises from adrenergic activation. Peritraumatic stress involves physiological symptoms such as trembling, sweating, and rapid heart rate or tachycardia (Vaiva et al., 2003). Meta-analytic studies demonstrate that levels of physical symptoms during a traumatic exposure and immediately after the exposure are associated with the development of symptoms of posttraumatic stress (E. Thomas, Saumier, & Brunet, 2012). For instance, those individuals that have *lower* cortisol levels following a traumatic event are more likely to experience PTSD weeks or months later (Yehuda, McFarlane, & Shalev, 1998). At first glance this finding may appear paradoxical. However, the answer likely lies in the fact that chronic stress exposure dampens general cortisol responsiveness, and thus those with lower cortisol response following a traumatic event are more likely to have had previous traumatic or high-stress exposures prior to the current event. For instance, with respect to cortisol levels obtained from recently sexually assaulted women presenting in an emergency room, those with previous sexual assault histories were found to have lower cortisol response than others who had not experienced previous sexual assault trauma. These women were subsequently three times more likely to develop PTSD (Yehuda et al., 1998).

By contrast, individuals with *higher* heart rates immediately following trauma exposure are more likely to develop PTSD than those with lower heart rates (Yehuda et al., 1998). Again, this may be related to prior exposure. Indeed, in our study of police recruits, those with previous histories of trauma exposure required more time for their elevated heart rate to return to baseline than those without trauma histories (C. Regehr, LeBlanc, Jelley, & Barath, 2008). Such research led to experimentation with pharmacological interventions and the important discovery that the immediate treatment of peritraumatic distress symptoms can lead to reduced risk of PTSD (Vaiva et al., 2003). For instance, in double-blind placebo trials, emergency department administration of propranolol (a β adrenergic blocker used to treat hypertension) to recently traumatized individuals was found to reduce the future incidence of PTSD and reduce physiological response when these individuals were later exposed to descriptions of their traumatic events. Similarly, administration of propranolol to healthy study participants reduces recall of recently presented emotionally disturbing material when compared to those who receive placebos. Other studies have found that hydrocortisone is also protective against the development of PTSD (Sijbrandij, Kleiboer, Bisson, Barbui, & Cuijpers, 2015).

Recent research has suggested that it is the combination of the psychological appraisal at the time of the event along with the biological response in the acute situation that best predicts the longer-term severity of posttraumatic distress. This psychological appraisal is influenced, among other factors, by previous experience and an individual's sense of control and mastery over the event. If the appraisal determines that risk of severe injury or death is high, the result may be emotional symptoms such as fear, helplessness, and horror (E. Thomas et al., 2012). These emotional reactions in turn influence the release of adrenalin and noradrenalin and hence heightened peritraumatic responses.

Let me now turn to other individual factors that influence traumatic stress reactions. As discussed in the previous chapter, resilience in the face of stressful and traumatic events is multifactorial. Originally studied in the context of children who were viewed to be "invulnerable" to highly abusive and neglectful life situations (Rutter, 1985), resilience, or the ability to bounce back, is now understood to be dynamic interaction between the individual and the environment (Earvolino-Ramirez, 2007). At the individual level, social work students with higher degrees of emotional intelligence, who had higher levels of social competence, and were more reflective were found to have higher levels of resilience (Grant & Kinman, 2012). Optimism and a tendency toward goal-directed problem-solving are other factors found to be associated with resilience in social workers (Collins, 2007). The nature of the social work organizational environment has also been found to support resilience. This includes factors such as workload, organizational climate, social support, and supervision (Bell, Kulkarni, & Dalton, 2003; Carpenter, Webb, & Bostock, 2013; McFadden, Campbell, & Taylor, 2015).

Chapter 2 describes the investigation that colleagues and I conducted into the impact of high-stress work on firefighters (C. Regehr, Hill, & Glancy, 2000) and child welfare workers (C. Regehr, Hemsworth, Leslie, Howe, & Chau, 2004b; C. Regehr, Leslie, Howe, & Chau, 2005). In these studies, we hypothesized that the factors that contribute to levels of post-traumatic distress in workers include: variables that are specific to the individual; factors that are related to the social environment, such as the organization in which the individual works; and factors related to the traumatic event itself. We evaluated the theoretical models using structural equation modeling (SEM), a statistical method that allows researchers to test hypothesized relationships between observed variables. SEM incorporates the benefits of a multiple regression analysis, in that it considers multiple factors that may simultaneously influence a phenomenon, and the benefits of path analysis, which allows for the influence of mediating variables. Further, SEM deals with one of the inherent difficulties of multiple regression analysis: measurement error arising from the multiple intercorrelations (Jaccard & Wan, 1996; K. Johnson, 1999). It is thus highly useful in evaluating relationships between complex and intersecting factors.

The first study was conducted with 164 firefighters from the Metropolitan Fire Brigade (MFB), Melbourne, and the Country Fire Authority (CFA) of Victoria, Australia (C. Regehr, Hemsworth, & Hill, 2001; C. Regehr, Hill, & Glancy, 2000) with a goal of understanding the nature of stress and trauma in the emergency services and factors that mitigate stress reactions. Our SEM analysis included two main predictors that we assumed interacted with one another: (1) relational capacity, or the ability to develop and sustain relationships, and (2) social support.

Social support was included in the model due to the consistent findings in earlier research regarding the relationship between posttraumatic symptoms and depression (C. Regehr, 2009). That is, social support within the organization, particularly from superiors, had been shown to be related to lower levels of distress following traumatic events encountered by rescue workers (Alexander & Wells, 1991; Burke, 1993; Fullerton, McCarroll, Ursano, & Wright, 1992; Weiss, Marmar, Metzler, & Ronfeldt, 1995). Similarly, social support of family and friends is significantly negatively correlated with scores on both trauma symptom scales and depression scales in emergency service personnel (Leffler & Dembert, 1998; C. Regehr, Hill, & Glancy, 2000; Weiss et al., 1995). Paramedics who had higher levels of family support were found to be less likely to take mental health stress leaves from work following a traumatic event (C. Regehr, Goldberg, Glancy, & Knott, 2002).

Relational capacity draws on attachment theory, which is the perspective that early attachment experiences become incorporated into perceptions of self and other and thus subsequently become the filter through which all future relationships are viewed. These mental templates of significant relationship patterns not only determine future interactions but are likely to be self-confirming as well (Hadley, Holloway, & Mallinckrodt, 1993). That is, expectations of other people influence the manner in which individuals interact with those people and who they select to become part of their support network.

According to van der Kolk (1996), secure attachment bonds serve as primary defenses against trauma-induced pathology. Indeed, in children exposed to severe stressors, a secure parental bond is the single most important factor in predicting negative outcomes. When early relationships with caregivers are marked with hostility, victimization, and blaming, relationships in adulthood are influenced by these filters and expectations, thus affecting social supports available following traumatic exposures (van der Kolk, Hostetler, Herron, & Fisler, 1994). In this regard, social support is viewed as a process of cognitive appraisal or a property of the person rather than an actual reflection of the transactions between individuals in a particular situation (Coyne & DeLongis, 1986). That is, individuals with limited relational capacity may possess cognitive structures or schemas that emphasize negative factors and consequently underestimate the amount of support they receive. Further, the nature of individual expectations and relationship skills play a large part in determining both the types of people with whom one will associate and how they will be accepted (Bowlby, 1979). Thus, the ability to garner and use social support is in itself a strength and an effective coping resource.

In testing the theoretical model, three components of relational capacity were included: alienation (the inability to feel close to others); insecurity (or anxious attachment); and social incompetence (the inability to establish relationships with others). Social support included the perceived support obtained from friends, family, and one's significant other. Distress was measured by intrusion and avoidance posttraumatic stress symptoms and by depressive symptoms. The results of our analysis supported the hypothesis that relational capacity is a significant factor in explaining perceptions of social support in firefighters exposed to critical events. Perhaps not surprisingly, those with stronger capacity to form close personal relationships and to relate to others also experienced greater support from others. Subsequently, perceived social support influences levels of depression and posttraumatic symptoms. Thus, while some emotional response to disturbing events may be normal, the severity of symptoms covaries with the ability of the individual to develop and sustain supportive relationships to buffer the impact of events. Individuals who are unable to trust others, are sensitive to rejection, are easily hurt by others, and experience difficulty in making friends are more likely to experience higher levels of distress following a critical event (C. Regehr, Hemsworth, & Hill, 2001). This analysis can be found in figure 3.5.

In a subsequent study, we compared social support in new recruits and experienced firefighters in a large fire and emergency service in the Greater Toronto area (C. Regehr, Hill, & Glancy, 2000). While it was hypothesized that experienced firefighters may have higher levels of social supports to protect themselves from the impact of exposure to critical events, this was not the case. Experienced firefighters reported significantly lower levels of support from family members and their employer and had lower scores on a general social support scale. This was of particular concern considering the fact that social support is often a

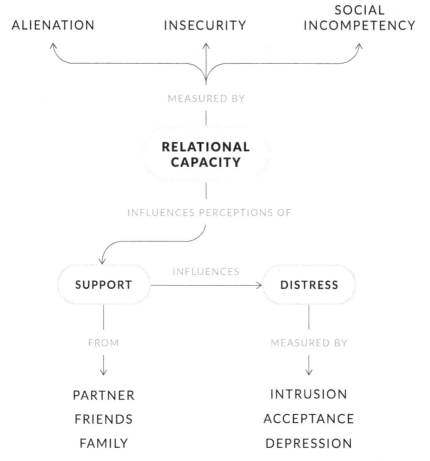

ALIENATION   INSECURITY   SOCIAL INCOMPETENCY

MEASURED BY

RELATIONAL CAPACITY

INFLUENCES PERCEPTIONS OF

INFLUENCES

SUPPORT ⟶ **DISTRESS**

FROM   MEASURED BY

PARTNER   INTRUSION
FRIENDS   ACCEPTANCE
FAMILY   DEPRESSION

FIGURE 3.5 The impact of relational capacity and social support on posttraumatic distress in firefighters

Source: C. Regehr, Hemsworth, & Hill, 2001.

protective factor in managing trauma reactions. Indeed, as might be expected, in this study those with lower levels of social support reported higher levels of traumatic stress symptoms and depression. A regression analysis revealed that social support and length of time on the job were the most important factors in predicting both depression and traumatic stress symptoms.

We surmised that the nature of the job may reduce the ability to sustain social supports. In two qualitative studies, one with spouses of firefighters (C. Regehr, Dimitropoulos, Bright, George, & Henderson, 2005) and one with families of paramedics (C. Regehr, 2005), we examined the impact of emergency service work on family life. One factor challenging family cohesion was shift work, which caused not only physical absence at important family moments but also emotional distance. In the paramedic study one spouse said, "One of the jokes we have is that we're married for 28 years but it only feels like 10 because of time we had apart" (C. Regehr, 2005, p. 103). In addition, once emergency responders return home, they are fatigued from long shifts that require a great deal of physical, emotional, and cognitive energy. Another spouse stated, "I'm very cut-off here. So when [my spouse] comes home, I am dying for company. . . . Can't have it. . . . Too tired" (p. 103). Spouses thus discussed the need to develop independent interests and friends to reduce their sense of dependence and isolation. Another factor that contributed to reduced support from family was the cohesiveness of the firefighting platoon in which team members will often spend leisure time with coworkers rather than family members. One spouse in the firefighter study said, "For him, always the first thing is his guys. They're like his family. His guys" (C. Regehr, Dimitropoulos, et al., 2005, p. 103). Wives of firefighters used terms like "boys club" and described how jokes and language acquired in the fire hall could contribute to shutting women out. In all, work-related stress and trauma exposure affected family life, creating emotional distance—what Ted Bober and I identified as the question, "How do you love a man of steel?" (C. Regehr & Bober, 2005).

EVENT AND ORGANIZATIONAL FACTORS

The second structural equation model analysis we conducted was with child welfare workers employed by the Children's Aid Society of Toronto, which sought to expand the previously tested model to include not only individual factors and social support but also factors related to the nature of the critical event experienced and the nature of the work organization (C. Regehr et al., 2004a). In defining individual characteristics, we drew upon the concept of cognitive schemas as a determinant of individual expectations and beliefs regarding one's own ability to manage crisis situations and about the capacity of others to assist (Horowitz, 1991). As described in chapter 2, McCann and Pearlman (1990a,b), suggested that key elements of self-schema that contribute to trauma are (1) safety and trust, and (2) power and control.

Locus of control is conceptualized as the patterned ways in which an individual perceives the sources of control over unforeseen stressors (Rotter, 1975). Locus of control ranges on a continuum between internal (all my successes and failures are the result of my own abilities and efforts) and external (everything that happens to me is a result of fate). Powerlessness or lack of control had previously been related to burnout in child welfare workers (Guterman & Jayaratne, 1994) and to levels of post-traumatic stress in victims (M. Gibbs, 1989; C. Regehr, Cadell, & Jansen, 1999). That is, individuals who, following a traumatic event, manage to retain a belief that they can control outcomes (even though they could not control the occurrence of the event) have been found to have lower levels of trauma than individuals who believed they were controlled by external forces. The measure of control that we used in this study was the Internal Control Index, a twenty-eight-item instrument designed to measure the general sense of control and autonomy that an individual experiences in life (Duttweiler, 1984). This measure is not specific to a particular event, but rather tries to capture a more general personality trait. Safety and trust were operationalized as relational capacity, or the ability to elicit and sustain supportive relationships with others in the aftermath of crisis.

The second set of predictors in our SEM model related to the organization. Based on previous research on burnout, we hypothesized that organizational factors included both ongoing workload stressors and social supports. Ongoing workload stressors in the jobs of child welfare workers had been found to include unwieldy caseloads, court appearances, overwhelming paperwork, and negative public perceptions (Collings & Murray, 1996; Guterman & Jayaratne, 1994; Vinokur-Kaplan, 1991). We gave the participants in our study a list of potential ongoing stressors in their jobs and asked them to indicate whether each item represented a stressor for them. The highest-ranked ongoing stressor was the quantity of work, which was rated as a stressor by 75 percent of respondents. Other highly endorsed items were documentation requirements (59.9 percent), dealing with difficult or disruptive clients (55.2 percent), and organizational change (50.6 percent). In addition, approximately one-third of participants indicated that job stressors included each of the following issues: conflicts with staff, supervisors, or managers; changing policies and standards; risk of civil or legal liability; court-related activities; public or media scrutiny; and/or lack of community resources. (See table 2.5 in the previous chapter.) In short, workload stressors were a significant concern for the majority of participants.

Previous research on social supports among child welfare workers found high perceived levels of support from coworkers, supervisors, and spouses and that supervisor and spousal support serves as a protective factor against burnout, anxiety, and depression (Davis-Sacks, Jayaratne, & Chess, 1985). Conversely, a study of social workers providing services in the aftermath of 911 did not find an association between social support and burnout, compassion fatigue, or secondary trauma (Adams, Boscarino, & Figley, 2006). A study on perceived social support in a national survey of 480 social workers perhaps sheds some light on these conflicting findings. This study found high levels of perceived social support among participants and that social support from coworkers and supervisors was associated with lower levels of burnout, anxiety, and depression. However, the *use* of social supports was not associated with symptom levels. The authors concluded that it was the *perception* that supports were available that was more important than actually reaching out and taking advantage of the supports available (Jayaratne, Himle, & Chess, 1988). I found a similar result in a study of women who had been sexually assaulted (C. Regehr & Marziali, 1999). In that study, women who reported lower levels of posttraumatic stress symptoms in the aftermath of rape identified support systems that were available to them but frequently did not confide in members of their support network. Thus, the capacity to develop strong social support networks and the knowledge that members of these networks can help in times of strife are more important than the actual use of these supports.

An additional factor is likely at play in the conflicting results regarding the influence of social supports on reducing distress in social workers (Davis-Sacks et al., 1985; Um & Harrison, 1998). My colleagues and I found high levels of personal social support among social workers when compared to other populations that we had studied. We concluded this high level of personal support may dampen the effects of social support found in other populations, in which individuals report a greater range of support from their personal networks. Dagan and colleagues more recently had a similar finding and reached a similar conclusion in a study of social workers in Israel (Dagan, Itzhaky, & Ben-Porat, 2015). That is, by their nature and training, social workers are effective in developing relationships and networks. Nevertheless, in the child welfare SEM study, we hypothesized that support coming from supervisors/managers and from the union may be influential.

Incident-related factors were hypothesized to include the length of time since the event and the number of traumatic events encountered in the past year. As noted earlier, an essential component of *DSM* criteria for posttraumatic stress is the duration of the symptoms (American Psychological Association, 2013). Symptoms lasting less than one month are classified as acute stress disorder, symptoms lasting one to three months are classified as posttraumatic stress disorder, while symptoms of lasting more than three months are viewed as chronic. This suggests that symptoms experienced following a traumatic event are expected to spontaneously remit within the first three months after the incident, and thus the length of time since the event is an important incident-related factor. As I discussed earlier, while there have been conflicting findings regarding the influence of the level of traumatic exposure (or dosage), some support exists for its importance in workplace trauma (Marmar et al., 1999; Mollica et al., 1998; Resnick, Kilpatrick, Best, & Kramer, 1992), and thus we wished to test its importance in this population. To quantify "dosage" in this study, we asked participants to report the number of critical events that they experienced in the previous year. Certainly, this approach is not perfect as it does not measure the magnitude of each event.

Since the early work on crisis theory, it has been assumed that crisis events not only cause distress but also present opportunities for growth and positive change (Caplan, 1964). That is, while posttraumatic stress symptoms are an expected outcome of exposure to traumatic events, increasingly studies of trauma also consider posttraumatic growth, including positive changes in perceptions of self, interpersonal relationships, and life philosophy (Tedeschi, Park, & Calhoun, 1998). As a result, the model examined for child welfare workers considered not only traumatic responses but also positive growth following trauma exposure on the job (C. Regehr et al., 2004a).

The results of our SEM analysis (figure 3.6) demonstrated that individual, incident, and organizational factors combined to predict post-

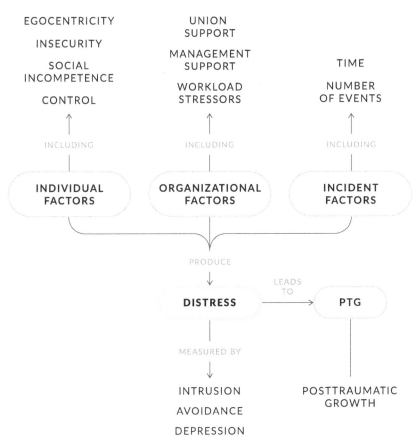

FIGURE 3.6 Predictors of posttraumatic stress in child welfare workers
Source: C. Regehr et al., 2004a.

traumatic distress in child welfare workers (C. Regehr et al., 2004a). Incident factors, including time since the last critical event and number of critical events experienced, did contribute significantly to the model for understanding distress. Those who had more recent and more frequent exposures reported higher levels of distress, lending support to the "dosage" model for understanding traumatic stress reaction. However, these factors were less salient than individual factors and organizational factors.

Individual factors, including relational capacity and sense of control, also contributed significantly to distress in the model. Individuals who were mistrustful of others, were shy and nervous in relation to others, or were sensitive to rejection were more likely to report higher levels of distress. In addition, the more control individuals felt they had over event outcomes, the lower the level of posttraumatic stress and depression symptoms they experienced. This finding was consistent with that of other research, which equated powerlessness and burnout (Guterman & Jayaratne, 1994).

Despite the importance of event and individual factors, organizational factors had the strongest association with distress in this model. These factors included the support of the union and ongoing work stressors. While reported posttraumatic stress symptoms related to a particular traumatic event, the existence of ongoing stressors related to workload, difficult clients, organizational change, and public scrutiny had a profound impact on the individual's experience of traumatic events. Interestingly, as union support increased, so did distress. We hypothesized that as workers felt increasingly distressed about workload issues, they turned to the union for support. Indeed, at the time of this study, a major issue that the union was dealing with was ongoing workload issues. Interestingly, social support from supervisors and managers appeared to be of limited value in relieving symptoms of distress in this study. Some studies have found social supports to be mediators of both burnout and posttraumatic distress in child welfare workers and other occupational groups (Davis-Sacks et al., 1985; Fullerton et al., 1992; Jayaratne & Chess, 1984). Others have suggested that perceived support from managers and supervisors is a poor predictor of stress and burnout in social workers (Collings & Murray, 1996; Um & Harrison, 1998). The findings of this study suggest that this form of organizational support does not significantly reduce the experience of posttraumatic distress.

We concluded that critical events in child welfare are encountered by individuals who are already coping with high levels of challenge and stress. In this context, individuals who consistently face adversity may no longer have the resources to manage and overcome posttraumatic stress reactions when faced with a traumatic event, such as the death of a child or the threat of personal injury. As a consequence, they report higher levels of traumatic stress and depressive symptoms. However, we also found that those individuals who experienced the highest levels of traumatic stress symptoms also reported the highest level of posttraumatic growth. This speaks to the resilience and creative capacity of these workers. This model can be found in figure 3.6.

Subsequently, Ted Bober and I sought to better understand the influence of the nature of trauma exposure and the influence of repeated exposure on posttraumatic stress reactions in counseling professionals. Previous research had suggested that factors that influence symptom level include: the number or percentage of trauma cases on a therapist's caseload (Brady, Guy, Poelstra, & Brokaw, 1999; Kassam-Adams, 1995; Ortlepp & Friedman, 2002; Schauben & Frazier, 1995); the availability of social support (Ortlepp & Friedman, 2002; Schauben & Frazier, 1995); personal history of trauma and abuse (Jenkins & Baird, 2002; Kassam-Adams, 1995; Pearlman & MacIan, 1995; Wall, 2001); and the perception that they had adequate training to assist victims effectively, thereby reducing the sense of hopelessness that may accompany this work (Ortlepp & Friedman, 2002). We conducted a survey with 259 trauma counselors (Bober & Regehr, 2006). Half of those participating in the survey were social workers who worked with traumatized individuals, and the remainder were mental health nurses, psychologists, and physicians. While our multivariate analysis contained a variety of possible factors identified in the literature—such as previous history of personal trauma, training, and supervision—the only significant factor for predicting traumatic stress reactions was the number of hours per week spent counseling traumatized individuals, a finding replicated by others (Dagan et al., 2015). In particular, the degree of exposure to traumatized individuals was associated with higher levels of intrusion symptoms, including nightmares and intrusive imagery. Of the various types of traumatic experiences that clients may have encountered—including workplace trauma, accidents, and being victims of violent crime—therapists working with victims of spousal violence, child abuse, sexual violence, and torture had the highest levels of trauma response.

PUBLIC AND SOCIAL ENVIRONMENTAL FACTORS

When tragic events occur in the course of an individual's professional practice, they not only impact the worker and his or her colleagues, but also have ripple effects that reach across the organization and into the public sphere. In exploring exposure to tragic and life-threatening events in the emergency services and social work, I became focused on the public response to these events and the impact of this response on workers and their organizations. In the case of emergency responders, this response was often initially highly positive as it focused on heroism; but for other workers, more often than not, it was mostly negative. For social workers, particularly those in child welfare, it was consistently negative. Franklin and Parton (2014) offered the following view of media coverage in the United Kingdom: "Social workers, especially those operating in the statutory sector, increasingly have been presented in the media as a metaphor or symbol for the entire public sector, personifying the 'evil' which the political new right presumes to be inherent therein" (p. 9). Ayre (2001) contends that the public opinions expressed in the media contribute to an organizational climate of fear, blame, and mistrust. Even if the initial public response to tragic events is an outpouring of support and admiration, this support inevitably wanes as society begins to consider what might have been done to facilitate a more positive outcome.

For example, emergency service workers regularly face life-threatening and uncontrollable situations where quick thinking and reasoned action are required. In many cases, these situations have favorable outcomes; many individuals are rescued or saved, but others may be lost. Failure to deal with these acute situations optimally may result in professional condemnation, community sanctions, and possible legal actions. For example, when the police use force to subdue an accused person or when a police shooting results in injury or death, civilian reviews, internal investigations, or criminal investigations are frequently invoked to examine the officers' actions. While public accountability is a reasonable expectation, the process has profound implications for all involved.

In child welfare, public inquiries—including coroners' inquests, public commissions, and criminal trials of workers—have become prominent and powerful institutions. In part, inquiries help society deal with moral panic. Public attention focuses on a phenomenon that is not necessarily driven by an increase in incidence, but instead a surge in attention. Further, inquiries themselves frequently take on a tone of moral righteousness. The motto of the Chief Coroner's Office for Ontario, for instance, reads, "We speak for the dead." All these political factors increase pressure on emergency responders whose actions may be the focus of the inquiry. Practice experience has shown that going through a postmortem review can be extremely stressful for workers. As a result of these observations, colleagues and I began a series of studies aimed at better understanding the impact of public inquiries, legal action, and media attention on emergency responders and social workers.

The first study in this series, involving 266 firefighters and paramedics, compared those who had been questioned in postmortem inquiries following a critical event in the workplace to those who had not been subject to such reviews (C. Regehr, Hill, Goldberg, & Hughes, 2003). We hypothesized that ongoing stressors related to the event, such as postmortem reviews, may serve to exacerbate traumatic reactions. Possible factors we thought might serve to contribute to traumatic responses as a result of postmortem reviews were (1) prolonged exposure to traumatic stimuli through the review process, (2) reduced control over the recovery process, (3) decrease in perceived social support as a result of questioning performance, and (4) stigmatization. We hypothesized that emergency workers involved in postmortem reviews would have higher levels of trauma and depression symptoms than those not involved. In addition, it was expected that public scrutiny in the form of media attention would be associated with higher levels of depression and traumatic stress symptoms.

As predicted, involvement in a review was associated with significantly higher levels of traumatic stress symptoms and depression in firefighters and paramedics. As another indicator of distress, those involved in reviews were significantly more likely to report taking stress leave from work than those who were not involved in reviews, although they did not report differing use prior to encountering a traumatic event. The length of time over which the review was conducted was significantly associated with traumatic stress scores. In fact, length of review was the sole predictor of trauma symptoms in the regression analysis, independently accounting for 19 percent of the variance in posttraumatic symptoms. In addition, media coverage of both the event and the review was significantly associated with depression scores (C. Regehr, Hill, et al., 2003).

A second study in this series aimed to assess the experiences of police officers facing a public inquiry following a traumatic work-related event (C. Regehr, Johanis, Dimitropoulos, Bartram, & Hope, 2003). Qualitative interviews were conducted with eleven individuals who had been subject officers in a postmortem inquiry process. Events leading to the inquiries included high-speed chases; shooting of civilians engaged in a crime; and the use of force to subdue accused individuals who were physically threatening police or were injuring a member of the public. Quantitative measures of social support and current level of distress were compared with the paramedics and firefighters matched for traumatic experiences and involvement in postmortem reviews. While the small sample size of police officers precluded statistical analysis, the officers in this study reported higher levels of support and lower levels of traumatic stress and depression than did firefighters and paramedics involved in reviews.

Figure 3.7 depicts the model that emerged for understanding stress and trauma reactions in police officers involved in public inquiries. This model begins with the critical event itself, after which officers suffered several reactions that are consistent with posttraumatic stress. Reactions stemmed in part from the realization that they had been in severe physical peril and/or had killed or caused harm to another human being. Stresses experienced in the inquiry process emanated from a number of factors: the undermining of officers' reputation, which overshadows all other career contributions and jeopardizes career advancement; the length of the review process, during which the officers may not know if they will lose their job, be held financially liable, or go to jail; and a sense that accusations were politically motivated and that they were the victims of an attempt to garner positive public opinion regardless of the cost to individual officers. Media attention surrounding their cases was frequently substantial and was viewed by officers as inaccurate and sensationalized. In the end, officers felt that regardless of being cleared, they would continue to be tainted long after the review process ended.

The process of the review not only impacted the officers involved but also had significant effects on their family members. In addition to stressors encountered by families of officers as a result of their chronic exposure to risk and trauma, family members had to deal with years of uncertainty about the outcome and the reactions of the officers under inquiry. Children were affected by media coverage and subsequent ha-

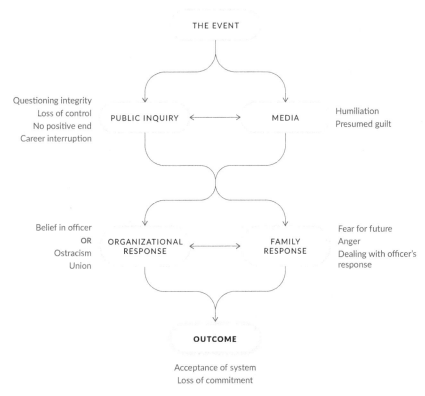

THE EVENT

PUBLIC INQUIRY ⟷ MEDIA

Questioning integrity
Loss of control
No positive end
Career interruption

Humiliation
Presumed guilt

ORGANIZATIONAL RESPONSE ⟷ FAMILY RESPONSE

Belief in officer
OR
Ostracism
Union

Fear for future
Anger
Dealing with officer's response

OUTCOME

Acceptance of system
Loss of commitment

FIGURE 3.7 Thematic model of police officers' response to public inquiries
Source: C. Regehr, Johanis, Dimitropoulos, Bartram, & Hope, 2003.

rassment at school. Spouses were angry that the system to which their loved one had devoted their life had now turned against them.

The organizational response to the allegations of wrongdoing and the public inquiry were viewed as highly significant to the officers in this study. Officers who felt supported by their superiors were highly complementary of management and continued to have a greater sense of commitment to the organization. Other officers felt humiliated and ostracized by the organization and continued to feel bitter about management's response. The support of the police association was also viewed as extremely meaningful. In the end, no officers in this study felt unaffected by the processes that they had endured. At best, officers felt resigned to learning the rules and preparing to defend themselves against possible future allegations. At worst, they felt that it was now "us against them." In many cases, their commitment to the job and the organization was diminished.

I present these earlier studies of the impact of media attention and postmortem reviews on police, paramedics, and firefighters to put the experience of social workers, and particularly child welfare workers, in context. Social workers and child welfare agencies are similarly responding to a societal system that has wide-ranging impacts for workers and their organizations, to which reactions are common and predictable.

In Canada, the social work community was rocked when child welfare worker Angie Martin was charged with criminal negligence causing death in connection to the death of baby Jordan Heikamp. Jordan was born in Toronto on May 18, 1997, and died five weeks later of chronic starvation, weighing just four pounds, two ounces. His mother, then nineteen, was estranged from her family, lived in shelters, and had no source of income. With the approval of Ms. Martin, Jordan and his mother moved to a shelter for homeless women, where he slowly starved to death. After a seven-month preliminary hearing, the charges against Ms. Martin were dismissed. Madam Justice Mary Hogan of the Ontario Court of Justice found that Ms. Martin had a reasonable belief that Jordan was being monitored by medical personnel and shelter staff and that the shelter itself was an appropriate residence. She further indicated that while Ms. Martin should have verified Ms. Heikamp's claims about the care of her child, there was no evidence that "Ms. Martin's acts or omissions were a contributing cause of Jordan's death by chronic starvation" (R. v. Heikamp and Martin, 1999, p. 20). Two years later, a coroner's inquest into Jordan's death highlighted problems in the system but ruled the death a homicide. Much of the press remained negative toward Ms. Martin, the child welfare agency that employed her, and social workers as a group (Kanani, Regehr, & Bernstein, 2002; C. Regehr, Kanani, McFadden, & Saini, 2015). One reporter concluded, "They proved if nothing else, that while you can fool all of the social workers some of the time and some of the social workers all of the time, you can't snow the ordinary Joe [on the jury]" (Blatchford, 2001, p. A10).

Public inquiries into child death are a phenomenon in which society attempts to deal with a serious issue that has lacked sufficient attention. At a time of prosperity in the Western world, large numbers of children continue to be victims of neglect, abuse, and murder. Nevertheless, addressing issues such as child poverty and societal structures, which limit the choices and opportunities available to some members, is overwhelming. In this environment, death inquiries become expedient ways to address public concern and guilt (C. Regehr, Chau, Leslie, & Howe, 2002b). These inquiries garner huge amounts of press interest. The Cleveland inquiry in England in 1988, for instance, resulted in over nine thousand press clippings within the first five weeks. Ayre, in reviewing the impact of media attention to child protection social workers in the United Kingdom, concluded that such attention resulted in a climate of fear, blame, and mistrust within organizations. Social workers are depicted as incompetent or ill-motivated "child stealers" (Ayre, 2001). Similarly, in examining representations of social work in the Russian immigrant literature in Israel, Khvorostianov and Elias (2015) asserted, "This study shows that Israeli social workers are portrayed in Russian-language online newspapers as undereducated, ignorant, and inefficient yet omnipotent and corrupt formalists, culturally alienated from the FSU [former Soviet Union] immigrants. Their professional activity is presented as inhumane, socially dangerous, criminal, and uncontrolled, motivated by greed or perverted desires" (p. 417). The impact of these depictions on decision-making will be addressed in a later chapter. Here, I consider the impact this attention has on trauma response.

As part of the larger study reported earlier with child welfare workers, we inquired whether participants had been involved in a formal review of the death of a child (C. Regehr et al., 2002b). Of the total sample of 175, 60 percent indicated that they had colleagues who had been involved in death reviews. Thirty-eight individuals (22 percent) had been personally involved as follows: internal agency reviews (100 percent); coroner's inquest (17 percent); and civil litigation (3 percent). Thirty-two people (18.5 percent) indicated that their actions had been questioned during the review, and fifteen of these (8.5 percent) had their actions criticized. Forty-three people (25 percent) stated that the actions of their coworkers had been questioned, and twenty-seven of these (15.5 percent) were criticized. Finally, fifty people (29 percent) indicated that there had been media coverage of an event in which they had been involved, and twenty-three (13 percent) characterized this coverage as "extensive."

We conducted qualitative interviews with twenty individuals to investigate the impact of inquiries into child deaths in this large child welfare agency (C. Regehr, Chau, Leslie, & Howe, 2002a; C. Regehr et al., 2002b). This impact was experienced at three levels: distress experienced by individual workers, radiated distress throughout the agency, and weakened public and community support. At the individual worker level, re-exposure to traumatic stimuli regarding the death of a child contributed to traumatic response. In addition to traumatic reactions to the death of a child in their care, repeated and prolonged exposure to the traumatic material throughout the inquiry process and through the media reports was described as the tearing off a scab and reopening of a wound. The all-consuming nature of inquiries was a second factor. Participants described the intense emotional focus that occurred during an inquiry and intensive work required for preparation. Further, by definition, inquiries try to assess what went wrong. This results in a critique of the system and of individual workers within the system. Participants reported feeling that their personal and professional integrity was being called into question. This parallels the experiences of health care providers who are associated with events that cause harm in patients. Expressed emotions such as guilt, anger, frustration, and fear have led one team of researchers to call these health care workers "second victims" of unfortunate patient outcomes (Seys et al., 2013).

Distress regarding the inquiry process did not end with individual workers; rather it radiated throughout the agency. Workers described a feeling of empathy for colleagues, subordinates, and managers who were under inquiry. They also reported discomfort with the scrutiny of the agency by the members of the inquest, and a feeling of guilt or blame by association. Further, the outcome of the inquiry resulted in an accountability-focused environment and strictly governed professional practices. As a consequence, workers described less satisfaction with their jobs, which no longer held many of the elements that attracted them to social work, and specifically child welfare, in the first place.

Finally, the experience of the inquiry into a child's death was intensified by the concentrated media attention on the issue and the resulting public opinion. At times this was experienced positively, but several respondents experienced this as hostile and isolating. There was a sense that all members of the organization had become tainted by the death and consequently that the competence and integrity of all workers was

FIGURE 3.8 Distress related to public inquiries into child deaths
Source: C. Regehr et al., 2002b.

being called into question. Factors associated with public inquiries into deaths in care are summarized in figure 3.8.

AN INTEGRATED MODEL OF TRAUMA RESPONSE

Acute stress disorder and posttraumatic stress disorder are common among social workers in many areas of practice. Workplace events leading to their development include direct traumatic exposures, such as threats and violence directed toward the workers themselves. They also include indirect exposures, such as bearing witness to the physical and psychological impacts on clients who are victims of spousal violence, child abuse, sexual violence, torture, and other horrific life experiences. While most individuals may experience symptoms of intrusion, arousal, and reexperiencing in the days and weeks immediately following certain high-impact events, the degree and nature of exposures do not predict the severity of symptoms over the longer term. Rather, there is a complex interaction between the individual, the organization, and the societal environment (figure 3.9). These factors will differentially affect professional decision-making.

As Kardiner observed in 1941, while vulnerabilities and resilience capacity do not predict the occurrence of acute distress immediately following exposure to a traumatic event, they have an important role in inhibiting the resolution or amelioration of posttraumatic stress symptoms over the longer term. These vulnerabilities and resilience capacities include genetic predisposition and characteristic patterns of interacting with others, understanding the world, and approaching challenges. Preexisting strengths and vulnerabilities set the stage for peritraumatic responses, that is, responses that occur during and in the immediate aftermath of a traumatic event. They are particularly salient when the event involves assaultive trauma, or trauma inflicted by another person, such as sexual violence or being held captive (Stein et al., 2002).

Physical reactions during the peritraumatic period, such as cortisol response and heart rate, are one factor associated with higher levels of PTSD in the weeks and months that follow an event (Thomas et al., 2012). Thus, administration of medications such as the beta blocker propranolol to recently traumatized individuals has been found to reduce subsequent PTSD symptoms (Sijbrandij et al., 2015). Physiological arousal is linked to psychological response, the degree of fear, panic, and helplessness the person encounters as the event unfolds. It is also linked to individuals' cognitive appraisal of the event, including perceived threat, the degree of control they believe they have over the event, and their behavioral response to it. This combination of cognitive appraisal at the time of the event and psychological and biological response predicts long-term symptom severity.

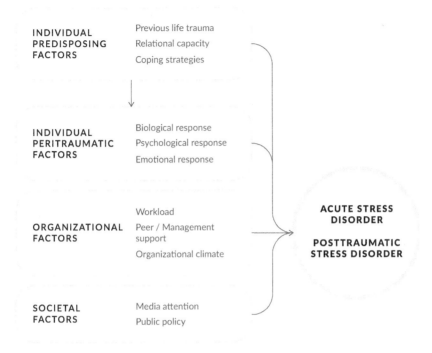

INDIVIDUAL
PREDISPOSING
FACTORS

Previous life trauma
Relational capacity
Coping strategies

INDIVIDUAL
PERITRAUMATIC
FACTORS

Biological response
Psychological response
Emotional response

ORGANIZATIONAL
FACTORS

Workload
Peer / Management
support
Organizational climate

SOCIETAL
FACTORS

Media attention
Public policy

ACUTE STRESS
DISORDER

POSTTRAUMATIC
STRESS DISORDER

FIGURE 3.9 A comprehensive model of factors influencing work-related acute stress and posttraumatic stress
Source: Author's own data.

In the longer term aftermath of a traumatic event, environmental factors contribute to resilience and lower PTSD symptom levels. For instance, the nature of the social work environment—including workload, organizational climate, peer support, and supervision—contributes to resilience (McFadden et al., 2015). The recovery environment also includes the larger society, social policies that require investigations when terrible outcomes occur, such as the death of a child, and the media, which reduce complex practice to heroes and villains.

Research also demonstrates that interactions between genetic and environmental factors as contributors to PTSD symptoms are moderated by personality (Yehuda et al., 2011). Resilience is predicted by optimism and a tendency toward goal-directed problem-solving (Collins, 2007). It is also highly related to the existence of social supports in an individual's life. However, research demonstrates that an individual's perception of available supports is more important than actually reaching out and taking advantage of the supports (Jayaratne et al., 1988; C. Regehr & Marziali, 1999). Indeed, resilient individuals will often indicate that they have a strong network of social supports but did not call on these resources in managing the crisis. In addition, social support networks exist for the individual, because they possess the relational capacity to develop such networks. Social workers by their nature have the capacity to develop relationships with others. They report high levels of social support, and thus the absence of social support is a less salient variable in research on traumatic stress in social workers than in other professions. Personality also affects the meaning that is later ascribed to a traumatic event. As noted in chapter 2, social workers feel pride in and commitment to the difficult work they do to improve the lives of others. Social workers are often able to turn difficult experiences into opportunities for learning and development. Indeed, those who report higher levels of PTSD symptoms following a traumatic workplace event also report higher levels of posttraumatic growth (C. Regehr et al., 2004a).

CHAPTER FOUR

Factors Contributing to Stress Response

Social workers regularly interact with highly distressed individuals who have complex histories involving trauma, violence, and abuse. These individuals may share their experiences in graphic detail; may demonstrate symptoms of posttraumatic stress, depression, anxiety, or other mental health symptoms; or may act out their distress in an aggressive or violent manner. The previous chapter discussed factors that contribute to the development of trauma responses, including the nature, intensity, and duration of trauma exposure; individuals' sense of control over events in their lives and their ability to establish supportive relationships with others; public response to the event, including public inquiry processes, media coverage, and social media; organizational supports; and other concurrent workload stressors.

A second issue identified in chapter 2 was chronic exposure to stressful and potentially traumatizing material. Repeated exposure to these situations can lead to ongoing stress reactions, depleting the resources of the individual worker and resulting in reactions that include changes to cognitive schemas (vicarious traumatization), allostatic load, and emotional burnout. Understanding factors that contribute to experiences of burnout and compassion fatigue also contributes to our understanding of influences on social work decision-making, particularly in high-intensity situations. This chapter reviews theories on the response to stress and empirical evidence supporting these theoretical models. The models considered fall into two broad categories: individuals' engagement with their work, including such factors as empathy, emotional labor, and coping style; and the nature of the work, including role conflicts and demands. The chapter concludes with a model for an integrated understanding of stress response.

EMPATHIC ENGAGEMENT

One factor that increases vulnerability to stress response in social workers relates to their empathic engagement with others. While professionals in the emergency services and other health care professions do engage with patients and clients with sensitivity and concern, empathy and relationship with clients are primary tools in social work, and the ability to engage with clients is viewed as a central skill. In social worker educational programs, this is referred to as "the use of self." For instance, Heath Walters, a field coordinator at Lewis Clark State College, recently wrote, "It is the use of self that enables social workers to strive for authenticity and genuineness with the clients we serve, while at the same time honoring the values and ethics we so highly value in social work practice" (2016). Carl Rogers, in his article "The Necessary and Sufficient Conditions of Therapeutic Personality Change" (1957), emphasized the centrality of unconditional positive regard and empathy as the foundation of the therapeutic relationship. Thus empathy can be understood to be a form of intervention.

Hojat recently summarized the research literature linking clinician empathy to a range of patient outcomes. Higher patient satisfaction, treatment adherence, and willingness to disclose problems are all outcome measures that have been repeatedly linked to empathy and empathic communications of health care providers (Hojat, 2016). For instance, primary care physicians with lower levels of empathy and poorer communication skills are more likely to be subject to malpractice claims than those with better empathy and communication skills, although this phenomenon was not found in surgeons (Frankel & Levinson, 2014; Levinson, Roter, Mullooly, Dull, & Frankel, 1997). Clinician empathy has been found to account for improvement in psychotherapy with an effect size of 0.2 (Hojat, 2016), and patients of physicians with higher levels of empathy have been found to have significantly better control of their diabetes (Hojat et al., 2011). In addition, physicians who used emotional components of empathy in their practice were more likely to order laboratory tests and performed CPR longer before declaring their attempts unsuccessful when compared to physicians who utilized only cognitive components of empathy (Nightingale, Yarnold, & Greenberg, 1991).

The concept of empathy has long been considered, debated, and examined by philosophers, researchers, and mental health professionals. But this work can be largely summarized as comprising two main elements: cognition and affect (Davis, 1983). The first component of empathy is seen to be a vicarious emotional process in which the person develops an affective connection with another and subsequently has an emotional response to the other's suffering (Hume, 1777/1966; Keefe, 1976). In this conceptualization, through witnessing another's emotional state, an individual is prompted to imitate the emotional response of the other and thereby experience a similar, although weaker, reaction (Davis, 1994).

This may be seen as akin to the concept of emotional contagion, an adaptive evolutionary response allowing groups of animals to avoid danger and ensure survival. From this perspective, emotion is transformed into physical changes that are perceived by another, resulting in neurological and biological responses that ultimately culminate in behavioral response. De Gelder and colleagues, for instance, describe the manner in which "fear spreads through a crowd as body postures alter in rapid cascade from one to the next" (De Gelder, Snyder, Greve, Gerard, & Hadjikhani, 2004). Indeed, fear induced through social observation engages similar neural mechanisms as direct personal experience with adverse events (Olsson, Nearing, & Phelps, 2007).

Moving from the crowd level to the individual level, those in close interaction with others often spontaneously and unconsciously copy one another's facial expressions and postures, referred to as *mirroring* or *mimicry*. This copying not only has social roots but also is the result of our hard wiring in the brain. Rizzolatti (2005) was the first to describe the existence of a particular type of neuron discharged when an individual performs an action or observes an action performed by another, which he dubbed "mirror neurons." Such neurons have been associated with the manner in which an infant acquires language and motor skills such as grasping with two fingers rather than an entire fist. Sounds are perceived, or movements observed, provoking imitative responses by the firing of mirror neurons. Mirror neurons provide a pre-reflective, unreasoned, and automatic mechanism to mirror the activities in the brain of others (Iacoboni, 2009). In this way, individuals learn from the behaviors and actions of others. This process also occurs in the coding of facial actions, particularly with the mouth, originally associated with survival skills such as sucking and biting, but also with communicative actions. It also facilitates the process of understanding the emotions of others. Movements or facial expressions that mimic that of another person and stimulate emotional response act as somatic markers and are experienced as "gut" sensations (Rothschild, 2006). That is, feelings that occur in response to stimuli usually happen without a cognitive awareness of what provoked them. Empathy can thus be understood as a simulation of the mental states of others through the activation of the mirror neuron system, the insula, and the limbic system (Gallese, 2001; Iacoboni, 2009). These emotional responses begin in early infancy before the development of the ability to differentiate one's own distress from that of others (Shamay-Tsoory, Aharon-Peretz, & Perry, 2009). Thus emotional empathy related to another individual who is suffering has deep physiological and developmental roots.

It turns out, however, that not all emotions are experienced similarly. Through examination of MRIs, De Gelder and colleagues demonstrated that viewing bodily expressions of fear in others produces higher activity in areas of the brain known to process emotional information (the amygdala, orbitofrontal cortex, cingulate cortex, and the insula). In contrast, exposure to happy bodily expressions only results in activation of visual areas of the brain (De Gelder et al., 2004). As such, we are more prone to experience distressing feelings observed in another person than we are positive feelings such as happiness. Further, the mirror neuron system not only elicits emotional and behavioral responses mimicking that of another individual but is also implicated in pain (Gallese, 2001; Shirtcliff et al., 2009). That is, when an individual experiences pain, the brain activity stimulated is similar to that produced when one imagines, anticipates, or observes pain in others. The difference is the degree of activation, not the nature of the activation (Shirtcliff et al., 2009). While the mechanism of activation is the same, the activation is more intense when the pain is directly experienced rather than observed or imagined.

Damasio (2001) suggests that simulation mechanisms activate internal body maps and create a representation of emotion-driven body-related changes "as if" the person had experienced the pain directly themselves. Many people can recall hearing about an injury experienced by someone else, such as accidentally slicing a finger while cooking, and feeling themselves shudder or their stomach clench while picturing the image.

Empathic attunement, or establishing congruence between the worker and the client, is an important aspect of the therapeutic process, particularly in working with traumatized individuals. The therapist can help the client achieve emotional regulation by modeling emotion management (Wilson & Thomas, 2004). On the other hand, it can lead to empathic strain. This may include affective dysregulation on the part of the practitioner in response to exposure to violent imagery or other disturbing material; retriggering experiences in the practitioner's own history; depletion of energy; or cognitive disillusionment in the world. Wilson and Thomas (2004) suggest that unaddressed empathic strain can lead to prolonged disequilibrium, enmeshment, withdrawal, or empathic repression.

The second aspect of empathy is a cognitive process in which an empathic individual has the ability to accurately imagine the viewpoint of others and perceive their plight. From this perspective, empathy can be seen to be an objective, detached, analytical process (Kant, 1788/1949; Rogers, 1957), the result of which allows an individual to behave in a manner that conveys concern and caring. Rogers (1957), for instance, defined empathy as the ability to perceive another's internal frame of reference with accuracy, as if one were that person but without ever losing the "as if" condition. Thus the helper is able to consider the consequences of his or her actions on the welfare of others (Hogan, 1969) and act in their best interests without actually feeling their pain. This type of empathy relies on higher-order cognitive functions such as cognitive flexibility and is associated with activity in the ventromedial prefrontal (VM) part of the brain. Damage in this area has been associated with impaired higher-order decision-making, moral judgment, and metacognition (Shamay-Tsoory et al., 2009). In contrast to emotional empathy, cognitive empathy develops in later childhood and early adolescence.

In a fascinating study that examines deficits in cognitive and emotional empathy in individuals who have suffered brain legions,

Shamay-Tsoory and colleagues (2009) demonstrated that these two processes exist in different regions of the brain. One process can be impaired via brain trauma while the other remains intact. The determination that affective and cognitive empathy emanate from different areas of the brain has been replicated in several studies, confirming early theoretical models for understanding empathy as two distinct processes (Eres, Decety, Louis, & Molenberghs, 2015; Fan, Duncan, de Greck, & Northoff, 2011). Emotional empathy, or the ability to feel the emotion of another, is affected by the inferior frontal gyrus (IFG), inferior parietal lobule (IPL), insula, and anterior cingula cortex (ACC). The IFG and IPL are implicated in simulation or mirroring of the affect of others, while the insula and (ACC) respond to both felt and observed pain. Cognitive empathy, or the ability to understand the emotions of another, is affected by the temporoparietal junction (TPJ) and the medial prefrontal cortex (mPFC). The TPJ is responsible for transient mental inferences of others and self-other decoding, while the mPFC engages in self-reflection and autobiographical memory. Figure 4.1 by Shamay-Tsoory (2011) depicts this relationship.

Race and gender have an impact on empathy—influencing not only how individual practitioners rate their own empathy, but also how others experience them. Berg and colleagues conducted two studies of medical students performing objective structured clinical evaluation (OSCE) interviews with standardized patients (SPs). Empathy was evaluated both through self-assessments by students and assessments of students by the SPs, and analyses were conducted on the basis of race and gender. Consistent with other research, women were perceived to have higher levels of empathy both in self-assessments and by SPs. When race was considered, an interesting finding emerged. When students of different racial backgrounds were asked to rate their own empathy, there was no statistical difference based on race. However, standardized patients who interacted with the students rated the empathy of Asian American students as significantly lower than that of white students (Berg, Majdan, Berg, Veloski, & Hojat, 2011). In a subsequent study by Berg and colleagues, African American students were rated as having significantly lower levels of empathy than Asian and white students by both African American and white standardized patients (Berg et al., 2015). Thus socialization, cultural norms, and racialized stereotypes shape both the emotional expression

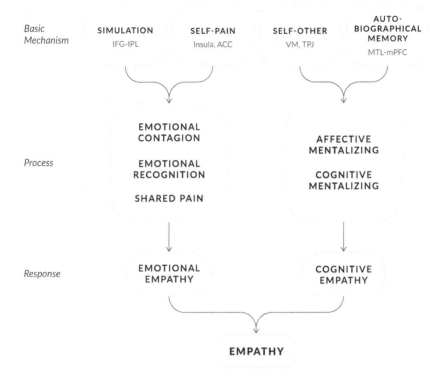

Basic Mechanism	SIMULATION IFG-IPL	SELF-PAIN Insula, ACC	SELF-OTHER VM, TPJ	AUTO-BIOGRAPHICAL MEMORY MTL-mPFC

EMOTIONAL CONTAGION

AFFECTIVE MENTALIZING

Process EMOTIONAL RECOGNITION

COGNITIVE MENTALIZING

SHARED PAIN

Response EMOTIONAL EMPATHY   COGNITIVE EMPATHY

EMPATHY

FIGURE 4.1 Elements of empathy
Source: Shamay-Tsoory, 2011.

and behaviors of individuals, as well as the manner in which they are perceived by others (Underman & Hirshfield, 2016).

The two elements of empathy have implications for the development of stress and trauma reactions in the helping professions. Empathy may be expressed as a cognitive understanding of clients' distress, while at the same time allowing the practitioner to maintain an emotional distance. Or it may involve an emotional connection with the individual. The latter form of empathy presumably increases vulnerability to symptoms of stress and trauma in the worker.

Some years ago, colleagues and I conducted a research project aimed at understanding traumatic stress responses in paramedics (C. Regehr, Goldberg, & Hughes, 2002). In this study, paramedics completed a variety of measures addressing exposure to traumatic events, supports, coping

strategies, and levels of posttraumatic distress. A subsample of paramedics participated in qualitative interviews designed to further explore
stressors encountered on the job, the effects of stress on participants,
organizational supports, and strategies for dealing with stress. Inter-
viewees were asked to describe the events in which they had been involved that they believed others would classify as traumatic. While most
discussed horrific events involving blood and gore, they were quick to
add that these were not the events that "have left me sleepless." It became
clear that the events that were most troubling for paramedics did not
involve multiple deaths in a dramatic incident, but rather the death or
injury of someone that the worker contextualized in relationship to
others—for whom the paramedic developed emotional empathy. Contex-
ualized relationships included situations where an individual died alone
without the support of others; a child who did not benefit from a loving
environment; a family devastated by loss; or the suicide of an alienated
individual. For instance, one paramedic stated, "Loneliness, people being
alone and very ill, that bothers me" (p. 507). Thus, in these situations, paramedics moved beyond a cognitive understanding of the loss or suffering
to experiencing an emotional connection. Cadge and Hammonds (2012)
describe a very similar finding in their qualitative study of intensive
care nurses. These personal observations can be understood within the
context of mirror neurons, discussed earlier. As a result of observing the
embodied emotions of others, such as loneliness and despair, these
same emotions are then mirrored in the worker in a sort of emotional
contagion. Gallese (2001) suggests that the crucial element is a meaningful relational link between the agent and the observer.

Paramedics in our study similarly reported that this type of concern
for others does not come without consequences. The outcomes of emotional empathy, or identification with victims, were described in terms
of intrusive imagery of the event, sleeplessness, anger, and emotional
blunting (C. Regehr, Goldberg, & Hughes, 2002). This finding was supported by previous research with emergency responders. For instance,
police officers confronted with the vulnerability of victims, such as in
cases of abuse or murder, have been found to experience higher rates of
posttraumatic stress disorder (PTSD) (Carlier, Lamberts, & Gersons,
2000); and firefighters have been found to experience increased psy-

chological distress as a result of identifying with victims of disaster (Fullerton, McCarroll, Ursano, & Wright, 1992). On the positive side, such experiences also led some paramedics to view their own relationships more positively and value them more (C. Regehr, Goldberg, & Hughes, 2002).

In our study of paramedics, the coping mechanism that participants most frequently described involved the deliberate use of cognitive strategies. During a traumatic event, paramedics described conscious attempts to shut out the emotional reactions of the victim's family members and to visualize the next technical step to be accomplished. They also discussed the need to shut down their own emotions. Following the event, an additional cognitive strategy involved reviewing the event from a technical standpoint and identifying learning opportunities (C. Regehr, Goldberg, & Hughes, 2002). These strategies do not necessarily represent an absence of empathy for victim and their families. Rather, they may be consistent with "detached concern" (Fox, 1959), a process akin to cognitive empathy. The concept of detached concern emerged in medicine in the 1950s. It arose from the notion that emotional responses in physicians threatened objectivity, as well as the suggestion that physicians should neutralize emotions and exercise "neutral empathy" (Halpern, 2003). In a research study of physicians in a medical ward of patients with novel illnesses, sociologist Renee Fox (1959) described the manner in which physicians maintained a dynamic balance between being sufficiently detached or objective to exercise sound clinical judgment while at the same time being sufficiently concerned about the patient to provide compassionate care. The strategy of detached concern has similarly been identified in mental health and social service professionals (Pines & Maslach, 1978) and forensic mental health nurses (Fluttert, van Meijel, Nijman, Bjørkly, & Grypdonck, 2010). I will return to this later in the chapter when I discuss coping strategies.

In presenting models for empathy in social work practice, Gerdes and Segal (2009) and King (2011) add a third dimension that goes beyond affective and cognitive empathy. Gerdes and Segal describe this third dimension as conscious decision-making toward empathic action. Such actions include helping, advocacy, organizing, and social action (Gerdes & Segal, 2009). King similarly presents a behavioral dimension of social work empathy manifested as altruism and the therapeutic relationship (King, 2011). In this way, empathy embodies social work values by consciously taking action to assist another.

EMOTIONAL LABOR

An alternative view of emotion in the professional or workplace environment was presented by sociologist Arlie Russell Hochschild in her important book *The Managed Heart* (1983). In this work, Hochschild proposed the term *emotional labor* to refer to an individual's efforts to regulate emotions in the workplace in order to achieve goals. While the term was originally applied to individuals in service roles, such as flight attendants, one can easily see its applicability to social work. For example, a social worker conducting a court-ordered assessment of a client accused of child sexual abuse must understand the extent and nature of the crimes committed. While details of the offenses are likely to be highly distressing, displaying shock or disgust would be counterproductive both for obtaining information and for engaging with the client to modify behavior. Thus social workers manage their negative emotions, drawing on their ability to empathize with the distress of the alleged offender. Guy and colleagues in fact suggest that emotional labor is a necessary component of effective human services work and can be thought of as a specialized form of knowledge or skill application (M. Guy, Newman, Mastracci, & Maynard-Moody, 2010).

Individuals are thought to employ two primary emotional labor strategies to regulate emotion: deep acting and surface acting (Hochschild, 1983; Hülsheger & Schewe, 2011). Deep acting as a strategy for managing emotional labor involves cognitive reframing of the situation. Such cognitive reframing in clinical social work can, for instance, occur when a social worker understands a client's aggressive or confrontational behavior as a response to frustration with systematic barriers and not a personal attack, or when the social worker understands that a sexual abuser's behavior is consistent with the offender's own treatment as a child—while still not excusing or condoning it. As a result, the worker's genuine emotional response is modified.

The act of managing emotional labor or adjusting the emotional response by suppressing negative emotions, amplifying emotions deemed to be appropriate for the situation, or faking emotions has been called *surface acting*. Surface acting is expressing an emotion that the individual does not actually feel (Hülsheger & Schewe, 2011). It is suggested that surface acting comes with costs. When the felt emotion is inconsistent with the emotion that must be displayed, the individual experiences a sense of dissonance. This dissonance has been associated with a number of negative outcomes, including self-estrangement or alienation, lowered sense of professionalism, poorer job satisfaction, exhaustion, burnout, and depression (Pugliesi, 1999).

The extent to which emotional responses are regulated, and the level of effort required to manage negative emotions, affects a worker's well-being. Those in more emotionally demanding roles, characterized by higher frequency and intensity of interpersonal interactions, have been found to have higher levels of burnout (Brotheridge & Lee, 2002). For instance, a study by Mann and Cowburn (2005) of mental health nurses in England revealed that nurses expended considerable emotional labor in daily interactions and that increased emotional labor was correlated with higher levels of experienced stress. In this study, nurses used deep acting (cognitive reframing) strategies in 82 percent of communications and surface acting (suppression of negative emotions) in 74 percent. This clearly demonstrates that both strategies can be employed in any given interaction—that is, the techniques are not mutually exclusive. Surface acting, however, was associated with more negative outcomes and higher levels of stress (Mann & Cowburn, 2005). Other studies have found that suppression of negative emotions requires greater effort and is associated with impaired performance on memory and complex decision-making tasks (Hülsheger & Schewe, 2011). Deep acting, or the use of reappraisal and reframing techniques, requires fewer cognitive resources than emotional suppression and thus has less impact on cognitive performance (Hülsheger & Schewe, 2011).

Like emotional empathy, empathic engagement with clients over a period of time can put social workers at risk of burnout because they are unable to separate personal emotions from professionally required emotions. The inability to detach oneself and in effect depersonalize can increase risk of burnout (Wharton, 1999). From this perspective, jobs that facilitate or encourage identification with the role, and workers who are most at ease with emotional labor, are theoretically at higher risk

(Wharton, 1999). Indeed, human service workers that exert emotional labor worry that the work hardens them and that they will be personally affected (Guy et al., 2010). However, the effective management of emotions through deep acting can elicit positive reinforcement and subsequently reduce levels of stress and burnout (Brotheridge & Grandey, 2002). Effective emotion management can be experienced as enhancing and empowering (Pugliesi, 1999). To this end, individuals in jobs that require higher levels of emotional labor have been found to experience higher job satisfaction and lower levels of stress—and the negative impacts of emotional labor are diminished by greater job autonomy (Guy et al., 2010; Wharton, 1993).

One aspect of the differential outcomes of deep acting and surface acting on the individual is the experience of authenticity. An individual who uses cognitive reframing strategies, and thus is able to express emotions that they truly feel, does not carry the personal burden of dissonance; their emotional displays match their internal experiences (Coté, 2005). In addition, however, their interpersonal interactions are likely to be different: other individuals are able to differentiate between real and faked emotional displays and will react accordingly (Hülsheger & Schewe, 2011). This is true not only in interactions with clients or the public, but also in relationships within the workplace—those with coworkers and supervisors (Pugliesi, 1999). Emotional expression through deep acting is positively rated by coworkers, while emotional expression through surface acting is negatively rated. Surface actors are viewed as unlikable and untrustworthy. Other studies suggest that people interpret inauthentic displays of emotions by others as attempts to control them (Coté, 2005). This in turn results in an increasingly negative interpersonal interactions and higher stress for the worker.

It is important to note that systemic issues also affect emotional labor. Gunaratnam and Lewis (2001) for instance explore the manner in which systemic racism in child welfare agencies requires that workers engage in emotional labor to manage emotions of guilt and anger triggered by policies and practices that perpetuate inequities. In addition, emotional labor is differentially experienced based on factors such as occupational status, gender, and race. Those in positions of higher occupational status are less likely to experience emotional labor due to what Hochschild (1983) referred to as "status shield," whereby they are less likely to have others express negative emotions toward them. Male nurses have been found to perceive less pressure to conform to expectations of emotional expression than female nurses, and if they do engage in surface acting, they feel less dissonance and distress (Cottingham, Erickson, & Diefendorff, 2015). Although this may make intuitive sense, other research in human service organizations has not found gender disparities in emotional labor (Guy et al., 2010).

APPROACHES TO COPING AS MEDIATORS OF STRESS AND BURNOUT

A large body of research and theory considers an individual's coping style as a mediator between stressful situations and the development of physical and psychological symptoms. One approach has defined coping styles as arising from stable personality traits, including fatalism, inflexibility, or hardiness. This approach assumes that enduring personality characteristics predispose an individual to cope in a way that either impairs or facilitates adaptation. A second approach views coping as an interactive process between the individual and the environment, or what has been called the *transactional model* (Folkman, Lazarus, Gruen, & DeLongis, 1986; Lazarus, 1993). In the transactional model, stress is thought to be determined by the degree to which a particular situation is appraised by the individual as exceeding resources and threatening well-being (Folkman et al., 1986). Lazarus and Folkman (1984) propose two types of appraisals: a primary or emotional appraisal of harm, threat, and challenge; and a secondary or cognitive appraisal of what, if any, actions can be taken to mitigate the risk. These appraisals are influenced by generalized beliefs held by the individual about risk, personal competence, and available resources. As a result of these generalized beliefs, individuals respond to challenges and threats in habitual ways, referred to as *coping styles*. Although there are many approaches to categorizing coping styles, they are often divided into three groups: task-oriented, emotion-oriented, or avoidant-oriented (Endler & Parker, 1994; Folkman & Moskowitz, 2004). Task-oriented coping includes attempts to modify or eliminate the sources of stress through action. Emotion-oriented coping includes behavioral and cognitive responses primarily aimed at managing emotional reactions to a stressor and maintaining emotional equilibrium.

This may involve cognitive reframing of an event or can involve distraction or relaxation strategies. Avoidant-oriented coping refers to attempts to actively avoid confronting the problem or engaging in behaviors aimed at avoiding emotional tension caused by the event. Often avoidant-oriented coping is associated with maladaptive behaviors such as overeating or alcohol use (Billings & Moos, 1981).

In any given situation, one coping style may be more effective than others, and thus coping styles should be considered with respect to the stressful situations at hand. For instance, in light of a situation that cannot be changed, such as receiving a terminal diagnosis, emotion-focused coping may be most effective. In other cases, taking action to alter the situation causing stress may be most effective. In line with the traits approach to coping, some coping strategies have been found to be fairly consistently applied by a particular individual; others less so. For instance, seeking social support is highly variable based on the stressful situation, whereas cognitive reappraisal tends to be more stable and applied by an individual across situations (Lazarus, 1993). Effective coping with any situation is associated with reduced psychological and emotional distress; it also mediates the physiological response to stress (Folkman & Moskowitz, 2004).

To assess the impact of coping on stress and trauma responses, my colleague Vicki LeBlanc and I conducted a series of studies with three different populations of emergency responders: police recruits, paramedics, and police communicators in an emergency call center. In each of the three studies, participants completed a series of questionnaires prior to participating in a simulated stressful scenario. Acute stress was measured throughout the individuals' study participation. The stressful workplace situations were designed to simulate actual workplace events. Our goal was to realistically create a workplace challenge in order to measure (1) factors that mediated stress responses and (2) the impact of stress on professional decision-making. Chapter 7 describes the aspects of the studies involving decision-making. In this chapter I outline the studies and discuss the findings with respect to symptoms of distress.

In all three studies, questionnaires elicited demographic information, trauma exposure in the workplace, posttraumatic stress symptoms, and coping strategies. The stress responses of the workers were assessed with a subjective anxiety measure, the State-Trait Anxiety Inventory (STAI) (Spielberger, 1983), and two physiological measures, salivary cortisol and heart rate. As discussed in chapter 2, under stress, the sympathetic nervous system is activated, epinephrine and norepinephrine are released into the blood stream, and heart rate increases. At the same time, the hypothalamic-pituitary-adrenal (HPA) axis is activated, leading to the release of the hormone cortisol into the bloodstream, which is then diffused to the saliva and eventually excreted into the urine (Dickerson & Kemeny, 2004). Salivary collection is a simple, noninvasive procedure (Sanchez-Martin et al., 2001), and as salivary cortisol levels show a close linear relationship with plasma cortisol levels (Ansseau et al., 1984; Cook et al., 1986; Harris et al., 1990), it was chosen for our biological measure of cortisol. Baseline measurements of perceived stress and cortisol were taken at the start of the study sessions, and response measures were obtained at specific times following each simulation. Heart rate was continuously measured throughout the study through the use of a Polar heart rate monitor (www.polarusa.com). The monitor consists of a watch-like receiver worn on the wrist and a transmitter worn around the chest. The transmitter picks up the signals from the heart and sends it to the watch-like receiver. The information from the monitor is then downloaded into a computer system to obtain a profile of the participant's continuous heart rate (LeBlanc, Regehr, Jelley, & Barath, 2007).

In the first study, eighty-four police recruits participated in a scenario utilizing a Firearms Training Systems (FATS) simulator (LeBlanc, Regehr, Jelley, & Barath, 2007). FATS simulation involves the projection of a realistic situation onto a blank screen in a specially designed simulation room. The simulation is programmed to respond to the police recruits' actions (i.e., communications, chemical spray, and firearms). The scenario constructed for this research involved a 911 call for a domestic dispute in which the officer's entry is first barred by an aggressive male, who subsequently allows the officer into the home and down a blind hallway. Upon entering a room at the end of the hallway, an unresponsive female is discovered lying on the floor, and the officer must determine the correct line of action. Possible considerations involve the ongoing presence of the perpetrator, the victim's need for medical attention, and the safety of the officer. Participants were videotaped during the simulations for later evaluation. Three expert raters at the Ontario Police College independently assessed the videotaped performance of each participant on two measures: one measuring specific behavioral competencies in the scenario, and a second ranking performance against peers.

For the purpose of the second study, a high-acuity event was created with the use of a high-fidelity mannequin placed in an ambulance simulator (LeBlanc, C.Regehr, Tavares, Scott, McDonald & King, 2012). Twenty-two paramedics were required to manage a simulated cardiac patient complaining of chest pain, in both low-stress and high-stress scenarios. To create a high-acuity situation, several stressors were added to the scenario. Auditory noise was introduced by setting the volume and alarms on monitors at maximum and by having constant two-way radio communication noise. A socioevaluative stressor was simulated by an actor playing the role of the patient's partner, presenting as visibly distressed and challenging the participants' actions and decisions. Patient presentation and treatment expectations for the scenario were developed by consensus with four experts in the field of prehospital care.

The third study sought to better understand the experiences of psychological distress and physiological stress in a relatively unexamined group of emergency responders, that of police communicators (C. Regehr, LeBlanc, Barath, Balch, & Birze, 2013). One hundred and thirteen police communicators responded to simulated 911 calls from members of the public in a large computer room designed to resemble an active dispatch center with the sounds of other communicators in the background. Scenarios in this study were masked recordings of actual 911 calls. An initial routine call was followed by a call that contained strong emotional content involving injury to a police officer.

The first question to be answered was whether the scenarios in these three studies were effective in creating acute stress responses in the emergency service workers. Indeed, both psychological and biological measures confirmed that we were able to do so. For instance, in the police recruit study, the State-Trait Anxiety Inventory was administered at baseline, just prior to the simulation, just after the simulation, and twice in the follow-up at twenty and thirty minutes post-scenario (C. Regehr, LeBlanc, Jelley, Barath, & Daciuk, 2007). As shown in figure 4.2, mean scores on this self-report inventory were highest immediately following the scenario and then diminished with time after the scenario. In addition, scores at each time period were significantly correlated with one

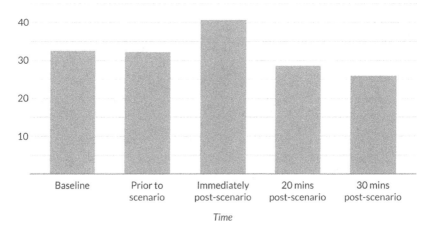

STAI Score

FIGURE 4.2 Pattern of self-reported stress response
Source: Regehr, LeBlanc, Jelley, Barath, & Daciuk, 2007.

other, suggesting consistency in self-reported stress among individual participants.

Heart rate was averaged across discrete two-minute segments of time prior to the exposure to the scenario (baseline and immediately prior to the scenario), during exposure, and after exposure (immediately after the scenario and twenty minutes post-scenario). There was a significant increase in heart rate during and immediately following the scenario in comparison with the baseline and pre-scenario intervals. The participants' average heart rate returned to the pre-scenario baseline within twenty minutes following completion of the simulated scenario, as shown in figure 4.3.

Salivary samples were collected twice at baseline and twice in the follow-up at twenty and thirty minutes post-scenario. As individuals have cortisol peaks at different times following a stressful event (twenty to forty minutes following the *onset* of a stressor; Kemeny, 2003), the peak cortisol level post-scenario was selected for subsequent analyses. Peak cortisol levels following the scenario were significantly higher than the cortisol levels at baseline, indicating that individuals did indeed have a physiological response to the stressful scenario (figure 4.4). Increases in cortisol level from baseline to peak were positively correlated with increases in subjective anxiety.

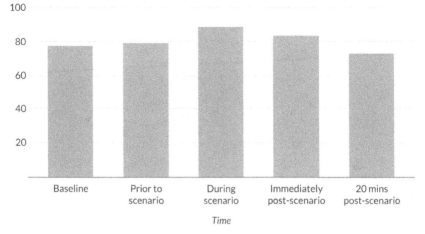

FIGURE 4.3 Pattern of heart rate response
Source: Regehr et al., 2007.

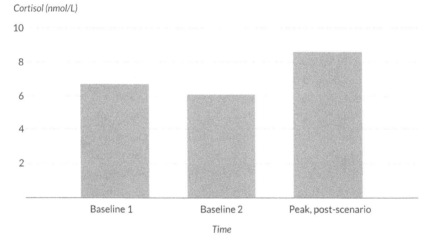

FIGURE 4.4 Pattern of salivary cortisol response
Source: Regehr et al., 2007.

Having determined that we had indeed created a realistic stress-inducing situation, the next question was whether there was an association between coping strategies and stress response. The first result of these collective studies pertains to coping strategies and posttraumatic stress symptoms. Among the three groups of police recruits, paramedics, and police communicators, coping style was associated with the presence of trauma symptoms. Participants that used either emotion-oriented or avoidant-oriented symptoms had higher levels of posttraumatic stress symptoms and were more likely to fall in the range of trauma symptoms consistent with a diagnosis of posttraumatic stress disorder than were individuals who did not use these coping strategies. This is consistent with previous research on emergency responders exposed to traumatic events in the workplace which have associated emotion and avoidant-oriented coping styles with the development and maintenance of posttraumatic stress symptoms (Beaton, Murphy, Johnson, Pike, & Corneil, 1999; J. Brown, Mulhern, & Joseph, 2002; Marmar et al., 2006). Task-oriented coping styles were not associated with the presence of trauma symptoms.

With respect to subjective ratings of acute stress, coping styles were associated with reported anxiety in all three groups of emergency responders. That is, those who used task-oriented coping styles and avoidant-oriented coping styles reported lower levels of anxiety following the scenarios. Emotion-oriented coping was not associated with subjective anxiety levels at any point in police but was associated with higher levels of distress in communicators and paramedics. In all three studies, participants' coping styles were also associated with their physiological responses to the stressful scenario. The use of emotion-oriented coping styles was associated with a greater heart rate response. In addition, those individuals who used emotion-oriented or avoidant-oriented coping styles were more likely to have larger cortisol responses to the stressful scenario compared to those who did not. The use of task-oriented coping styles was not associated with physiological responses to the scenarios.

Thus avoidant-oriented and emotion-oriented coping styles were associated with higher levels of long-term reactions to traumatizing events, as measured by posttraumatic stress symptoms, whereas no association was found with task-oriented coping. In the immediate situation, however, task-oriented coping appeared to serve a protective role both in terms of decreased subjective anxiety and decreased physiological response to a high-acuity event. Emotion-focused coping resulted in higher levels of physiological stress response. This replicates the findings of others that task-oriented coping is an effective method of dealing with stressful, high-stakes situations in the emergency service workplace and that emotion-oriented coping may be ineffective in this realm (Beaton et al., 1999; Bramsen, Dirkzwager, & van der Ploeg, 2000; Fortes-Ferreira, Peiro, Gonzalez-Morales, & Martin, 2006).

The results with respect to avoidant-focused coping bear some further discussion. Avoidant-focused approaches were associated with lower levels of subjective distress, but higher cortisol response. Lazarus (1998), in a review of the costs and benefits of denial, discussed situations in which denial may be an adaptive response. Noting that denial is not a single act but rather a diverse set of processes that respond to different external and internal conditions, he points to the utility of denial as part of the process of challenges like grieving or anticipating a negative event such as surgery. Fully appreciating the gravity of the situation or the magnitude of the loss at particular times can overwhelm resources and adaptation. This brings us back to the concept of detached concern in the management of stressful or traumatic workplace events (McCammon, Durham, Allison, & Williamson, 1988; C. Regehr et al., 2002). Coping mechanisms that allow for the avoidance of emotions may be perceived as helpful during a high-acuity event. They allow the emergency worker to control strong emotional reactions and to do their work. In the longer term, however, strategies aimed at suppressing and avoiding the strong emotions of trauma are thought to contribute to ongoing psychological harm and physical harm such as allostatic load, resulting from traumatic experiences and stress exposures (Folkman & Moskowitz, 2004; McCammon et al., 1988; Thoits, 1995; Wastell, 2002).

Studies in policing have found that coping style is also a factor predicting job satisfaction and less acute forms of distress, such as generalized job stress (Cooper, Kirkcaldy, & Brown, 1994). Research on coping strategies in social workers has yielded similar results. For instance, in a study of 151 frontline child protection workers, Anderson (2002) found that use of disengaged (avoidant) coping was significantly associated with higher levels of emotional exhaustion, depersonalization, and lower levels of personal accomplishment on burnout scales. In contrast, engaged (task-oriented) coping was significantly associated with lower depersonalization and higher accomplishment scores but had no significant association with exhaustion scores. In a mixed sample of 249 female nurses, social workers, and psychologists, task-oriented coping was associated with lower depersonalization scores and higher accomplishment scores, while emotion-focused coping had the reverse associations. Exhaustion was not associated with any form of coping (Ben-Zur & Michael, 2007). Gellis (2002) compared job stress, job satisfaction, and coping in a sample of 168 social workers and 155 nurses. Nurses reported significantly more job stress and significantly lower job satisfaction than social workers. In both groups, however, avoidance-oriented coping was associated with higher ratings of stress and lower ratings of job satisfaction. Task-oriented problem-solving was associated with greater job satisfaction (Gellis, 2002).

ROLE CONFLICT AND ROLE AMBIGUITY

Role conflict occurs when workers are faced with incompatible demands regarding their behavior in any given situation. Role conflict, for instance, can emerge when the best interest of the client does not fit with the required institutional role of the social worker. Beverley Antle and I discussed this some years ago when examining the role of social workers in court-mandated practice (C. Regehr & Antle, 1997). One such example is the manner in which the therapeutic alliance that develops between a social worker conducting a court assessment and a client who is accused or found guilty of a violent crime. We suggested that social workers are selected to perform the role of assessors in court-mandated situations because of their relationship skills. However, while the ability to form a therapeutic alliance and obtain relevant information supports the outcome valued by the court, the therapeutic alliance may not always serve the best interest of the individual being assessed. The client may not be aware of the complexity of the relationship and may assume that the social worker will provide an assessment that is in his or her best interest, in spite of the nature of the referral and the social worker's obligation to address the needs, interests, and safety of others (C. Regehr & Antle, 1997).

Role ambiguity occurs when a worker is uncertain about what to do or questions whether the work is effective. Acker (2003) describes the changes in mental health social work as a result of the implementation of managed care in the United States as an example, suggesting that the erosion of traditional roles for social work has led to a devaluing of past roles and lack of clarity of current roles. An interesting cross-cultural comparison revealed differences in the effects of role conflict and role ambiguity between Norwegian and American social workers (Himle, Jayaratne, & Thyness, 1986). Norwegian workers overall reported higher levels of stress related to role ambiguity, role conflict, job challenge, value conflict, and financial rewards than did American workers. Regression analyses demonstrated that in both samples, the strongest predictor of burnout and turnover was the challenge of the job—specifically, lower levels of challenge were associated with higher levels of burnout and turnover, whereas increased challenge was associated with higher job satisfaction. Thus experiencing a job as challenging is a protective factor.

However, although role conflict was identified as a problem among social workers in both the United States and Norway, it was only a significant predictor of emotional exhaustion and depersonalization in American social workers. Similarly, role ambiguity was inversely associated with personal accomplishment in American social workers, although it was not in Norwegians. The authors speculate that this may be due to the fact that American social workers tend to work in more highly specialized agencies (Himle et al., 1986). Another American study using structural equation modeling found that role stress interacted with job autonomy in predicting burnout (Kim & Stoner, 2008). Acker (2004) found the same associations in a study of American mental health workers. Thus as work is experienced as more meaningful and challenging and as workers have the scope to address these challenges in a creative manner, chronic stress associated with the job is reduced.

Role conflict can result in moral distress or shame in two situations: when needs and expectations conflict (such as between the client and the organization); or when there is a conflict between what is required and the available resources—including the worker's skills. Gibson (2014a, 2014b) conducted a scoping review of shame, inadequacy, failure, and the struggle to practice humanely. In this review he found that for workers in a complex environment, the failure to live up to expectations (personal, organizational, and clients') can lead to negative self-judgments, a sense of inadequacy, and shame. The workers' shame may be primarily focused on not living up to personal expectations of self, concern about harming the client, fear of being ostracized by others in the organization or profession, or fear regarding their broader public reputation. In a study of Australian social workers, Stanford (2009) identified the fear and shame engendered by the conflict of harming clients by either being ineffective or by being overly controlling, overly protective, and/or punitive. Furthermore, social workers experience moral distress when institutional structure and available resources (including time to adequately address the problem) create obstacles to pursuing what is judged to be the morally right course of action (Jameton, 1992). This distress is believed to linger, creating a moral residue that, in the long term, impairs work-related well-being.

As social workers are not entirely autonomous decision-makers, but are rather bound by policies, laws, and organizations, they face moral dilemmas and consequently moral distress (Mänttäri-van der Kuip, 2015). In a survey of 1,215 nurses and social workers in the United States, one-third reported a sense of being powerless or overwhelmed, and almost one-quarter reported physical symptoms when dealing with ethical problems (Ulrich et al., 2007). In a study of 817 social workers in Finland, moral distress was associated with lower job satisfaction and lower commitment to the job. Interestingly, despite many factors considered as potentially contributing to moral distress, moral distress was most strongly predicted by insufficient resources, budget constraints, and work overload (Mänttäri-van der Kuip, 2015). This suggests that moral distress in this sample was most strongly connected to the relationship between job demands and resources available to provide adequate service.

WORKPLACE DEMANDS AND CONTROL

Chapter 2 discussed workload demands on social workers. In our child welfare study (C. Regehr, Hemsworth, Leslie, Howe and Chau, 2004), this included the following (in descending order of importance): quantity of work, documentation requirements, difficult or disruptive clients, organizational change, changing policy requirements, and conflicts with others in the organization. It also included societal demands placed on workers in terms of public inquiries and media attention to high-profile events, which were discussed in chapter 3. Our work and that of others clearly demonstrated the influence of these types of public factors on traumatic stress responses. It also pointed to the erosion of public faith when tragic events occur and when inquiries call into question the judgment and competence of workers. Accompanying this is increased stress related to liability. Recent decades have seen a substantial increase in the number of court cases being brought against social workers. Perhaps the most profound increase in the personal liability of social workers has emerged in child protection, where workers are forced to make critical decisions about apprehending children, often against the parents' wishes. When protection workers apprehend children, they can be faced with civil lawsuits from disgruntled parents claiming negligence and the violation of their rights. Conversely, when children are not apprehended, further abuse or even fatalities sometimes result, and the workers are blamed both civilly and criminally for the child's injury or death (Kanani, C. Regehr, & Bernstein, 2002; C. Regehr, Kanani, McFadden, & Saini, 2015). These challenges add to the many demands placed on workers by the organization and their clients, and undermine their sense of control over the nature of their work and their decisions.

The demand-control model of job strain, dating back to 1979, proposes that the level of stress experienced by workers is a consequence of both the demands placed on them and the degree of control, or decision latitude, they have (Karasek, 1979). The model contains two predictions: (1) stress increases if an increase in psychological job demands is not accompanied by a coinciding increase in decision latitude, and (2) competency will increase when job challenges are matched by an individual's skill or control in managing the situation (Karasek, 1979). Aspects of decision latitude include freedom to make or participate in decisions, creativity, an opportunity to learn new things, and the need for a high skill level. Aspects of job demand include quantity of work, time allowed to complete work, and consequently having to work quickly and having no time to finish tasks. Numerous studies since Karasek's in 1979 have confirmed that jobs with high demand and low control are the most stressful for workers both in terms of psychological distress and physiological distress (such as cardiovascular strain) (Van der Doef & Maes, 1998). A modification to the demand-control model that incorporates relationships with coworkers and supervisors is known as the *demand-control-support model* (S. Johnson et al., 2005). In this model, social support serves as a moderator of stress-related symptoms that may result from a mismatch between job demand and decisional control or latitude. This is consistent with research discussed in chapter 3 on social supports in the workplace environment.

Danielle Millar and I applied this analysis to interviews that my team conducted with paramedics (C. Regehr & Millar, 2007). Demand identified by the paramedics included physical issues, such as the risk of contracting a serious infectious illness and the ability to take a break or eat a meal given the pace of work. From a time-demand perspective, paramedics perceived the amount of work that they were assigned to be excessive. One said, "Right now our system is under-staffed as is every other system, so our workload is heightened; so you are doing more calls, more emergency driving, more patient contact; the more calls you do, the more stressors you pick up, and the more conflict you try to resolve, and that just plays on you by the end of the day" (p. 52). Paramedics also described an interaction between the demands of the work pace and the psychological demands of dealing with tragic situations, leaving little time for the physical rest or psychological processing of tragic encounters. Another paramedic described how one case immediately followed another: "You have just brought in someone who passed away; and then you are on the phone with someone asking if you are ready to go, and you don't think about it, you just keep doing it" (p. 52). With respect to control, paramedics described the hierarchical structure of the organization and the authoritarian model of decision-making. Some also indicated that the challenge of the job did not provide them with the opportunity to use their full range of specialized skills. Quantitative analysis confirmed that depression scores were negatively correlated with a sense of control and with self-efficacy, indicating that reduced sense of control was associated with increased distress. From a support perspective, paramedics reported a high degree of social and emotional support from their immediate coworkers, but an overall low degree of social cohesion in the organization—especially between workers and supervisors, who were perceived as distant. As a result of these factors, some paramedics experienced depression, were challenged with substance abuse, and had taken mental health stress leave. One reported, "I just basically burned out and fell into a pot of booze. Then I quit [drinking] because it was killing me, killing my family, killing my work" (p. 56). Other long-term effects described by some respondents included reduced capacity to manage stressful events and disengagement from family members: "You almost treat your family like another call. . . . There is an [emotional] deficit there" (p. 56). Overall, paramedics in this study perceived their work

DEMAND

Time pressures
Physical risks
Psychological stress
No time to recuperate

CONTROL

Low levels of
personal control

Low self-efficacy

Lack of recognition for
skills and knowledge

SUPPORT

No support from co-workers
No support from supervisors
Lack of organizational support

**WORK STRESS
AND DEPRESSION**

FIGURE 4.5 The demand-control-support model
Source: C. Regehr & Millar, 2007.

environment to be high in demand, low in control, and low in support. These factors interacted to create negative personal, family, and work effects. These are summarized in the model presented in figure 4.5. While this study was conducted with another high-risk profession, similar dynamics occur in the social work workplace.

The province of Ontario embarked on a sweeping process of child welfare reform following a series of inquests into the death of children under the care of children's aid societies. In an attempt to understand the effects of this reform on child welfare agencies and the social workers within them, colleagues and I conducted a series of interviews with agency supervisors and managers, applying the lens of the demand-control-support model (C. Regehr, Chau, Leslie, & Howe, 2002a).

Virtually all respondents in the study described the increase in workload subsequent to child welfare reform as being a key stressor for all child protection workers. For managers and supervisors, it was reported that workload had doubled in the past three years due to shorter timelines, increased recording, and increased need for supervision of new staff. New technology aimed at reducing workloads had actually added work time. Participants identified getting the same information from multiple sources, causing duplication of work as they sorted through priorities. The added pressures related to child welfare reform resulted in higher staff turnover and large numbers of new employees. One supervisor participant stated that half of the workers they supervised had less than one month's experience. The relative inexperience of a large percentage of the frontline workers meant that supervisors had to provide more and more in-depth forms of assistance. In some cases, this resulted in the feeling of being forced to "micromanage" the work of staff. As referrals increased, supervisors were reluctant to pass them on to already overburdened workers, but saw no option. The constant flow of new staff undermined efforts to encourage collegial support and mentoring for the frontline workers. Beyond concerns about the workload stressors on staff, and concerns focused on their staff's ability to do the job effectively, supervisors and managers were also concerned for staff's safety and well-being; they were acutely aware that they were sending young and inexperienced staff into highly volatile situations alone.

An additional stress was the respondents' perception of the critical nature of media attention and public opinion. This was fueled by the media's tendency to focus on negative news stories and investigate possible malpractice or negligence on the part of the child welfare system and its workers. Supervisors and managers, in their roles as representatives of the agency, felt the added pressure of speaking to the press and presenting a fair and accurate account of the event without breaching confidentiality. They avoided sharing the nature of their work with others in social settings, sensing disapproval of the agency and its workers.

Respondents felt the support of management and supervisors was important to workers, but many described a sense of dissatisfaction with being able to provide for all the support needs of their staff. One stated,

"It is my hypothesis that because of the work that we do, which is totally unpredictable on a regular basis, the place people get their security is in the office, back with their team, with their supervisors. That allows people to do their job. . . . On one hand it is exciting, on the other hand it can be very stressful [to hold this level of responsibility]" (p. 28). Another said, "I can see the impact on staff but I feel powerless in terms of what I can do to make it less stressful, less onerous for them to have to keep up with these changes" (p. 28). In the end, supervisors and managers conveyed a sense that no matter how hard they worked to support staff, many would leave shortly for better opportunities. Perhaps one of the most disturbing findings of the study is that these supervisors and managers, with many years of experience and tremendous wisdom, are giving up. This was partially due to their belief that others did not understand the magnitude of the problem and the changes required and that it was therefore unlikely that the situation would improve soon.

In all, the demands had increased significantly while the ability to control the environment had decreased; clinical judgment and expertise were replaced by rigid rules, timelines, and processes. Supervisors and managers were well aware of the importance of support for workers and sought to foster a supportive environment, but they felt that their efforts were undermined by workload and cyclical problems of inexperience and turnover. In this agency, demand was high, control was diminished, and support seemed unachievable.

AN INTEGRATED MODEL OF FACTORS CONTRIBUTING TO STRESS RESPONSE

The large body of research literature addressing occupational stress has long focused on the important interaction between the work, the workplace, and the worker. Work factors include the balance between demands and the control afforded to the worker to manage these demands, as well as the degree of role ambiguity and role conflict inherent in the work. In social work, this may not only involve client unpredictability and needs, but also societal demands in which deeply held beliefs are in conflict. These conflicting values may be the sanctity of the family versus the safety of children; the individual's right to determine how he or she will live versus the responsibility to assess and intervene when someone is suicidal; and balancing confidentiality of treatment with the duty to warn and protect those at risk of harm. The degree of control that workers have over their work despite the conflicts and demands is an important mediating factor. In addition, the degree to which demands are perceived as challenges can positively affect the experience of stress. As discussed in earlier chapters, workplace demands can be mediated by workplace supports, such as supportive colleagues and a belief that management is supportive and helpful. This is depicted in figure 4.6.

Importantly however, the manner in which individuals interact with their work can also exacerbate or moderate stress. The degree and

FIGURE 4.6 An integrated model for understanding stress response
Source: Author's own data.

nature of empathic engagement, the approach to managing emotional labor, and coping styles, are important individual mediators of stress. In all three cases, the balance of cognition and emotional regulation is critical. In the case of empathic engagement, a degree of emotional empathy may facilitate the therapeutic process and clinical decision-making. More important, however, is cognitive empathy, as it allows the social worker to understand the client's frame of reference while allowing for emotional protection. Similarly, in the case of managing emotional labor, cognitive reframing to facilitate understanding of the client's behavior results in lower levels of stress response than suppressing emotions and displaying ungenuine emotions. And finally, task-oriented rather than emotion-oriented coping strategies are associated with lower stress responses. In the next two chapters, I discuss the nature of expertise and decision-making to set the stage for addressing the intersection between stress and decision-making.

CHAPTER FIVE

Competence and Expertise

An expert is commonly understood to be a person with authoritative knowledge or superior skills in a particular area. This definition aptly captures the notion that expertise is domain-specific: being an expert in one area does not translate to expertise in another. The definition also conjures up images of experts studiously focusing their attention on amassing knowledge about a particular area and developing and honing their skills through repeated practice over a prolonged period. This image of expertise is consistent with theoretical models and research on its acquisition. What it does not fully capture, however, is the essence of expertise—not only the science, but also the art of great experts. The apparently effortless way in which true experts face problems or challenges—and arrive at solutions as if they were being guided by innate intuition—is something that not everyone achieves.

Researchin the area of expertise has in some part focused on the process of intuitive problem-solving and decision-making in which great experts engage. Intuition has been described as an unconscious process that is not mediated by reasoning. It invokes the use of rapidly produced holistic associations, and results in affectively charged decisions. This description includes several elements. First, while the final outcomes of intuitive problem-solving and decision-making are accessible to conscious thinking (experts can articulate the outcome), the rules and knowledge used for the inference are not accessible (experts cannot articulate how they arrived at the outcome). Rather, intuition involves linking disparate pieces of information in a rapid, effortless, and often effective way (Dane & Pratt, 2007). Information from the situation at hand is matched with a deeply held, yet unconscious, model or schema for organizing information. It produces rapid and holistic judgments based on complex patterns of temporal and conceptual relationships (Salas, Rosen, & DiazGranados, 2009).

Experts in any given domain are ideally situated to capitalize on intuition because they possess rich bodies of area-specific knowledge that foster rapid and sophisticated associative processes, thereby producing accurate, but seemingly instinctual, insights and conclusions (Dane, Rockmann, & Pratt, 2012). However, as intuition occurs outside conscious deliberation, the individual cannot articulate the steps, inductive thinking, or incremental decisions that lead to the result. Intuition is knowing without knowledge of the process by which the decision is made (Salas et al., 2009). This is reminiscent of the common observation of social work field instructors that teaching a student in the field practicum requires instructors to think about, and articulate, what they know and how they arrived at a particular assessment conclusion. Teaching others reveals to experts what they actually know.

Finally, the intuition that underlies expertise often carries with it an affective component, colloquially referred to as "following your heart" or "going with your gut." It can be understood to be experiential information processing (Dane et al., 2012). That is, the cognitive frameworks or schemas that underlie expert problem-solving and decision-making are inductively derived from emotionally significant experiences. In this way, the affective components of workplace experiences, including stress and trauma, may influence the unconscious schemas or patterns that underlie an individuals' expertise.

This chapter reviews the theoretical foundations of competence and expertise; models for understanding the development of expertise, the role of intuition and meta-competencies in expertise, factors influencing expertise in social work, and finally attending to factors that impact expertise.

THEORETICAL FOUNDATIONS OF COMPETENCE AND EXPERTISE

Ericsson and Smith suggested that "the study of expertise seeks to understand and account for what distinguishes outstanding individuals in a domain from less outstanding individuals in that domain, as well as from people in general" (1991, p. 2). These authors view expertise to be a stable characteristic of the individual that involves both inherited and acquired abilities. Inherited or innate abilities that contribute to expertise include intelligence and personality characteristics. Acquired abilities include general knowledge, experience, and domain-specific or task-specific knowledge.

When Sir Frances Galton published the treatise *Hereditary Genius* in 1869, he argued that innate characteristics limit the ability of an individual to excel in every domain in which they may wish to be great, despite the necessary correlates of motivation and perseverance. Galton begins with the example of individuals engaged in physical training who observe their strength and endurance increase incrementally with practice until they reach a plateau. At that point, no further improvement is achieved. For instance, individuals training to run can become faster and faster, and stronger and stronger, but at some point they realize they will never be Usain Bolt. Galton then likens this to the study of mathematics, in which many students will master initial concepts, but as the difficulty increases, fewer will attain mastery. At the top ranks (in his case study, those who obtained mathematical honors at Cambridge University), there is a marked difference in scores between the individuals who come first in any given year and those who come second or third. Galton referred to such abilities as *hereditary gifts* or *hereditary genius*. (An interesting side note is that Galton was the cousin of Charles Darwin, author of *The Origin of Species*.)

Galton nevertheless acknowledged that social structures (particularly the class system of England at the time of his writing) impacted the ability of individuals with inherent abilities to be socially recognized for their expertise. Some potentially brilliant mathematicians would never have the opportunity to develop and demonstrate their innate abilities at Cambridge. In this vein, research has demonstrated that standardized measures of general ability—for instance, IQ tests—have been remarkably unsuccessful in accounting for individual differences in levels of performance in arts, science, and professional practice as measured by factors such as income, prestige, prizes, and awards (Ericsson & Smith, 1991). Rewarded individuals may indeed have gifts that help them attain excellence and recognition, but not necessarily greater gifts than others who are not recognized. Rather, many remarkably gifted individuals will not be given the opportunity to rise to preeminence, while other decidedly untalented people do exceedingly well in terms of financial success and public accolades. This finding is not surprising to social workers, who are well aware that societal structures and systemic barriers limit the choices available to individuals and present varied blocks or enablers based on factors such as race and social class.

Nevertheless, Galton provided a situation-specific approach to exceptional performance during which systemic issues (in his example social status), which might be a limiting factor in ordinary circumstances, may prove less limiting. He contended that in extraordinary times of strife—such as civil war—individuals who rose to preeminence despite their social condition were "cool in danger, sensible in council, cheerful under prolonged suffering, humane to the wounded and sick, encouragers of the faint hearted" (1869, p. 48) Thus in addition to hereditary genius in the sense of *cognitive intelligence*, Galton identified a set of *personal characteristics* that allow certain individuals to rise to the level of expert or leader in their field despite being denied the social opportunities afforded to others. These personal characteristics resemble those of individuals who demonstrate resilience in the face of adversity or change, as discussed in chapter 2 (Rutter, 1985). Qualities that enhance resilience include self-confidence and a sense of self-worth, confidence in control over one's fate, social intelligence, openness to new experiences, and optimism (Collins, 2007; Earvolino-Ramirez, 2007; Grant & Kinman, 2012).

Arising from what Ericsson and colleagues described as the surprisingly unsuccessful search for stable inheritable characteristics that account for superior performance across fields (Ericsson, Krampe, & Tesch-Römer, 1993), more recent theories of expertise view it to be a process of amassing causal knowledge about a domain (Schmidt & Boshuizen, 1993). That is, through education and experience, individuals acquire information about relevant concepts, they then develop a richer understanding of the relations between these concepts, and ultimately this results in a personalized cognitive map for addressing practice issues that they face. From this perspective, the development of expertise is a linear process based on the acquisition of increased knowledge.

Schmidt and Boshuizen (1993) suggest a modified approach in which the development of expertise is a process characterized by distinct phases whereby the learner employs qualitatively different knowledge in different situations. Using the case of physicians, they suggest that in the course of medical training, students develop causal networks as to the underlying processes that lead to disease. Through repeated application of acquired knowledge within these causal networks, the knowledge becomes compiled into diagnostic labels—in which detailed concepts are clustered together into higher-level concepts. These higher-level concepts are narrative in nature, what Schmidt and Boshuizen call "illness scripts." Each illness script is characterized by three elements:

- enabling conditions (including heredity, biological determinants such as age and gender, and compromising factors such as drug abuse or travel)
- fault (pathogens, nutrient supply)
- consequences (complaints, signs and symptoms)

When confronted with an ill person, the physician searches for the illness script that best matches the current situation. Social workers will recognize this process. When confronted with a new client, our thinking about the situation and the questions we ask are directed by previous encounters. For example, this young person suffers from schizophrenia, has lost his housing, and seeks hospital admission. As we inquire about the young person's situation, new twists to the story emerge that differentiate his case from cases we have seen before. This novel encounter enriches our previously held script and becomes another layer or alternative to be considered when faced with the next case.

The illness script formulation builds on the foundational work of de Groot (1965), who sought to determine a model for understanding expertise through the study of chess grand masters. De Groot observed that while the thought processes and recall ability of grand masters did not differ significantly from that of other experienced players, they were much better and quicker at coming up with the right moves, seemingly by relying on pattern recognition. Building on this work, Chase and Simon (1973), through a series of experiments, determined that grand masters were unable to articulate the patterns they were perceiving and rather encoded information into relational structures consisting of familiar configurations of pieces. These structures developed through years of practice and resulted in unconscious perceptual processing. Chase and Simon went on to estimate the number of hours required to develop the skills required to attain top levels of expertise.

Subsequently, Ericsson and colleagues (1993) examined research on expertise across various domains including chess, music composition, writing, and science and conducted a series of studies on the acquisition of superior performance in music. While physical ability and intelligence may be necessary to attain a certain level of proficiency, the overriding factor in determining superior performance in all domains they studied was sustained and deliberate practice over a ten-year period. This practice was characterized by four elements:

- a preexisting knowledge of the nature of the task (in order that it could be done correctly)
- knowledge of the outcome of the task (in order to determine if it was it done correctly)
- immediate corrective feedback (how to do it better)
- repetition of the same or similar tasks after integrating the learning acquired from the last attempt

This lead to Malcolm Gladwell's popular characterization of the ten-thousand-hour rule (an approximation of Ericsson's ten years)—in which expertise is developed through deliberate and sustained practice for a prolonged number of years (Gladwell, 2008).

It is important to note, however, that while rejecting Francis Galton's claim that innate physiological ability or mental capacity differentiates those who are proficient in an area from those with superior expertise, Ericsson and colleagues (1993) allowed for the enabling influence of motivation and determination, personality characteristics identified by Galton. They argued that the capacity to engage in the hard work of deliberate practice is necessary for attainment of eminent performance.

This ability has recently been called *grit*, or the perseverance and passion required to attain long-term goals (Duckworth, et al., 2007). Duckworth and colleagues suggest that "grit entails working strenuously toward challenges, maintaining effort and interest over years despite failure, adversity, and plateaus in progress. . . . [The gritty person's] advantage is stamina. Whereas disappointment or boredom signals to others that it is time to change trajectory and cut losses, the gritty individual stays the course" (pp. 1087–1088).

Popular writer Malcolm Gladwell, however, reminds us that the manner in which individual characteristics intersect with the social environment further influences one's ability to achieve preeminence in a particular field. In his book *Outliers*, Gladwell provides the example of young people who excel in sports (2008). In each of the sports he reviews (baseball, soccer, and hockey), those young people who excel on junior teams are those whose birthdays fall shortly after the cutoff dates for participation based on age. For instance, in international junior soccer where the cutoff date is January 1, three-quarters of the players on the 2007 Czech junior soccer team were born in the first three months of the year, and none were born after September. Gladwell contends that this effect continues throughout life. As an example, in American baseball, where the cutoff date for a particular age level is July 31, more major league players are born in August than any other month. He thus suggests that kids who find themselves consistently in the older and more physically mature part of the cohort are systematically advantaged throughout their sports career, despite the fact that by the time they reach the professional leagues, month of birth is no longer an apparent issue. This seemingly random societal norm has a profound effect on opportunity, including spurring those with advantage to practice as their effort is more likely to lead to success.

In addition to social structures such as birthday cutoffs, societal attitudes may strongly influence perseverance, performance, and the eventual outcomes for any individual. In his exceptional book *Whistling Vivaldi*, Claude Steele (2011) presents the pervasive influence of what he terms "stereotype threat" to self-evaluation and ultimately performance. Drawing on his own extensive research and that of others, he demonstrates that when individuals confront the possibility that stereotypes of a group to which they belong could actually apply to them as an individual, the affective response to this possibility can be threatening enough to have disruptive effects on their performance in a particular domain. Applying this to racialized students in the United States, Steele suggests that when faced with the threat of being judged and treated stereotypically, students may internalize the fear of fulfilling the stereotype and ultimately perform in a manner that confirms the stereotype. Specifically, he demonstrated in a series of experimental design studies that making students vulnerable to judgment arising from negative racial stereotypes, such as those about intellectual ability depressed standardized test scores when compared to students of races that do not carry that stereotype. Conversely, when conditions were designed to alleviate the threat, or when stereotypes evoked suggested superior ability, students improved performance (Steele & Aronson, 1995). Thus he demonstrates the manner in which social context and group identity influence behavior. Racial and other stereotypes can undermine effort, performance and the achievement of mastery through the erosion of confidence in one's own personal ability. On the other hand, Steele also demonstrates that if one happens to be a member of a group that is viewed as having unique aptitude for a certain skill or in a certain area, one's performance and effort can be enhanced.

Finally, the individual characteristics of conceptual capacity and flexibility also intersect with practice in the development of expertise. In a tongue-in-cheek commentary in the scholarly journal *Academic Medicine* entitled "Chickens and Children Do Not an Expert Make," Glenn Regehr (1994) described the experience of attending a livestock fair and witnessing a chicken playing tic-tac-toe. He reports, "Despite going up against some of the greatest tic-tac-toe minds at the livestock fair, the chicken never lost a game and often won. . . . By any simple definition, the chicken was an extremely competent tic-tac-toe player. She was a veritable tic-tac-toe grand master" (p. 970). While trying to discern the difference between the chicken and a medical expert, he noted that the chicken was likely responding in a rapid, reflexive, and unreflective manner to a familiar pattern. We might consider this a type of overlearned behavior aimed at having a predictable response to situations. In many domains this is important. For instance, as I will discuss later in this book, individuals in emergency service professions, such as firefighting, learn standard responses to situations. This allows colleagues who may be in another part of a burning building to predict how each member of the team is likely to behave. Regehr noted that, unlike the chicken, a child at the age of eight may understand the concepts of tic-tac-toe but, lacking the experience derived from practice, would likely lose regularly to the chicken. Thus, although conceptual understanding is useful, it is not sufficient without practice and experience at recognizing patterns. He concludes that it is the combination of conceptual understanding and experience that allows an expert "to demonstrate cognitive flexibility and adaptability when faced with novel situations in a given domain, rather than a ritualized set of responses to a predictable set of stimuli" (p. 970).

DEVELOPMENT OF EXPERTISE

Dreyfus and Dreyfus (2005) brought together their respective perspectives from engineering and philosophy to describe a staged model of expertise development. Their original 1986 volume *Mind over Machine: The power of human intuition and expertise in the era of the computer*, sought to explain the "failure of artificial intelligence" in the late 1970s and the observation that computers could outperform beginners but could not rival experts. They proposed a developmental process of acquiring expertise in a stepwise manner. The five-stage model, depicted in figure 5.1, describes the manner in which individuals move from rule-guided knowing to experience-based intuitive knowing, in which responses are experienced as automatic. In the early stages, rules are learned as absolutes to be memorized and applied. In chess, this may be understood to be the rules of the game. Over time, these rules become second nature and are no longer in conscious awareness. The highest stage, expertise, is evidenced by the performance of a chess grand master in a lightning round, in which the entire game must be played in two minutes. At this speed, the grand master relies entirely on immediate perceptions rather than analysis and comparison of alternatives (Dreyfus, 2005).

Scardamalia and Bereiter caution, however, that expertise is not an end state "in which abundant knowledge and skill make it possible to accomplish with ease things that the non-expert can do, if at all, only with difficulty" (1991, p. 172). Rather, citing examples of writers and physicists, they suggest that experts spend their days working carefully

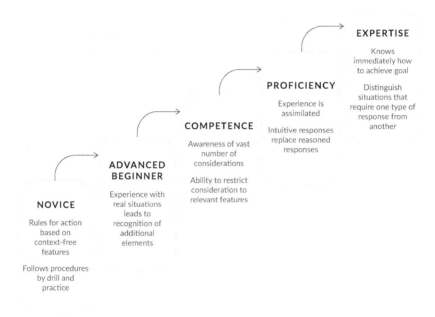

EXPERTISE

Knows immediately how to achieve goal

Distinguish situations that require one type of response from another

PROFICIENCY

Experience is assimilated

Intuitive responses replace reasoned responses

COMPETENCE

Awareness of vast number of considerations

Ability to restrict consideration to relevant features

ADVANCED BEGINNER

Experience with real situations leads to recognition of additional elements

NOVICE

Rules for action based on context-free features

Follows procedures by drill and practice

FIGURE 5.1 Five-stage model of the acquisition of expertise
Source: Dreyfus & Dreyfus, 2005.

and deliberately on problems that are difficult for them. They extend their knowledge and expertise by working on problems that are outside their area of competence, and in doing so, they resist repeated execution of familiar routines. Zilbert and colleagues describe this in terms of working at the boundary of the comfort zone. In a qualitative study of surgeons, participants described factors involved in their assessment of risk in novel situations including patient features, environmental features, and their perceptions of their own competence in that domain (Zilbert, Murnaghan, Gallinger, Regehr, & Moulton, 2015). When they decided to perform an operation despite viewing it to be on the edge of their expertise, they adopted strategies to enhance success, including optimizing the team by asking senior colleagues rather than trainees to participate in the procedure; optimizing the environment, for instance by using a head lamp; taking personal time to plan the procedure; arranging time for team-based planning; and mentally rehearsing the procedure (Zilbert et al., 2015).

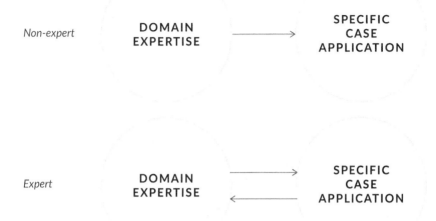

FIGURE 5.2 Dialectical process of expertise
Source: Adapted from Scardamalia & Bereiter, 1991.

Scardamalia and Bereiter (1991) contend that while experts do rely on domain knowledge and apply this knowledge to a particular case, they do so in a dialectical process. That is, not only is domain knowledge applied to a specific situation, but the learning from that novel situation is extracted and generalized into the individual's knowledge base. According to these authors, nonexperts are generally focused on a unidirectional process of using existing knowledge to solve a problem and then move on without pausing for the integrative element.

Schon (1987) identifies the complexity of professional practice, commenting that problems are interconnected, environments are turbulent, and practitioners are faced with conflicts of goals, purposes, and interests. In the real world of practice, notes Schon, problems do not present themselves in a clearly definable form; instead, they are constructed of elements that are puzzling, troubling, and uncertain. He thus describes a process in which some practitioners are able to bring art and intuition to situations of uncertainty, instability, uniqueness, and value conflict. Schon describes two interrelated processes:

knowing in action and reflecting in action. *Knowing in action* can be understood to be the actions and judgments that occur spontaneously. These actions do not require deliberate thought; individuals may not be aware that they have learned them, and they may not be able to articulate what they know that lead to these actions—much as Chase and Simon (1973) described with chess players. *Reflecting in action* involves improvisation and consists of varying, combining, and recombining understanding and possible actions from a variety of schemas. The reflective practitioner can articulate and question tacit understanding that has emerged from repetitive experiences and make sense of new situations, perhaps arriving at a novel understanding in a reflexive manner, as identified by Scardamalia and Bereiter and indeed creating a new "illness script" (Schmidt & Boshuizen, 1993). In this way, Schon defines two processes that occur in professional practice: the automatic response to routine problems and the creative response to new problems.

In his book *How Can I Help? A Week in My Life as a Psychiatrist*, David Goldbloom describes the process of teaching a trainee the skill of "listening for a diagnosis." He describes how the path to diagnosis is determined through a physician's history of taking observations, suggesting that "a physical exam or lab tests should mainly serve to confirm what the physician already suspects after taking a careful patient history" (Goldbloom & Bryden, 2016, p. 22). He suggests that trainees need more time to conduct an assessment "as they learn the longhand of interviewing; clinical experience will teach them the shorthand" (p. 24). He likens the discovery of the diagnosis to solving an Arthur Conan Doyle mystery, a process that requires the use of all five senses. One of the things that developing psychiatrists will learn is the importance of the first few seconds of the interaction with the patient: "Everything is fair game in our medical sleuthing—appearance, clothing, grooming, facial expression, speed of movement, style of interaction—as long as it does not lead to premature judgment" (p. 26). In some ways, these elements will be very familiar to everyone who has learned to conduct a standard mental status exam (C. Regehr & Glancy, 2014). Goldbloom, however, draws attention to the rapid and apparently automatic manner in which this occurs. Finally, as he outlines the process of the interview, he describes something akin to an illness script: "A map has started to emerge of [the patient's] relational universe that a few minutes ago had been terra incognita" (p. 38).

Moulton and colleagues consider a model of expertise that accounts for the transition from automatic cognitive resources to intentional analytic processes (Moulton, Regehr, Mylopoulos, & MacRae, 2007). Drawing on theories that address how individuals effectively use cognitive resources to select relevant information for attention, processing, and ultimately direct action, they consider how individuals use the limited cognitive "space" available to them. In the course of increasing experience, complicated and complex activities become automated, freeing up cognitive resources for other purposes, including meta-cognition. (*Meta-cognition* is a familiar term in education research and can be understood to be a higher order form of thinking that involves awareness, consideration, and ultimately control over personal cognitive processes.) Experts are able to attend to situational differences and then slow down their automatic reactions and use cognitive resources in an effortful way (Moulton et al., 2007). Slowing down may be initiated in two ways. In the first instance, slowing down is proactively planned, such as what a surgeon does while preparing for the surgery. During the preparation, possible challenges are considered and an advance decision is made to slow down should an anticipated challenge occur. In the second instance, slowing down is situationally responsive to an unanticipated occurrence (Moulton, Regehr, Lingard, Merritt, & MacRae, 2010b).

Moulton and colleagues then went on to examine their theory in the context of the operating room. Through observation and interviews with surgeons, they identified four cognitive strategies that expert surgeons used when facing novel and challenging situations:

- stopping a surgical procedure when more information was needed
- removing distractions during critical slow-down moments
- focusing more intently by withdrawing from extraneous conversations or distractions, without removing them
- fine-tuning or adjusting to emergent cues (Moulton, Regehr, Lingard, Merritt, & MacRae, 2010a)

Using the concept of meta-cognition, Ge and Hardré suggest that the development of expertise occurs in three sequential stages.

1. *Discovery and exploration of new concepts.* During this stage, learners are preoccupied with learning new information and have limited ability to integrate concepts through meta-cognition.
2. *Knowledge integration.* As knowledge becomes solidified, cognitive capacity is made available to engage in meta-cognition. The learner thus proceeds to integrate information into new schemas and restructure existing schemas. In this second stage, learners' confidence diminishes as they identify gaps in their knowledge, leading to an awareness of where they are not professionally competent. Ideally this is rectified as feedback from others and is integrated, thereby addressing gaps in knowledge. In this way, experts continue to adapt their knowledge and approaches.
3. *Automation and tuning.* Over time, knowledge and skills become more automatic and efficient. More complex and detailed tasks can be completed, and individuals are able to ground their approaches in a theoretical framework (Ge & Hardré, 2010).

Chi, Glaser, and Farr (2014) identify several characteristics of experts that arise from the literature. First, experts excel mainly in their own domains and generally are not advantaged over nonexperts when faced with problems in a different domain. Second, as noted earlier, experts perceive large meaningful patterns in their domain. Over time and with experience, they organize knowledge into clusters against which they weigh new situations. Third, experts perform tasks more quickly and with fewer errors than novices. In part, this relates to practice as well as pattern recognition, which allows them to solve a problem without an extensive search of relevant knowledge. Next, when solving novel problems, experts step back from the immediate application and consider the issue qualitatively—developing mental representations from which they can infer relations. And finally, experts have strong self-monitoring skills; when compared to novices, experts are more likely to know when they make errors and to check their solutions. Another characteristic of experts is that they possess "strategically-organized context knowledge that reflects a deep understanding of their subject matter" (Ge & Hardré, 2010, p. 24). That is, experts are able to discern when models of understanding are applicable to the context and when they are not, and they adapt accordingly.

Social work professor Michael Eraut (2004) notes that expertise in the field is not developed in a vacuum; rather, the work environment gives rise to the learning that culminates in expertise. He has identified four types of work activities that contribute to this process:

1. Teamwork and other group activities in which people work toward a common outcome
2. Observing and listening to others, allowing the individual to learn from the expertise and tacit knowledge of others
3. Tackling challenges with the support of others
4. Seeking consultation from others with respect to insights and challenges regarding specific cases

This process can be augmented by workplace practices and procedures that facilitate learning. Such processes include direct supervision from managers; the provision of designated mentors; coaching; formal shadowing opportunities where others can be observed; attending and contributing to professional conferences; opportunities to work toward additional qualifications; and encouragement of independent study (Eraut, 2007).

EXPERTISE AND COMPETENCE IN SOCIAL WORK PRACTICE

Fook and colleagues propose a social work–specific adaptation of Dreyfus and Dreyfus's model of expertise (2005) by which an individual progresses from conscious analytic behavior using context-free rules, to skilled behavior based on the unconscious and intuitive recognition of patterns. Their research involved qualitative interviews with thirty expert social workers in Australia, combined with an analysis of the participants' responses to standardized vignettes (Fook, Ryan, & Hawkins, 1997). Based on this research, they identified several themes related to the practice of expert social workers in addressing challenging situations:

• rather than applying overall theoretical frameworks, social work experts selected particular theoretical concepts to guide their work

- while social work experts were continually aware of context and complexity at both the micro and macro levels, their focus remained on the client
- subsequent interventions employed by expert social workers were also focused on the individual and not the surrounding systems
- and finally, while expert social workers were confident in their abilities and their capacity to influence the situation, they remained guarded about the effectiveness of their interventions due to awareness of situational constraints

Consistent with the model proposed by Dreyfus and Dreyfus, a comparison of experts and students revealed that expert social workers were more likely than students to take into account situational characteristics, were more confident in their professional identities, and were more positive about the ability of social work to influence change. While informative, one challenge of cross-sectional studies such as this is that it is not possible to determine whether those abilities inevitably grow in all individuals, or whether certain individuals have the requisite characteristics to become expert social workers over time, while others leave the profession.

In this vein, colleagues and I wondered whether it was possible to determine prior to admission whether some individuals lacked the characteristics that would allow them to attain competence or expertise in social work (Pelech, Stalker, Regehr, & Jacobs, 1999; C. Regehr, Stalker, Jacobs, & Pelech, 2001). This investigation took two forms: (1) analyzing quantitative data in admissions files, and (2) conducting a content analysis of personal statements prepared by applicants to the program. In each study, a comparative analysis was performed between students who did not encounter difficulties in the program, and those who experienced placement breakdown, required an extended practicum, had repeated difficulty meeting academic expectations, and/or demonstrated significant problems in interpersonal relationships. These students were identified independently by the director of the practicum and faculty members not involved in the research analysis. In analyzing quantitative data from admissions files, we determined that students who were later identified as experiencing problems in the program were on average older than other students, were more likely to be male, had lower entering grade point averages (GPAs), and (perhaps paradoxically) had more social service workplace experience. These findings were consistent with some earlier findings regarding the value of age and gender as predictors of difficulty in student social workers (Cunningham, 1982; Duder & Aronson, 1978; Pfouts & Henley, 1977) and with our subsequent research on the association between entering GPA and performance in the practicum (Bogo, Regehr, Hughes, Power, & Globerman, 2002).

Clearly, however, unlike GPA, demographic-based findings could not be considered particularly helpful for establishing screening criteria in admissions. Therefore, another faculty member researcher, Carol Stalker, and I, with combined clinical experience of forty years, conducted a content analysis of personal statements written by applicants as part of the admissions process. As one might expect, a tidy list of characteristics that describe the personal statements of students who later encountered difficulties in their graduate social work studies could not be identified. Nevertheless, in comparison to other students, issues identified in the statements of students who later encountered problems in the program included a focus on personal histories of abuse, injustice, or neglect, and plans to work with others with similar experiences. These students were four times as likely to report that they had experienced sexual abuse, spousal violence, parental neglect, or personal alcoholism. They were less likely to identify concern about injustices toward others, were less likely to note areas of personal weakness, and were more than twice as likely to report having received personal therapy (C. Regehr et al., 2001). Given the important objective of diversifying students in social work programs, these findings point to the need to consider resources and programmatic elements that may better assist students with troubling histories to develop into experts.

In a series of research studies, our team at the University of Toronto investigated the nature of social work expertise and competence. These studies are described in detail by Marion Bogo in her recent book, *Achieving Competence in Social Work Through Field Education* (2010). One study sought to understand core elements of competence and expertise in social work through eliciting field instructor's depictions of exemplary and struggling students (Bogo et al., 2006). A purposive sample was drawn from all of the field instructors of the University of Toronto graduate program in social work who offered placements in health, mental health, or child welfare. Inclusion criteria were being an experienced field instructor (i.e., five years or more); possessing strong competencies as a field instructor as determined by the practicum director; and recent supervision of students (i.e., within the last three years). Analysis of the qualitative interviews revealed four important areas discussed by field instructors that differentiated exemplary students from those viewed to have problems or struggles in the practicum: personal qualities, approach to learning, practice skills, and behavior in the organization.

An overarching theme of this research study was the tendency of field instructors to describe innate characteristics or personal qualities as key distinguishers between students and critical elements for predicting future success. Important attributes identified in both exemplary and struggling students are highlighted in the following statements: "She exuded *confidence*, which wasn't over-confidence." "She brought a kind of personal *maturity* with her. She in fact did not have very mature clinical skills but she was a *risk taker* and learned quickly." "She was *bright* and very knowledgeable and she was *motivated* and *interested*" (p. 583). On the other hand, struggling students evoked opposite responses: "Didn't work independently, constantly *needed reassurance*." "He was a little messy on his *boundaries* and he was a terrible *procrastinator* so any program he would have been in it would have been an issue." "The more complexity the person was faced with, the more *overwhelmed* they would become, [stating] that's just too complicated and it's too difficult" (p. 583). Field instructors also identified some very challenging behaviors in struggling students, such as hostility, dishonesty, and sleeping in meetings. One field instructor clearly identified the importance of core characteristics when selecting students for this site: "I am not looking at . . . assessment and those kind of skills, but I am looking for the qualities of the person" (p. 583).

Similarly, as field instructors described the students' approach to learning, they invoked terms that suggested innate or characterological traits. Exemplary students were viewed to have *initiative*, a desire to learn skills, and conceptual sophistication. When faced with corrective feedback, they were seen to be *adaptable, flexible, and motivated* to find solutions. Struggling students were seen to overestimate their abilities and "didn't know what [they] didn't know." Thus they were *resistant* to corrective feedback, were unwilling to "start with the basics," and wanted "to be seen as a peer" even though they "did not have the knowledge" (p. 584). While these skills were viewed to be inherent to the individual, it is important to acknowledge that they are also contextually bound, as suggested by the work of Claude Steele (2011).

Students' practice skills were linked to their ability to conceptualize practice and connect the dots between information gathered, allowing them to set goals and determine appropriate interventions. Finally, *relational skills* both with clients and with others in the organization were described as fundamental elements that differentiated exemplary students from struggling ones. Specific descriptions can be found in table 5.1

Specific practice skills of a more technical nature, such as conducting assessments and implementing interventions, were seen by field instructors within the context of personality characteristics. Indeed, field instructors were often forgiving of skill deficits in exemplary students, believing that, due to the student's inherent abilities and motivation, these deficits would be overcome. For instance, the deficits of an exemplary student were attributed to lack of prior exposure to the area. Similarly, when a struggling student was viewed as a "nice person," the field instructor worked harder and invested more energy in teaching, to the extent that they worried about compromising expectations. Conversely, good practice skills such as assessment and or report writing in problematic students were overshadowed by problems in relating interpersonally, having poor boundaries with staff, being overly critical of others, being unable to work within organizational rules, personalizing feedback they received, or being overly dependent on the field instructor.

This is not to suggest that learned practice skills such as assessment, report writing, communication, and intervention plan implementation are not important. Indeed, most competency-based models are reliant on these very skills. However, our research suggests that expert social workers describe a hierarchy of competencies that includes both overarching personality characteristics and procedural or operational skills. These overarching personality characteristics have been referred to as *meta-competencies*. Drawing from the management literature, Cheetham and Chivers (1996) applied this concept in the development of a professional competence model, modifying a model used in the United Kingdom to determine occupational standards that focused on job-specific tasks. They critiqued the existing model, suggesting that in the effort to

TABLE 5.1

Field instructors' depictions of exemplary and problematic students

	Exemplary Students	Problematic Students
Personal qualities	• Mature, quick, energetic, independent, conscientious, responsive • Go beyond: engage with staff, produce work beyond expectations • Take risks, meet challenges • Relational capacity	• Poor judgment • Mental health problems • Major personal issues in own lives • Dishonesty • Issues with self-identity
Approach to learning	• Committed to learning • Seek new opportunities to learn • Engaged in learning before the practicum begins (literature searches) • Accept and integrate feedback • Self-reflective	• Not open about practice (withholding tapes) • Unaware of learning needs • Not receptive to new ideas • Passive
Practice skills	• Ability to conceptualize link between theory and practice • Positive relationship skills (able to engage and challenge) • Excellent interviewing skills • Can work with content and process	• re "lost," can't conceptualize • Don't have basic personal skills to connect with clients • Disrespectful of client or process • May have excellent assessment and report-writing skills
Behavior in organization	• Understand role of student • Communicate well and get along with team • Can work with other systems • Keep personal issues separate from work • Work within boundaries and ethics	• Trouble grasping social work role • Difficulty with professional boundaries • Raise concerns among team members due to poor judgment or overinvolvement in politics

(Bogo et al., 2006)

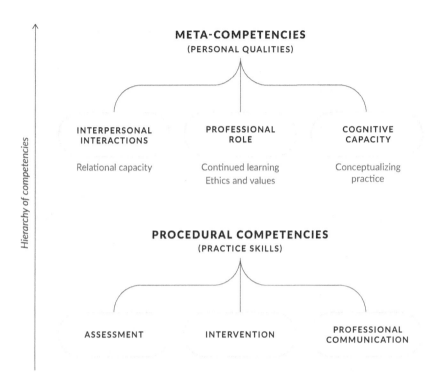

FIGURE 5.3 A hierarchy of competencies
Source: Modified from Bogo, 2010; Bogo et al., 2006.

judge competence based on performance of specific routine tasks, personal behaviors that underpin performance were being ignored. In their model, meta-competencies include communication, self-development, creativity, and problem-solving ability. In the management literature, meta-competencies include attitudes, leadership, innovation, communication, and the ability to create a team-oriented culture (Tubbs & Schulz, 2006). Building on our team's research with students, Marion Bogo suggested that meta-competencies in social work practitioners occur in four areas: cognitive-conceptual meta-competencies, including the professional's knowledge base and ability to conceptualize practice; interpersonal and relational meta-competencies with clients and members of the organization; personal and professional approaches to learning and assuming a professional role; and ethics and values related to the profession. Procedural competencies include assessment, intervention, and communication. These are depicted in figure 5.3.

Edward Thorndike, a professor of educational psychology at Columbia University Teachers College, originally proposed the concept of social intelligence in a 1920 edition of *Harper's* magazine. He proposed three types of intelligence: mechanical, social, and abstract. Mechanical intelligence is the ability to learn and manage concrete elements—such as a car or the land. Abstract intelligence is the ability to manage ideas and symbols—such as words, numbers, or legal decisions. Social intelligence is the ability to understand and manage within the realm of human relations (E. Thorndike, 1920). Seventeen years later, Robert Thorndike and Saul Stein, also of Columbia's Teachers College, lamented that no tool to adequately measure the construct of social intelligence had yet been developed. They suggested that this was in part due to the fact that social intelligence was a multifaceted concept that may also intersect significantly with abstract intelligence (R. Thorndike & Stein, 1937). This early conceptualization reinforces our findings regarding meta-competencies—or the interrelatedness of conceptual ability and relational ability as core features of social work expertise.

Building on this concept, Salovey and Mayer proposed a subset of social intelligence that they called *emotional intelligence*, which they defined as "the ability to monitor one's own and others' feelings and emotions to discriminate among them and to use this information to guide one's thinking and actions" (1990, p. 189). Emotional intelligence includes both the capacity to identify and draw on one's own feelings in order to understand and guide behavior, but also includes interpersonal intelligence or the ability to identify the emotions of others for the purposes of predicting future behavior.

SELF-APPRAISAL OF COMPETENCIES

Interestingly, it is the very characteristics that are seen to be most important for the development of expertise that are blind spots for individuals with deficits in those areas. This became clear in another area of inquiry in our work on the ability of social work students to self-assess their areas of competence and areas of weakness, as measured by the level of agreement between the student and the supervisor. In the first study, we designed a relative-ranking instrument (C. Regehr, Regehr, Leeson, & Fusco, 2002) that built on previous work conducted in medicine seeking to move the notion of self-appraisal from asking "How good am I?" to "What aspects of my professional performance require the most improvement?" (G. Regehr, Hodges, Tiberius, & Lofchy, 1996). In using this instrument, students were asked to select ten of the learning goals that they had identified at the beginning of their practicum and place them in a random list from A to J. Students were then asked to rank-order each skill relative to the other skills. The field instructors were subsequently asked to independently rank the same ten learning goals. Fifty-eight student/supervisor pairs completed the evaluation forms. Thirty-seven of these students allowed their data to be used in the study.

The mean correlation between student self-assessment and field instructor assessment found in this study (0.53) was consistent with findings for psychiatric residents (G. Regehr et al., 1996) but was higher than that generally reported for professionals in the self-assessment literature. However, there was considerable difference in the agreement for different types of goals. Goals with high agreement focused on practical skills such as communication skills, individual and group treatment skills, and community knowledge (table 5.2). This suggests that students are quite accurate in assessing their abilities in more concrete domains of practice. Conversely, considerable disagreement was evident in three goals: (1) dealing with resistance, ambivalence, or conflict in the therapeutic relationship, (2) ability to function on a team, and (3) adherence to social work ethics. Thus students were strikingly less able to assess their strengths in meta-competencies.

Not only are students less able to identify deficits in meta-competencies, but they are more reluctant to receive corrective feedback on these issues. In a paper entitled "When Values Collide," we described an analysis of qualitative data accrued across four research studies that addressed the experiences of field instructors in evaluating students and providing corrective feedback (Bogo, Regehr, Power, & Regehr, 2007). We reported that conflict occurred both between students and supervisors and within individual supervisors themselves when providing feedback in these domains. Supervisors noted difficulty in giving feedback when students do not accept it. They described a range of student reactions, including arguing, becoming defensive, attacking the instructor's teaching style, and becoming silent and avoidant. Three types of circumstances were identified by instructors as limiting students' acceptance

TABLE 5.2

Agreement between students and supervisors on level of skill ($N=37$)

Skill	Level of Agreement (Pearson's Correlation)	Number of Students Identifying This Learning Goal
High agreement		
Communication skills	0.86	17
Community systems knowledge	0.75	12
Intervention planning and evaluation	0.74	15
Individual counseling skills	0.71	12
Group work skills	0.69	17
Low agreement		
Dealing with resistance or conflict	−0.01	7
Ability to function on a team	−0.02	10
Adhering to social work ethics	−0.24	7

(C. Regehr, Regehr, Leeson, & Fusco, 2002)

of feedback: (1) where students had difficulty understanding the role of social work and the nature of practice and hence could not accurately assess their behaviors or skills, (2) where students had worked before entering the educational program, believed themselves to be competent, and were not open to a new view of their skill level, and (3) where students' personality style was such that problematic behaviors were a pervasive part of their interactions with clients, colleagues from related professions, or both. Indeed, when confronted with corrective feedback, some students became fearful and cautious, and their struggles in learning were exacerbated. A downward and deteriorating cycle ensued, with negative feedback producing more anxiety and concern, which in turn interfered with students' ability to learn and progress (Bogo et al., 2007).

FACTORS THAT INTERFERE WITH EXPERTISE

Two core concepts underline the analysis presented in this chapter. First, expertise is domain-specific. An individual develops the requisite knowledge and cognitive abilities in a particular area, and these skills and abilities may or may not be transferable to other areas. Second, while expertise and competence develop over time, some individuals are better equipped to develop expertise than others are. This capacity to develop expertise is founded on the possession of meta-competencies, or overarching abilities such as cognitive flexibility, relational capacity, and openness to learning (see figure 5.3).

Unlike many other professionals, social workers acquire expertise in the context of high-stress work environments characterized by risks to personal safety, repeated exposure to distressing material involving interpersonal abuse and violence, public oversight, and media scrutiny. These environments lead to incident-related traumatic stress responses (chapter 3) and chronic stress responses such as burnout and compassion fatigue (chapter 4). They can also result in increased resilience and posttraumatic growth, which includes such elements as enhanced compassion, an improved sense of self (including one's own limitations and vulnerabilities), and greater insight (Arnold, Calhoun, Tedeschi, & Cann, 2005; Cadell, Regehr, & Hemsworth, 2003; Tedeschi, Park, & Calhoun, 1998).

Perhaps not surprisingly, factors that predict the development of stress and trauma reactions closely map onto the meta-competencies identified for social work, as well as factors that contribute to the development of expertise. In chapter 3, I noted that relational capacity, or the ability to develop and sustain relationships, was among the various factors that predicted longer-term posttraumatic and stress reactions. Relational capacity allows an individual to approach difficult situations with a greater sense of personal esteem and self-efficacy, as well as a healthy ability to appraise others critically and realistically. Further, relational capacity allows individuals to develop social support networks that will be available in times of distress. These same abilities allow an individual to develop a network of mentors and colleagues who can be relied on when managing difficult cases, who can be consulted when novel situations are presented, and who contribute to the ongoing learning and development of expertise through a reflective process.

Relational capacity also allows for empathic engagement with others. Empathic attunement can help an individual examine all aspects of a situation from a client's point of view, including the affective considerations involved in contributing to the current situation and in shaping the client's view of any potential solutions. However, the ability to balance emotional and cognitive aspects of empathy ensures that the professional is able to fully consider the wide range of factors affecting the situation and not exclude some due to emotional clouding of the issue.

As noted earlier in this chapter, professional intuition, the automatic and unconscious process in which experts engage, is based on schemas that are derived from emotionally significant experiences (Dane & Pratt, 2007). Indeed, Dane and Pratt suggest that evidence from organizational, cognitive, and neurological psychology all point to the fact that affect and emotions are an integral part of intuitive judgments. Where a social worker's experiences have included traumatic or high-stress exposures that continue to invoke affective and autonomic reactions, we would expect that these experiences will have shaped their expert schemas. As a result of their "gut feeling" reactions, these experiences will also shape their professional judgments. For instance, situations reminiscent of highly emotional experiences may highlight perceptions of risk, which may or may not be useful in final clinical decisions.

An individual's approach to his or her professional role and learning impacts both vulnerability to stress and trauma as well as the ability to develop expertise as a social worker. As noted in chapter 2, McCann, Sakheim, and Abrahamson (1988) suggest that upon encountering traumatic situations, an individual attempts to cope with arousal in one of three ways: (1) by failing to be sensitive to the discrepant input; (2) by interpreting the meaning of the input in a manner that is consistent with existing schemas; or (3) by altering existing schemas. Those who are able to employ meta-cognition to modify existing knowledge schemas (Ge & Hardré, 2010; Schon, 1987) can continually develop their knowledge and abilities, thereby achieving greater levels of expertise. Conversely, those who fail to be aware of discrepant information will continue to use rule-bound models of professional problem-solving that may or may not apply in a given situation.

Another central feature of expertise is emotional intelligence. Emotional intelligence is the capacity to access one's own feelings, to discriminate among those feelings, and to draw on them in guiding behavior, combined with the ability to monitor the moods and behaviors of others and integrate this knowledge to predict future behavior (Salovey & Mayer, 1990). Those with the superior ability to harness their own emotions for solving problems will be advantaged in developing and exercising expertise in social work practice. Social work scholars and educators Yorke, Grant, and Csiernik (2016) describe a process using what they call "the third eye." Building on Schon's model of response in action, these authors discuss the acquisition of active self-reflection, a sophisticated and subtle multilayered approach in which the professional simultaneously observes, interacts, and reflects on the encounter. Using the third-eye imagery, they suggest that the first eye is objective and theoretically informed; the second eye is attunement to the professional's own anxieties, reactions, and responses; and the third eye is the ability to disconnect and appraise the situation from a suspended vantage point. While Yorke and colleagues focus their discussion on unconscious biases related to race, class, age, or gender, this analysis can easily be extended to preexisting expectations and schemas informed by prior trauma experiences.

Thus experts develop intuitive knowledge that guides their approach to practice. This intuitive knowledge is shaped by the integration of new knowledge into existing schemas, thereby developing an increasingly rich framework for addressing both familiar and novel situations. This framework also incorporates affective experiences that may help, or potentially hinder, decision-making. Salas and colleagues (2009) have asserted that expertise is at the root of effective intuitive decision-making. In the next chapter, I turn to the process of professional decision-making.

CHAPTER SIX

Decision-Making

Professional judgment in complex clinical situations encompasses a multifaceted cognitive process that incorporates professional knowledge, accumulated expertise, and critical thinking. While evidence-based practice has been emphasized in many forums, including professional guidelines and accreditation, government policy, and educational programs, there is nevertheless considerable research to suggest that when exercising judgment, professionals continue to rely on tacit knowledge consisting of their own experience, professional values, and consultations with colleagues. This in part arises from concerns that characterize evidence-based practice as the rationing of resources disguised as science (Porta, 2004; Saarni & Gylling, 2004); as being overly rigid and constricting (Rosenfeld, 2004); and as being based on an aggregation of cases that do not necessarily reflect the individual about whom a professional judgment must be made (Lipman, 2004). As David Naylor opined in *The Lancet*, "Sound clinical decisions should ideally be driven by an amalgam of evidence, values or preferences, and circumstances. . . . A rigorous decision analysis can indeed delineate for typical patients the available options, clinical consequences, and any associated degrees of uncertainty. But to paraphrase Voltaire, typical patients are far from typical" (2001, p. 523). Thus as I discussed in chapter 5, professional decision-making is both a science and an art.

One of the challenges identified in professional decision-making is the wide variation in judgments not only between professionals, but even for a particular professional at different periods of time. A number of factors have been proposed to explain differences in clinical judgment (or errors in clinical judgment). These factors include inadequate training, knowledge, experience, and problem-solving capabilities; ambiguous, missing, or contradictory information; fear of making the wrong decision; guilt in breaching client trust; and sympathy for clients in situations of hardship (Gambrill & Shlonsky, 2000; Horwath, 2007; Van de Luitgaarden, 2009). This chapter will review the research literature on cognition and decision-making, including theoretical models of decision-making, as well as the literature on decision-making and risk in social work.

MODELS FOR UNDERSTANDING DECISION-MAKING

"Most important decisions are based on beliefs concerning the likelihood of uncertain events, such as the outcome of an election, the guilt of a defendant, or the future value of the dollar" (Tversky & Kahneman, 1974, p. 1125). Theories of decision-making have thus emerged from an examination of how individuals make choices in the face of risk, where *risk* is defined as the uncertainty about the probability that each of several possible outcomes will occur (Mohr, Biele, & Heekeren, 2010). Several models have been suggested for understanding the processes people engage in to make decisions in times of risk, which range from deliberate cognitive processes to unconscious intuitive approaches that arise in the manner discussed in chapter 5. Slovic and colleagues defined this in three ways: *risk as analysis*—involving logic, reason and scientific deliberation; *risk as feelings*—referring to fast, instinctive, intuitive reactions; and *risk as politics*—those who control the manner in which risk is defined have the power to define the outcome (Slovic, 1999; Slovic, Finucane, Peters, & MacGregor, 2004).

Each of these models is evident in social work decision-making. Take, for instance, the decision of whether a child is at risk of harm at the hands of her parents. Standardized risk assessment measures and structured professional judgment (SPJ) tools have been developed to guide social workers in making the decision based on common risk factors (risk as analysis). In addition, experienced child protection social workers will consider other factors, such as their ability to form a relationship with the parents, which is discussed later in this chapter (risk as feelings). Finally, as discussed earlier, the context in which the decision is made includes societal outrage over child deaths, recent public inquiries into the deaths, and new agency mandates or legislation arising from political reactions to high-profile cases (risk as politics). These factors intersect with one another in the decision-making process.

RATIONAL CHOICE THEORY

Rational choice theory emerged from the discipline of economics as a means for understanding choice behavior where outcomes are uncertain. At the end of World War II, Von Neumann and Morgenstern proposed the *expected utility model* in their classic book *Theory of Games and Economic Behavior* (1947). According to this theory, an individual compiles a mental list of the range of possible costs and benefits of any given choice and then considers the likelihood that each possible outcome will occur. Considered broadly, utility may be a financial gain (as in the case of gambling), a health outcome (such as when considering surgery), or a moral value (such as balancing individual rights and freedoms and community safety). Expected utility is calculated by multiplying the probability of an outcome by its utility, or in other words how important, desirable, or undesirable it is to the individual. The rational individual will then make a choice that maximizes possible positive outcomes and minimizes possible negative outcomes.

$$\text{Desirability (utility)} \times \text{likelihood (probability)} = \text{decision}$$

While this began as a mathematical model applied to individual decision-making in games of chance where complete information is available (for instance, there is a one-in-six chance a dice will roll a 3), Von Neumann and Morgenstern asserted, "It will be seen that many economic and social phenomena which are usually ascribed to the individual's state of 'incomplete information' make their appearance in the theory and can be satisfactorily interpreted with its help" (p. 30).

The theory is a more sophisticated mathematical (specifically, multiple-regression) approach to a model of decision-making proposed by Benjamin Franklin in a 1772 letter to Joseph Priestly, an eighteenth-century English theologian and scientist who is credited with the discovery of oxygen and the invention of soda water (Decision Science News, 2012). In the letter, Franklin described his method for making difficult decisions. He divided a sheet of paper into two columns, one for pro and one for con, and added thoughts relevant to the decision over the next few days. When all considerations were noted, Franklin assigned a weight to each item, considered the balance of pros and cons, and reached a decision. Franklin indicated that while the weight of reasons did not have algebraic precision, he felt he was less likely to take a rash step using this form of what he called "moral or prudential algebra."

Despite the intellectual appeal of rational choice theory, people often do not make choices in the manner the theory would predict. Rather, according to rational choice theory, people are quite likely to "misbehave" (Thaler, 2015). For example, Thaler describes an experience where undergraduate students in his class were unhappy with the fact that the average score on an exam was 72 points out of 100, despite the fact that actual points were irrelevant when the marks were changed to bell-curved letter grades for the transcript. Nevertheless, in light of student unhappiness, Thaler decided to make the exam worth a total of 137 points instead of 100. What transpired was that students were much happier when the average class score was 96 out of 137, even though the score translated to only a 70 percent average, rather than the original 72 percent average. Observations such as these have led to an entirely new field of scholarly activity that incorporates psychology and economics, called *behavioral economics* (Thaler, 2016).

Behavioral economics seeks to better understand common ways in which individuals diverge from a mathematical or logical appraisal of choice and make judgments based on other factors. For instance, Tversky and Kahneman (1981) identified the importance of both the decision frame and the assessment of prospects in affecting an individual's perceptions of options and outcomes. They suggest that factors that influence these perceptions are shaped in part by the manner in which the problem is presented, but they also include the norms, habits, and personal characteristics of the decision-maker. For instance, from an economic perspective, people are considerably more comfortable using a credit card for an item costing $100, if those who use cash are given a 5 percent discount (resulting in an actual cost of $95), than if the item costs $95 and there is a $5 surcharge for using a credit card. Same cost, different frame. Further, as demonstrated by prospect theory, many people are willing to drive ten minutes to another store in order to save money when a $30 item is on sale for $20 at the other location. However, those same people are less likely to drive the ten minutes if a $130 item is on sale for $120. In each case the drive is worth $10, but the prospect is different. In this way, rational behavior is bounded by other factors (Tversky & Kahneman, 1981).

Slovic, Monahan, and MacGregor (2000) demonstrated the effect of framing in a series of studies in which forensic psychiatrists and psychologists were presented with case summaries of hospitalized patients with mental disorders. Participants were asked to judge the likelihood of a patient harming someone after being discharged. In this case, the framing involved presenting risk as a percentage versus presenting risk in a manner that compared the current patient to other violent individuals. When clinicians were told that twenty out of every one hundred patients similar to Mr. Jones are estimated to have committed an act of violence, 41 percent indicated they would refuse to discharge the patient. However, when they were told that patients similar to Mr. Jones have a 20 percent chance of committing an act of violence, only 21 percent indicated that they would refuse to discharge. Thus, when all other factors are held constant, the manner in which risk is framed changes clinician behavior.

Mandeep Dhami and colleagues demonstrate further flaws in the real-life application of the rational choice model in a series of studies related to criminal justice, both in the decisions of individuals to engage in risky and illegal behavior, and in the decisions of judges overseeing court proceedings. In one study, eighty Canadian and eighty-seven Spanish undergraduate students were asked about the potential benefits and drawbacks of driving under the influence of alcohol (DUI) and riding with a drunk driver (RDD), as well as their actual recent experiences in engaging in these activities and the likelihood they would do these in the year ahead (Dhami, Mandel, & Garcia-Retamero, 2011). This issue has obvious implications for the safety of the young people engaged in this risk-taking activity and of society at large. As a result, many countries have focused on educating youth about the risks of drinking and driving, including both Canada and Spain, where the study was conducted. Further, penalties for drunk driving are stiff in both countries, including license revocation and incarceration. The researchers found that one-fifth of Canadian participants and over one-half of Spanish participants had engaged in driving while impaired in the past year, and one-half of the Canadians and just under one-half of the Spaniards reported riding with a drunk driver. Participants were well aware of the risks of drunk driving. Chief drawbacks they identified included the death or injury of others, property damage, and legal sanctions. On the other hand, participants noted that DUI and RDD are cheaper, faster, and more convenient than other options for getting home from a bar or party, including taxis and public transit.

Each benefit and drawback identified by participants was weighted according to the level of importance and likelihood of occurrence, as suggested by rational decision-making theory. The theory predicts that the resulting equation would determine decision-making. However, while the drawbacks identified by participants were significantly greater than the benefits in terms of importance and number, nevertheless the factors of convenience and cost led to the participants' prediction that they would continue to engage in both DUI and RDD. The authors concluded that there was no support for rational decision-making theory in this instance and that crime-reduction strategies that focused only on negative outcomes were doomed to be ineffective (Dhami et al., 2011).

Turning to professional decision-making, Dhami (2003, 2005) investigated the process of judicial decisions. Noting that such decisions are guided by formal rules and principles of due process, she suggested that, in theory, judges should search through the information pertaining to guilt and innocence, weigh it according to its reliability and validity, and combine it into a verdict. In the case of a bail hearing, such factors as the alleged offender's ties to the community, the seriousness of the offense, and the strength of the evidence in the case might predict an accused's risk of skipping bail and not returning to court if released into the community. Dhami observed 342 judicial bail hearings in two courts in London, England, and coded them according to the defendant's personal characteristics and previous criminal record, the nature of the offense, and the conditions of the bail hearing itself. Dhami found that the average bail hearing lasted seven minutes, during which three questions correctly predicted 96.3 percent of decisions in Court A and 94.6 percent of decisions in Court B:

1. Does the prosecutor oppose bail?
2. Did a previous court impose conditions or remand into custody?
3. Did the police impose conditions or remand into custody?

In each case where there was a previous punitive approach, the judge similarly denied bail. Dhami concluded that judges employed a *fast and frugal strategy* and did not use a rational decision-making model (Dhami, 2003, 2005).

HEURISTICS

Heuristics are just such a fast and frugal strategy. Most important decisions are based on beliefs concerning the likelihood of uncertain events, such as stock market performance, the guilt of an offender, or the risk that someone may harm themselves (Tversky & Kahneman, 1974). The challenge with such decision-making is that the list of possible influences on the outcomes of such events is seemingly endless, and predicting the likely outcome is thus a daunting task. A *heuristic* is an approach to problem-solving that employs a practical method that is not guaranteed to be optimal or perfect but is sufficient for the immediate goals. "Heuristics are efficient cognitive processes, conscious or unconscious, that ignore part of the information" (Gigerenzer & Gaissmaier, 2011, p. 451). Heuristics can be understood to be mental shortcuts or simple rules of thumb that ease the burden of decision-making.

Heuristics are integral to what Gigerenzer refers to as "gut feelings"— unconscious inferences of woven-together data from the senses using prior knowledge about the world. As discussed in the previous chapter on intuitive expertise, gut feelings appear quickly in the consciousness, triggered by external stimuli in an automatic manner. The underlying reasons and rationale for gut feelings are not known to the individual, but they are strong enough to act on (Gigerenzer, 2007). Examples of unconscious heuristics include the ability of baseball players to accurately predict the trajectory of pop-up fly balls and be at the right spot to catch it. Players do not calculate the velocity, wind direction, and air resistance in a differential equation. Rather, accomplished players have learned to fixate their gaze on the ball, start running, and adjust speed to ensure that the angle of gaze remains constant (Gigerenzer, 2007). Similarly, as I discuss below, experienced child welfare workers judge future risk to a child at the hands of a parent in part by the quality of the relationship the worker is able to establish with the parent. In a sense, their decision depends on whether they think they can keep their eye on the ball through this relationship.

Tversky and Kahneman (1974) describe three common heuristics: representativeness, availability, and anchoring. *Representativeness* is the method individuals use to determine if a person, object, or other construct is likely to be a member of a particular group. In this heuristic, individuals rely on stereotypes associated with the category in question. Tversky and Kahneman provide the example in which people are told that Mr. X is meticulous, introverted, meek, and solemn, and then they are asked whether Mr. X is likely to be a farmer, salesman, or librarian. Many people answering this question will rely on biases and suggest that he is a librarian. Yet in doing so they are making inferential errors, one of which is simply based on probability. In the absence of any other information, the fact that there are more farmers and salesman than librarians would suggest that Mr. X is more likely to be a farmer or salesman than librarian. The fit between biases and the decision made creates an illusion of validity, instilling confidence in the individual decision-maker (Tversky & Kahneman, 1974).

Availability heuristics occur when individuals assess the probability of an event based on the ease with which they can recall instances of the event (Tversky & Kahneman, 1973). For instance, a person may assess the risk of cancer based on the number of individuals in that person's acquaintance that have been diagnosed with the disease. Similarly, when the media is focusing on a particular type of occurrence, such as child abuse or sexual violence, members of the public believe the incidence of such violent offenses to be higher. In a clinical setting, when social workers assessing a particular form of risk, such as suicide, are acutely aware of recent tragedies on their own caseload or among colleagues at their institution, they may perceive that the probability of suicide is greater. Thus while availability heuristics may be useful—for instance, someone is more likely to suffer from a common illness than something extremely rare and thus should be treated for the common illness first—they may also lead to systematic errors.

Anchoring is the process by which a final determination is based on the first impression in any situation (Tversky & Kahneman, 1981). In clinical assessments, it involves weighting initial assessments more heavily in final assessments (De Bortoli & Dolan, 2015) or interpreting subsequent information in light of earlier information obtained. Thus if an initial diagnosis or formulation is reached quickly, clinicians are more likely to attune to information that confirms that diagnosis and ignore or minimize conflicting information.

Gigerenzer (2007) adds another potential pitfall in heuristics: the tendency to explain behavior internally without analyzing the environment, which can result in a fundamental attribution error. That is, behaviors are attributed to some innate quality of the individual, rather than an environment that shapes behavior or offers few other options. This was evident in the descriptions that field instructors provided of exemplary and struggling students in chapter 5. In summary, while heuristics can be extremely useful for practitioners, they also carry risks of bias. Heuristics need to be learned in an environment that provides timely, helpful, and corrective feedback and that can shape experience (De Bortoli & Dolan, 2015). In addition, however, heuristics can form the basis of decision tools to aid practitioners.

Fast and frugal heuristics can be codified into simple decision trees that become part of the decision-maker's repertoire for addressing decisions. Such decision trees limit the information search and do not involve computation. Fast and frugal decision trees specify (1) how the information is to be searched (what to look for and in what order cues should be considered); (2) when the information-seeking will be stopped (as the sufficient factors on which to base the decision have been ascertained); and (3) how the information results in a decision (if important factor X is present, the odds are sufficient that decision Y should be made). Gigerenzer and Gaissmaier (2011) assert that this process, involving both less time and less information, can improve decision-making as it reduces distraction caused by less relevant variables.

Despite the potential drawbacks of fast and frugal methods, Naylor has asserted that "the best lessons in fast and frugal rules of thumb may well come from understanding the cognitive processes of those master clinicians who consistently make superb decisions without obvious recourse to the canon of evidence-based medicine" (2001, p. 523). Similar to the fast and frugal decisions made by judges in London in the study conducted by Dhami, studies of physicians demonstrate the effective use such methods. For example, Green and Mehr (1997) sought to understand the behavior of physicians when faced with coronary care decisions. Initially, these researchers noted that when physicians in the emergency room were confronted with the possibility that individuals were suffering from a cardiac arrest, they behaved in an overly cautious manner in admitting individuals to a coronary care unit. When questioned about their diagnostic criteria, the physicians had developed their own experience-based fast and frugal approach, tending to admit individuals with histories of hypertension and diabetes, despite the fact that empirical evidence does not support these criteria as the best indicators of risk. As a result, Green and Mehr developed a pocket probability calculator in which physicians entered certain criteria into an electronic program and then a probability was calculated to determine whether admission to coronary care was indicated. Decision-making improved significantly. Next, to further test the benefits of the electronic calculator, they took the tools away from physicians but were surprised to discover that decision-making continued at the improved level even without the tool. It was revealed that physicians had learned the criteria to be entered into the calculator and continued to apply the criteria as a new rule of thumb. From this observation, Green and Mehr developed a new fast and frugal approach consisting of three questions (figure 6.1):

1. Does the electrocardiogram indicate a particular abnormality (called ST segment changes)?
2. Is the chief complaint chest pain?
3. Is any one of a number of specified factors present?

The results of each question lead either to the ultimate decision or to the next question. This approach proved highly accurate and efficient and was easily accepted by physicians.

Similarly, Brown and Rakow (2016) sought to understand clinician judgments with respect to violence risk assessments. In their study, nine clinicians were presented with case vignettes in which eight violence cues from standardized measures of violence prediction were integrated.

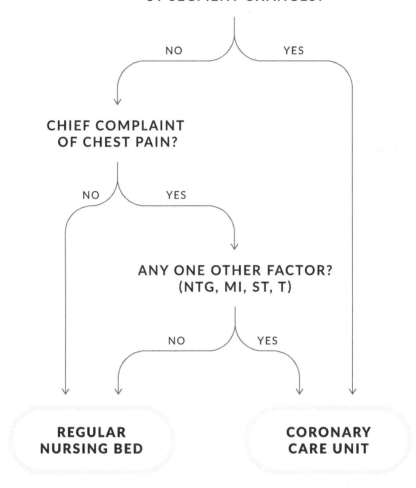

ST SEGMENT CHANGES?

NO   YES

CHIEF COMPLAINT
OF CHEST PAIN?

NO   YES

ANY ONE OTHER FACTOR?
(NTG, MI, ST, T)

NO   YES

**REGULAR
NURSING BED**

**CORONARY
CARE UNIT**

FIGURE 6.1 A fast and frugal decision tree for cardiac risk
Source: Gigerenzer, 2007, p. 174.

Clinicians were then asked to predict future risk of violence. In each of the cases, the risk assessments of clinicians could be correctly predicted by one to four cues, which were remarkably consistent across clinicians. The cues commonly identified as most relevant were more recent and less historical indicators (Brown & Rakow, 2016). Thus, despite the availability of more complex models, clinicians relied on a simplified but unarticulated heuristic.

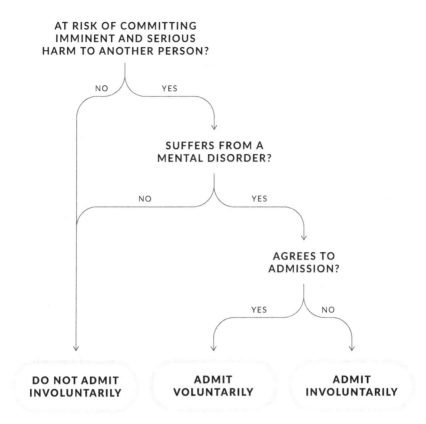

FIGURE 6.2 A fast and frugal decision tree for involuntary admission
Source: Modified from C. Regehr & Glancy, 2014.

In our book, *Mental Health Social Work Practice in Canada*, Graham Glancy and I suggest the use of a decision tree in determining whether an individual is eligible for involuntary admission to hospital under mental health legislation in most Canadian provinces (C. Regehr & Glancy, 2014). Such a model provides a simple means for both remembering criteria and for training others in learning the criteria (figure 6.2).

ACTUARIAL RISK ASSESSMENT TOOLS

As discussed in previous chapters, recent years have been fraught with high-profile inquiries throughout North America, Europe, and Australia into the deaths of children under the supervision of child welfare services (C. Regehr, Chau, Leslie, & Howe, 2002b) and attempts to hold child welfare workers and their organizations legally responsible (Kanani, Regehr, & Bernstein, 2002). Child protection professionals face some of the most difficult decisions in social services. Specifically, they must choose whether to remove children from their birth parents or potentially leave them in harm's way. In an effort to improve the performance of child welfare agencies and individual workers with these agencies, child welfare services throughout North America moved to using highly standardized risk assessment models in the hopes of more accurately identifying children at risk of harm (Gambrill & Shlonsky, 2000). The assumption of these models is that uniform measures and training will result in consistent and accurate assessments.

Actuarial risk assessment tools are statistical algorithms intended to predict specific risk outcomes, such as child abuse, sexual violence, or suicide. They are based on large data sets consisting of individuals who have committed the violent acts in question and identifying commons variables among these individuals. Each variable is statistically weighted according to the strength of the relationship with the outcome. Scores are then combined to determine a general probability score (Brown & Rakow, 2016; De Bortoli & Dolan, 2015). The algorithms used in risk assessment tools are transparent and explicitly outline factors involved in the decisions. Theoretically, they also simplify the decision-making process considerably by outlining the relevant factors, ensuring that these factors are considered each time such a decision is to be made, and simplifying the analysis by providing weights for each item. Given the method of development, actuarial measures are often based on historic and stable factors such as previous history of violence, mental health history, family history, and developmental history. As a result, many researchers report higher degrees of consistency in decisions made—although as I will demonstrate in chapter 7, stress and trauma responses do have an impact on the manner in which individuals complete the tools.

In social work, actuarial risk assessment tools have been applied to a number of contexts. For example, the objectives of risk assessment processes in child welfare are to identify, from cases referred to child welfare authorities, the subgroup of children at high risk for future abuse or neglect. This is done so that action can be taken to prevent abuse or neglect and to determine the relative risk for subsequent maltreatment in children who have been abused (Fluke et al., 1995; Pecora, 1991). The appropriate assessment of risk to children is critical given the enormous consequences for them and their families of both over- and underestimation of risk. Risk assessment instruments thus provide a mechanism for targeting treatment resources to the highest-risk children through the use of explicit criteria and uniform approaches to assessment (Camasso & Jagannathan, 2000; DePanfilis & Zuravin, 2002; English & Pecora, 1994).

The importance assigned to standardized risk assessment tools in child welfare practice sparked considerable controversy given that they have been implemented throughout the world despite concerns about their reliability and validity (Baird, Wagner, Healy, & Johnson, 1999; Camasso & Jagannathan, 2013; Lyons, Doueck, & Wodarski, 1996). For example, in comparing actuarial and consensus-based models used in three states, Baird and Wagner (2000) determined that over 71 percent of high-risk cases in Michigan were rated as low or moderate risk by the model used in the California system, even though the rates of substantiated abuse were identical. Despite efforts to create reliable and valid measures, workers must employ a certain level of subjective judgment given the nature of the phenomenon being predicted, and opportunities for bias exist. For example, in each of the states considered in the Baird and Wagner study, racial differences were found in classifications. Fewer African American than white families were identified as high risk. This difference was greatest in Washington, which classified 8.3 percent more African American families as low risk.

Similarly, as a result of legislative changes in both the United States and Canada regarding sexually violent predators (Glancy, Regehr, & Bradford, 2001), mental health practitioners are called on to predict the future dangerousness of convicted sex offenders. Because predictions of dangerousness based solely on clinical assessments of offenders of any kind, and in particular sexual offenders, have proved to be remarkably inaccurate and to result in very low rates of inter-rater reliability between professional assessors (Hilton & Simmons, 2001), considerable effort has been focused on the development of actuarial tools with the aim of improving predictive accuracy. The original actuarial instruments focused exclusively on "static" or historical factors such as the age at first offense and the nature of violent offenses. The developers suggested that these tools for the prediction of dangerousness were accurate enough to be used in isolation and that adjunctive clinical assessments may not only fail to add to the predictive validity, but in fact may be detrimental (Quinsey, Harris, Rice, & Cormier, 1998; Quinsey, Khanna, & Malcolm, 1998). Other authors stated that actuarial instruments should only be used in association with other clinical methods of evaluation. From this perspective, it has been argued that the use of risk appraisal instruments may not only fail to meet the standard for admissibility in court, but may also be unethical according to some professional associations (Sreenivasan, Kirkish, Garrick, Weinberger, & Phenix, 2000). One criminal court judge, after reviewing the use of actuarial instruments in a case before him, stated, "None of these actuarial instruments seem to include whether the person has been or is being treated, whether he has been or is still incarcerated, is under house arrest or is comatose, although to the unsophisticated one or more of these would seem to bear heavily on future conduct" (In re Valdez, Smith et al., p. 6). Consequently, more recent actuarial instruments have included a clinical component.

In sex offender risk assessment, actuarial scales are designed following retrospective research for factors associated with recidivism in offender populations. Typically, the files of violent offenders are reviewed and factors associated with violent behavior are determined. These factors are then combined and weighted, producing a score that is assumed to give an assessment of risk. Next, a particular violent offense is selected as the "index offense," and again through the process of chart review research, the degree to which the weighted factors predicted subsequent offending is assessed. The model of analysis used to evaluate predictive validity typically employs a receiver operating characteristic (ROC) analysis. In this analysis, the true positive rate (TRP = sensitivity) and the false positive rate (FPR = 1- specificity) are plotted on a graph and result in a curve. The area under the curve (AUC) is the probability that the detection method will give a randomly selected violent person a higher score than a randomly selected nonviolent person. A perfect detection method would give an AUC score of 1.0, and a test that was no better than chance would give an AUC score of 0.5. The standard error scores are also reported to assist the reader in determining the accuracy of the assessment of the measure. In addition, the correlation, or r, is also frequently reported by researchers. This is the average correlation between test scores and sex offense recidivism. Studies addressing the predictive validity of tools have found variable results in part due to differing populations studied, differing definitions about what constitutes recidivism, and differing lengths of time between the index offense and follow-up (Glancy & Regehr, 2004).

The assessment of suicide risk has also seen considerable controversy regarding the relative value of clinical assessments based on expertise compared to standardized, evidence-based risk assessment measures based on actuarial data. A study conducted at the Centre for Addiction and Mental Health compared a variety of scales to clinical assessments (Cochrane-Brink, Lofchy, & Sakinofsky, 2000). While several scales have strong psychometric properties, these researchers and others (Harriss & Hawton, 2005) have found that while scales are important adjuncts to clinical assessment, no scale reliably predicts whether clients will ultimately die of suicide. In large part, this is due to the fact that scales are based on predictive data acquired at the group level that may not accurately reflect the characteristics of the client in question (C. Regehr, Stern, & Shlonsky, 2007), reflecting back on the earlier comment by Naylor (2001) that "typical patients are far from typical."

To better understand the use and utility of standardized tools in suicide risk assessment, researchers conducted two studies of hospitals in England. In the first study, they sampled 6,442 patients presenting with self-harm over a three-month period at thirty-two hospitals, including teaching and nonteaching hospitals in urban and rural settings (Quinlivan et al., 2014). All but one mental health service reported conducting a risk assessment if a patient presented with self-harm behavior. However, despite the fact that health care has central oversight in the United Kingdom through the National Health Service, there was no uniformity on which scales were used for assessing suicide risk. Among emergency departments, 41 percent used only locally developed tools that had not been tested for validity, and 37.5 percent used standardized published scales. Of those using published scales, 66 percent also used a locally developed tool. Among mental health services, 69 percent used locally developed scales, and 9.5 percent used standardized published scales. In examining repeated self-harm at six months in patients assessed, those hospitals that used standardized published measures as part of their assessment had significantly lower rates of repeated self-harm. The authors concluded that there was cause for concern when services are relying on tools that have not been empirically validated, although they acknowledged possible confounds, including setting and patient mix (Quinlivan et al., 2014).

The researchers followed up with a study evaluating the performance of standardized risk scales, in this case focusing on the patient level, not the institutional level. Using a prospective cohort-based approach, they examined 483 cases of self-harm in which specific empirically validated measures were used. Overall, they found that risk scales performed poorly in predicting repeated self-harm. While they noted that self-harm is a broad definition of suicide risk, they concluded that "risk scales following self-harm have limited clinical utility and may waste valuable resources. Most scales performed no better than clinician or patient ratings of risk. Some performed considerably worse" (Quinlivan et al., 2016, p. 429).

On the other hand, in the area of suicide risk, clinical expertise alone has been proven to be a remarkably inaccurate predictor. A study examining professional judgments of suicide risk determined that participating psychiatrists and nurses had ratings of risk that ranged from 25 to 100 percent for a single case. Also concerning in this study was that 42 percent of individual psychiatrists and 78 percent of individual nurses had significantly different ratings of risk when confronted with the same paper-based case vignette at different time periods (Paterson et al., 2008). Thus while actuarial measures have considerable drawbacks—including rigidity, lack of sensitivity to change, and most importantly failure to inform prevention and risk management (Douglas, Ogloff, & Hart, 2003)—decision-making based on professional knowledge and expertise is highly variable.

As noted throughout this section, actuarial risk assessment tools have a wide range of benefits and drawbacks. However, while proponents argue that they eliminate subjective bias, prejudice, and arbitrary decision-making, perhaps the most troubling drawbacks are the failure of actuarial risk assessment tools to consider context, particularly context as it relates to gender and ethnicity (Shaw & Hannah-Moffat, 2000). Cross-cultural assessments of dangerousness are challenged by the fact that the manner in which psychological constructs are measured and the fact that they have been normed on Western populations may introduce bias when used with members of other groups (Haag, Boyes, Cheng, Mac-Neil, & Wirove, 2016). Långström (2004), for instance, reviewed the predictive accuracy of two well-known tools aimed at determining the risk of recidivism among people charged with sexual violence in Sweden. His results determined that while the tools accurately predicted recidivism among Nordic and European offenders, they were unable to distinguish African and Asian recidivists from non-recidivists.

The use of actuarial violence risk assessment measures with Indigenous offenders has recently been challenged in the Canadian courts in the case of *Ewert v. Canada*, 2015. Ewert, who was serving two concurrent life sentences for second-degree murder, attempted murder, and escaping custody, was deemed to be at high risk of reoffending on the basis of actuarial tools administered while he was in custody. As he believed that the risk assessment would be highly prejudicial at his parole hearing, he did not apply for parole. Ewert then challenged the actuarial tools, charging that they were culturally biased against him. Although meta-analyses and large sample studies have demonstrated that the major risk factors and commonly used scales do predict recidivism for Indigenous offenders, the predictive accuracy is weaker than for non-Indigenous offenders (Gutierrez, Helmus, & Hanson, 2016).

In reviewing Ewert's claims, the Supreme Court of Canada ruled that actuarial risk assessment measures were sufficiently unreliable when applied to Indigenous inmates that their continued used was a breach of the right of liberty and security of the person under the Canadian Charter of Rights and Freedoms. The Court thus issued an order preventing Correctional Services Canada from using actuarial risk assessment measures to determine the disposition of Indigenous inmates until their reliability in predicting dangerousness in this population had been demonstrated.

While testifying in the *Ewert* case, Stephen Hart, the leading developer of several actuarial tools, acknowledged that the tools did not take into account the substantially higher rates of social distress in Indigenous communities, including poor infrastructure and resources, family disruption, chronic poverty and unemployment, trauma and substance abuse, and higher rates of incarceration, many of which are considered important risk factors for violence. Later, when reflecting on the implications of this process, he stated definitively:

I think those of us working in the field of violence risk assessment here in Canada should acknowledge that we have not demonstrated the cross-cultural validity of the actuarial tools in question with respect to Indigenous Peoples. . . . But one can also acknowledge that, in light of the concerns raised by Mr. Ewert, the situation is no longer tenable, and therefore we must take responsibility to change it. . . . Personally, I feel a sense of responsibility and regret for the lack of attention devoted to this issue. (Hart, 2016, pp. 89–90)

Hart (2016) calls on threat assessment experts to deal squarely with the issue of cultural bias in actuarial tools and to take reasonable steps to deal with diversity issues that might arise in practice, including identifying potential diversity issues that might bias their threat assessment; seeking to educate themselves regarding how diversity issues may impact their effectiveness in risk assessment; and in cases where diversity issues may result in bias, indicating this clearly in their rendering of their professional judgment.

STRUCTURED PROFESSIONAL JUDGMENTS

As a result of drawbacks in both actuarial tools and clinical judgment alone, a newer approach to assessment of risk has emerged that blends research evidence and clinical practice and incorporates concepts of risk management with risk assessment. This approach has been termed *empirically validated structured decision-making*, or *structured professional judgment (SPJ)*. The SPJ approach focuses on the development of evidence-based guidelines or frameworks that encourage systemization and consistency but allow for flexibility in incorporating case-specific and contextual factors that influence risk. It recognizes that risk is dynamic and sensitive to changing conditions (Doyle & Dolan, 2002) and allows for "overrides" of actuarial measures when justified (Webster, Haque, & Hucker, 2013). In many ways, the SPJ tool serves as an aide-mémoire, providing a list of empirical items that allow information to be broken down into manageable pieces (De Bortoli & Dolan, 2015). The practitioner then exercises judgment in identifying factors, weighing them, and combining them in a manner that best responds to risk (Brown & Rakow, 2016).

Structured professional judgment tools share a number of common features (Guy, Packer, & Warnken, 2012):

- Items and factors are included in an SPJ following a systematic review of the scientific research and a consideration of the professional and legal literature related to a specific population.
- SPJs provide guidance on how to carry out the assessment, which factors to consider, and how to rate the factors.
- Judgments are not directed according to a predetermined numeric formula; rather, the decision-maker determines the relevant weight of each factor.
- The determination of risk is not cumulative, linear, or a particular cluster of factors. Indeed, at times one factor alone should be disproportionately weighted as contributing to risk.
- Conclusions are communicated in a categorical manner—low, moderate, or high—rather than an absolute score.
- SPJs are not strictly predictive but also contribute to prevention. Upon making a determination of current risk, decision-makers identify specific interventions that will manage or reduce risk.

While SPJs have largely been directed at the risk of harm to others, Bouch and Marshall (2005) apply the model of SPJs to suicide risk assessment. They observe that suicide risk factors can be categorized as static, stable, dynamic, and future. Actuarial methods rely on static and stable risk factors and consequently provide an indication of a person's general propensity for suicide. However, they do not capture the dynamic and future factors that inform risk prediction and more importantly direct clinical management of risk (table 6.1). Thus, SPJs have been developed that incorporate these various elements.

One such tool is the Short-Term Assessment of Risk and Treatability (START), which is intended to address multiple domains of mental health practice including risk to others, self-harm, substance abuse, and suicide (Webster, Nicholls, Martin, Desmarais, & Brink, 2006). Unlike most SPJ tools, the START is intended to address a number of risks at

TABLE 6.1

Categorization of suicide risk factors

Factor	Nature	Examples
Static	Historical	History of self-harm
	Fixed and unchanging	Family history of suicide
		Childhood adversity
Stable	Long-term	Personality disorder
	Likely to endure for many years	Character traits
		Addiction
Dynamic	Uncertain length of duration	Suicidal ideation
	Fluctuating intensity	Hopelessness
		Substance use
		Psychosocial stress
Future risk factors	Anticipated, based on changing circumstances	Access to preferred method of suicide
		Service resources and contact
		Response to intervention
		Further stress

(Modified from Bouch & Marshall, 2005)

one time with the realization that these risks often compound one another. The tool includes twenty dynamic factors that are to be coded as risks or strengths, and provides an opportunity to identify particularly critical risks or key strengths. On the basis of this assessment, the clinician works with colleagues, often with the assistance of the client, to develop a risk management plan. The clinician can complete the tool independently or in a team meeting.

In child welfare practice, an SPJ model called structured decision-making (SDM) combines actuarial tools with clinical judgment. For instance, the manual for the Saskatchewan Structured Decision Making System for Child Protection Services includes cultural considerations, screening criteria, service-level guidelines, and decision trees (Children's Research Center, 2015). The model includes provisions for policy overrides such as incident seriousness or child vulnerability factors that warrant the highest level of service regardless of overall risk score. It also includes provisions for discretionary overrides when the worker believes that the score is too low based on their own clinical judgment. However, discretionary overrides can only increase the risk level by one level (e.g., from low to moderate, but not low to high) and must be approved by a supervisor. Recent reports suggest that thirty-three U.S. states have now adopted this model (Bosk, 2018).

A number of researchers have evaluated the various SPJ instruments and their ability to assess the fluctuating risk of self-harm and violence toward others. Meta-analyses have suggested that SPJs have the same predictive validity as actuarial measures, with the caveat that actuarial measures are most effective when used with individuals who most closely resemble the population on which the tool was validated (Singh, Bjørkly, & Fazel, 2016; Singh, Grann, & Fazel, 2011). Further, when actuarial or SPJ risk assessment tools are used to inform treatment and management decisions, they perform moderately well in identifying those at higher risk of violence. However, they are less effective when relied on as the sole determinants of high-impact decisions such as sentencing, release from jail, or discharge from high-security facilities (Fazel, Singh, Doll, & Grann, 2012). Psychologists, nurses, and psychiatrists are split on which method (SPJs or actuarial measures) are more accurate or useful (Singh et al., 2016). Either set of tools can serve as useful augmentations to clinical experience in high-risk professional decision-making.

DECISION-MAKING IN SOCIAL WORK

At times in social work practice, all of the decision models—expert intuition or heuristics, actuarial tools, and SPJ aids—are used either independently or in concert with one another. Research conducted by our team sought to understand how social workers use each of these models. In two studies, one on suicide risk assessment and one on risk assessment in child welfare, we asked social workers to interview standardized patients performing as clients and offer professional judgments on the level of risk presented. We attempted to replicate an actual clinical encounter as closely as possible. Standardized patients are healthy individuals trained to portray the personal history, physical symptoms, emotional characteristics, and everyday concerns of actual patients. They are trained to give consistent information and maintain a consistent level of emotional intensity and engagement. However, the nature and quantity of information they provide is dependent on the questions posed by the interviewer.

In the first study, ninety-six child welfare workers employed at twelve different child welfare offices located in a large urban center, smaller cities, and rural communities interviewed two mothers suspected of child abuse, completed risk assessment measures, and then participated in interviews regarding their subjective views of their decision-making and performance (C. Regehr, Bogo, Shlonsky, & LeBlanc, 2010; C. Regehr et al., 2010). The first scenario involved an interview with a mother (Ms. Smith) of an infant following a report by the child's day care provider of welts observed on the child. The second scenario involved an interview with a mother (Ms. Samuels) of a latency-aged child following the report by a school that the child had disclosed physical abuse. Each scenario was presented in one of two forms, with the parent being confrontational and with the parent being nonconfrontational. Each worker conducted two risk assessment interviews, either with Ms. Samuels as a confrontational client and Ms. Smith as a cooperative client, or vice versa. The order of interviews was modified and randomly assigned in a 2×2 design to allow for examination of various order effects.

At the end of each scenario, participants completed three risk assessment measures commonly used in child welfare agencies. The Ontario Risk Assessment Measure (ORAM) is an SPJ tool that was used in Ontario from 1998 to 2007 and was based on the California Risk Assessment Model. Workers use their clinical judgment to arrive at an overall rating from 0 (no/low risk) to 4 (high risk). The Ontario Safety Assessment (OSA) is a consensus based tool with fourteen threats addressing the caregiver's current and previous behavior, ability to supervise, and attitude toward the child. On the basis of this measure, workers make a final judgment, referred to as the safety decision, as to whether the child is safe or unsafe. The Ontario Family Risk Assessment (OFRA) is an actuarial-based instrument that assesses the future risk of maltreatment. It is important to note that this was a study on decision-making and was not intended to determine the reliability and validity of the various instruments. While many of the participants were trained on the measures, the training was not consistent. In addition, the participants only completed the tools at the end of the interviews and did not use them as aids during the interviews.

There was considerable variation in professional judgments regarding the safety of the children regardless of the tool considered. Using the OSA, which dichotomizes judgment into safe (safe and safe with intervention) and unsafe, 66.3 percent of the workers indicated that "one or more safety threats are present and placement is the only protecting intervention possible for the children" in the Smith case with the young child; 33.7 percent of workers did not have this finding. In the Samuels case, 94.7 percent of workers did not find the child unsafe based on the above criteria, while 5.3 percent of workers did decide that the child was unsafe (figure 6.3). On the actuarial measure, the OFRA, which has a possible abuse score that ranges from 0 to 18, the highest score given to the Smith child was 15, and the lowest was 1. More than 60 percent (62.4 percent) of respondents had a rating of 4 to 6. The highest score given to the Samuels child on the OFRA was 7, and the lowest was 1. Scores were generally 3 or 4, with 66.6 percent of scores in this range. The SPJ measure (ORAM) has five levels of risk; 8.5 percent of workers

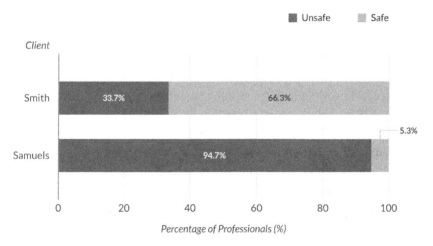

FIGURE 6.3 Percentage of professionals judging risk of child abuse on the consensus-based tool

Source: Regehr, Bogo, Shlonsky, & LeBlanc, 2010.

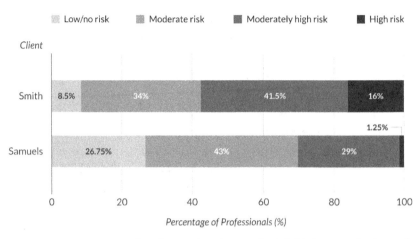

FIGURE 6.4 Percentage of professionals judging risk of child abuse on the SPJ tool
Source: Regehr et al., 2010.

found the Smith child to be at low or no risk, 34 percent found the child to be at intermediate risk, 41.5 percent found the child to be at moderately high risk, and 16 percent found the child to be at high risk. For the Samuels child, 26.75 percent of workers found the child to be at low or no risk, 43 percent found the child to be at moderate risk, 29 percent found the child to be at moderately high risk, and 1.25 percent found the child to be at high risk (figure 6.4).

Workers' level of education and age were not associated with the scores they gave on the risk assessment measures. Risk assessment scores between the Smith and Samuels cases were associated with one another ($p \leq .001$), indicating that workers who attributed higher risk in one family also tended to attribute high risk in the other family. I will discuss this study and the next in greater detail in chapter 7 and focus on stress and trauma factors associated with risk assessment.

Qualitative interviews following the completion of risk assessment measures in the child welfare study provided some additional insights into decision-making processes. Many participants spoke about historical and event factors commonly associated with risk, such as the severity of the injury, the nature of the report from teachers judged to be credible sources, past histories of abuse, and previous involvement with child welfare. Other participants focused on the context as contributing to risk or safety, such as the possibility of intimate partner violence perpetrated by the mother's boyfriend and poverty in the Smith case; the recent death of the father and the mother's difficulty coping with work and other stressors in the Samuels case; and the presence or absence of social supports in both cases. However, a sizable number of workers focused on less tangible factors. Many commented on the mothers' body language and demeanor, the mother's emotional attachment to the child, the mother's emotional reaction to the allegation, and the interviewer's sense about whether the mother was telling the truth. While most workers were not personally affected by the mothers' emotional reactions (see chapter 7), some workers referred to their own emotional reaction, as depicted by one worker who said, "I felt unsteady." In the end, several of those who felt the situation was safe relied in large part on their ability to develop a relationship with the mother. These workers spoke about needing to spend more time with the mother, "feeding her," getting to know her, and keeping her calm. Thus professional expertise, or the art of practice, is evident in the qualitative comments.

The second study on suicide risk had seventy-one participants—thirty-seven final-year MSW students who were specializing in mental health (52.5 percent of participants) and thirty-four experienced social workers employed primarily in large mental health facilities in three different cities (47.9 percent of participants) (C. Regehr et al., 2016; C. Regehr, LeBlanc, Bogo, Paterson, & Birze, 2015). One client was an adolescent (Karolina) presenting with a situational crisis. The second client was a depressed middle-aged woman (Margaret) who was a victim of intimate partner violence. At the end of each scenario, participants were asked to determine whether the client required hospitalization due to imminent risk of suicide. Participants then completed three standardized suicide risk assessment measures: the Beck Scale for Suicide Ideation (BSS), the Hamilton Rating Scale for Depression (HRS-D), and the Columbia Suicide Severity Rating Scale (C-SSRS). The standardized measures were not used as clinical guides in this study, but rather were used to assess factors that workers included in their judgment. The BSS and HRS-D have items that sum to a total score, while the C-SSRC is a structured professional judgment tool.

As with the child welfare study, there was considerable variability in the assessment of suicide risk in the second study. Seventy percent of participants believed that the adolescent patient in acute crisis (Karolina)

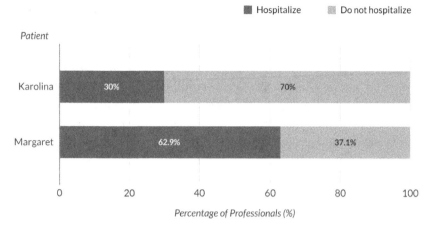

FIGURE 6.5 Percentage of professionals judging risk of suicide
Source: Author's own data.

did not require hospitalization as a result of suicide risk, while 30 percent believed that she should be hospitalized. Similarly, 62.9 percent of participants believed that the depressed middle-aged woman (Margaret) should be hospitalized, whereas 37.1 percent believed she did not require hospitalization (figure 6.5).

Professional judgment that Karolina should be hospitalized was associated with four factors in T-test analyses: the age of the respondent, scores on the BSS, scores on the HRS-D, and scores on the C-SSRS. That is, in addition to the association between scores on the suicide scales and judgment that hospitalization was necessary, younger respondents were less likely to believe that the adolescent patient required hospitalization. Logistic regression analysis revealed that only two factors were significantly associated with the judgment that Karolina required hospitalization when the influence of other factors was taken into account: the BSS, which independently accounted for 47 percent of the variance, and the respondent's age, which accounted for an additional 8 percent of the variance.

Professional judgment that Margaret should be hospitalized was associated with only one factor in T-test analyses: scores on the BSS. Higher scores on the BSS were associated with a judgment that hospitalization was necessary. In a logistic regression analysis, the BSS accounted for 24 percent of the variance. Thus, scores on standardized risk assessment measures were the strongest predictor of judgments regarding the need for hospitalization to ensure the safety of the patient in both cases, although patient age was also significant in the case of Karolina. Nevertheless, participants completing the risk assessment measures arrived at very different scores. In chapter 7 I will discuss the influence of stress and trauma on risk appraisal in professionals.

CONFIDENCE IN PROFESSIONAL JUDGMENT

A different question exists with respect to the certainty or confidence with which a clinician makes a judgment about situations involving risk to a child. Baumann, Deber, and Thompson (1991) identify the possible co-occurrence of micro-certainty with macro-uncertainty, a situation in which a clinician feels certain or confident in a field where no absolute answers exist. Research has demonstrated that individuals working under conditions of uncertainty tend to overestimate the probability (or be overly confident) that their judgments are correct (J. Smith & Dumont, 2002). Other research cautions that overconfidence can cause people to underestimate the magnitude of their uncertainty and the cost of their error (Mamassian, 2008). Similar to errors in judgment based on heuristic processes (Gambrill, 2006), sources of overconfidence in clinical judgment include: (1) confirmation bias, where an individual attends to information that confirms early impressions; (2) dispositionism, in which people overestimate the impact of personality characteristics and underestimate the importance of situational variables; (3) representativeness, where it is believed that the client represents the classic case; and (4) calibration errors, where the probability of an outcome is underestimated (Arkes, 1981; Baumann et al., 1991; Glascoe & Dworkin, 1993; J. Smith and Dumant, 2002). Not surprisingly, research suggests that confidence in professional decision-making increases with experience (Hay et al., 2008), yet it is not clear whether this is related to the accuracy of judgments.

In both our studies described above, following each scenario and completion of risk assessment measures, participants were interviewed to determine their subjective views of their decision-making and performance. Each participant was asked to rate their confidence in their performance on a scale of 1 to 5, as well as their confidence in their final determination of risk on a scale of 1 to 5, for each client interview. They also were asked to discuss how they felt about their performance, what they may have done differently, and what information they used in assessing risk. Interview data was transcribed and then divided according to the distributions of scores. Groupings of high confidence, moderate confidence, and low confidence were formed and subjected to thematic analysis. High confidence was defined as level 4.5 or 5, and low confidence was level 1 or 2 on the five-point scale.

In the child abuse study, confidence in performance and confidence in the assessment of risk were positively associated with age. Consistent with other research (Gambrill, 2008; Hay et al., 2008), as age and experience increased, confidence also increased. There were no significant differences in either confidence in performance or confidence in assessment of risk based on gender in either study. Further, confidence in performance and confidence in risk were positively associated with one another in both scenarios. As a general rule, participants were equally confident in both their performance and judgment across scenarios. Of note in the suicide study, which included both experienced social workers and students, was that seven students reported high confidence in their risk assessment of Margaret while only three experienced workers reported high confidence (table 6.2). Of particular importance in both studies, however, was that confidence was not related to the appraised level of risk to the child, and participants felt equally confident whether they appraised the child to be at high risk or low risk. That is, some par-

TABLE 6.2

Confidence in appraisal of suicide risk

	High-Confidence Risk Assessment		Low-Confidence Risk Assessment	
	Client			
	Margaret	Karolina	Margaret	Karolina
Experienced worker	3	4	2	6
MSW student	7	0	9	4
Total	10	4	11	10

(Author's own data)

ticipants were highly confident that a client was at high risk, and other participants were equally confident that the client was at low risk. These findings, emerging from our clinical simulation study, replicate that of a paper-based scenario study examining psychiatric hospitalization. That study concluded, "Staff expressed high levels of confidence in the accuracy of their treatment choices, but their particular choices were distributed over a range of treatment options that did not correspond to confidence levels" (Hendryx & Rohland, 1997, p. 71).

High Confidence

Workers who felt confident in their performance felt that they used the time effectively and quickly collected data. Confident workers felt they had moved the interview along well and had been able to gain enough information to make an assessment of risk. Worker engagement with the client was also important in determining the level of confidence workers had in their performance. In the child welfare study, workers who were confident felt they were able to build a rapport despite safety concerns and indicated that they remained calm despite the mother's emotional state. Confident workers indicated that they felt comfortable and did not feel threatened even when the mother was confrontational. For example, one worker reported being able to overlook "jabs and remarks" made by a confrontational mother as the worker moved toward building rapport. Another reported trying to accommodate the mother's mood and body language. Several participants also noted that getting the client's agreement or cooperation increased their sense of confidence in their performance. That is, the ability to establish a safety plan with the client's cooperation increased workers' confidence in their performance.

When the risk of child abuse was judged to be high, workers that were confident in their risk appraisal focused on the seriousness of the abuse (such as the child getting hit with a belt or being burned) and the child's fear. Collateral information, such as medical corroboration or a report from the day care provider, also increased confidence. The perception that the mother denied or minimized the abuse or did not appreciate the child's distress increased the workers' confidence that the child was at risk. When the risk was perceived to be low, the cooperation of the mother increased confidence in the appraisal, even when the mother was confrontational. One worker overlooked the confrontational behavior, noting that the confrontational mother took ownership and responsibility. Indeed, some workers viewed being confrontational as a good sign. One worker wished the mother had been more confrontational, as this would demonstrate that she loved her daughter.

In both studies, workers who highly rated their confidence in risk appraisal drew on both generic knowledge and specific experiences (such as working with people struggling with substance abuse and depression). Workers attributed high levels of confidence in the level of risk assessed to training, past supervisions, and experience. One worker indicated the tools and guidelines helped with decision-making. Another reported being very familiar with the tools and therefore had high confidence. These workers comfortably applied their knowledge of assessment and social work interventions and tried "to tease through what was relevant and what interventions could help with different needs of the client." (Regehr, Bogo, LeBlanc, Baird, Paterson & Birze, 2016, p. 39)

Interestingly, workers who highly rated their confidence in risk appraisal described experiencing varied emotional states. That is, some discussed feeling "confident," while others discussed "anxiety." However, these emotions did not seem to impact workers' impression of their ability to appraise the risk of the client. For instance, one worker reflected on feeling "anxious. A bit uncertain. Not confident." One worker reflected feeling "under pressure to solve [the client's] problem; felt obligated to help and do the session 'perfectly'—this was a source of anxiety." (Regehr, Bogo, LeBlanc, Baird, Paterson & Birze, 2016, p. 40) Not only did the nature of their emotions not shake the confidence of these workers regarding their assessment of risk, they seemed to use their own feelings as indicators of client risk.

Highly confident students in the suicide study also referred to training and past experience involving direct work with suicidal people when articulating risk factors and dimensions that affected their decision. For instance, one student identified having "lots of experience working with suicidal people in some capacity [since the age of 16]." Decisions regarding assessment and hospitalization were expressed assertively, such as one student who "knew right away of my decision" and "decided quickly that the client was someone to take to the hospital," and another who stated that the client "definitely needs to be hospitalized/seen by a doctor immediately." Interestingly, many of these students (five of seven) responded that there was not anything they might have done differently within the allotted time. These students attributed high levels of confidence to training or similar client encounters in the past. They appeared to make their judgments quickly and did not believe that they would have benefited from additional time to gather more information. Their responses are consistent with research and literature on possible inferential biases that affect confidence and judgment (Arkes, 1981; Baumann, Deber, & Thompson, 1991; J. Smith & Dumont, 2002). What might be called *overconfidence*, since suicide risk cannot be definitively judged, has been associated with quickly making judgments and believing that all relevant data has been collected. Previous research with psychiatrists has similarly found this to be twice as prevalent in trainees as in experienced clinicians (Mendel et al., 2011).

Low Confidence

Participants who felt low confidence in their performance indicated that they felt unprepared and disorganized. They felt they could not engage the client or get her to answer questions effectively. They felt they did not ask the right questions or enough questions. One worker reported being too critical. Low confidence workers indicated that they felt caught off guard, flustered, out of control, and uncomfortable. One worker felt "really bad," scrambled, nervous, and "psychologically trapped for words." These emotional states led them to comment that they could not stay focused or engage the client. Contrary to high-confidence workers, low-confidence workers reported a further eroding of confidence when the client was confrontational, a finding confirmed by previous research (Horwath, 2007). Feelings were also noted as a source of confusion. For instance, one worker in the child abuse study felt positively toward the mother and had difficulty reconciling this with the severity of the abuse.

Workers with low confidence in their risk appraisal felt that they were unable to obtain sufficient information in their interview with the client. This is consistent with previous research that found that workers who were less confident were unable to acquire information necessary to assess risk (Van de Luitgaarden, 2009). Some workers attributed this to time restrictions, while others attributed it to the client's resistance to providing information or their own inability to engage the client. One worker attributed low confidence to a lack of experience, while another attributed it to passivity in the interview. One worker suggested that a further reason for low confidence in the risk appraisal is that the risk assessment tools are not robust. Another worker indicated that different findings of risk on the three assessment tools decreased the level of confidence.

THE CENTRAL ROLE OF THE PROFESSIONAL IN PROFESSIONAL JUDGMENTS

Social workers in many areas of practice make decisions that are critical to the health, safety, and life of clients, their families, and other vulnerable members of society. Such decision-making carries a burden in that predictions of future risk will never be perfect, and tragedies will inevitably occur. To improve the ability of professionals to accurately identify children at risk of harm, individuals who may commit violent crime, or individuals who may commit suicide, organizations, professional guidelines, and professionals themselves have moved toward highly standardized risk assessment models. While research in a variety of fields has demonstrated that carefully validated actuarial models outperform clinical judgment in estimating future risk (Grove & Meehl, 1996), clinical judgment nevertheless remains critical to the complex process of predicting risk (van de Luitgaarden, 2009). Our research confirms that social workers are highly variable in their assessment of both future child abuse and suicide risk—with some workers viewing risk to be high, and others viewing it to be low.

Interestingly, however, the confidence with which social workers viewed their decisions was not related to the actual risk assessment. That is, different workers could be equally confident in higher and lower risk assessments for the same case. The assessment of risk of child abuse and suicide could be considered classic examples of micro-certainty with macro-uncertainty (Baumann et al., 1991). Predicting which children are at risk is a near impossible task. Similarly, the ability of any clinician to accurately judge whether a specific client who presents with suicidal ideation will indeed attempt suicide in the immediate future is highly questionable. A number of excellent actuarial tools exist that can aid in gathering information and making decisions, yet no scale can accurately predict suicide or violence or offer a clear point where intervention is imperative (Cochrane-Brink et al., 2000; Harriss & Hawton, 2005).

In the end, actuarial tools, standard professional judgment tools, and fast and frugal decision trees remain guides for professional decision-making. However, other individual worker factors appear to override these guides, directing professional judgment in one way or another. Regardless of how much we wish to make professional decision-making "rational," people will continue to "misbehave" according to rules of rational decision theory. Understanding the factors that influence individual differences in professional decision-making raises the possibility that professionals will be able to design their own fast and frugal methods that take into account three elements: their own unique application of empirically validated tools; gut feelings that inform experiential knowledge; and the social and political context in which the risky decision is being made.

CHAPTER SEVEN

Stress, Trauma, and Decision-Making

As discussed earlier, social work decision-making often involves high stakes, and errors can result in significant harm or death for a client or others. These decisions, daunting in the best of circumstances, are often not made in optimal conditions. The events surrounding the decision itself are stressful, often occurring in the context of high emotion and, at times, risk to the safety of the social worker—resulting in what was referred to in chapter 2 as "white-knuckle care work" (Baines & Cunningham, 2011).

In addition, social workers themselves do not approach these situations as clean slates. The history social workers bring to complex, high-risk decision-making is a great benefit. They have acquired experiences that contribute to expertise—the ability to recognize not only similar patterns, but also novel features that must be taken into consideration. This expertise allows the social worker to sift through multiple factors and arrive at a decision that is, as discussed in chapter 5, seemingly intuitive, experienced by the expert as a "gut feeling" (Gigerenzer, 2007). Indeed, these gut feelings tap into the social worker's cognitive, emotional, and physiological reactions and can contribute to a richly nuanced heuristic understanding to guide decision-making. However, as discussed in chapters 2 to 4, many of the work-related experiences of social workers can be stressful and traumatizing, resulting in psychological and physiological distress and harm. This chapter explores the impact of these experiences on professional decision-making.

EMOTION AND DECISION-MAKING

Research on the neuroscience of judgment and decision-making has focused on the role of emotion when making choices under conditions of risk and uncertainty (Vartanian & Mandel, 2011). Emotions interact with cognitive evaluation in situations of risk, and this interaction ultimately guides behavior (Mohr, Biele, & Heekeren, 2010). Mohr and colleagues demonstrate this in a meta-analysis of fMRI studies conducted to examine whether (1) risk processing is influenced by emotions; (2) neural processing of risk is influenced by context; and (3) risk is processed differently when an individual faces potential losses. On the basis of their analysis, they conclude that adverse emotions affect risk processing independent of the context in which decisions are made, especially when individuals face possible loss. Thus, despite the nature of the decision—choosing a restaurant for dinner, choosing a method to save for retirement, or deciding whether to undergo treatment suggested by a physician—emotions drive our decision-making processes. When the decision will result in not only a possible gain, but also a possible loss of something we already possess, the effect of emotion is intensified.

While a number of brain regions are implicated in decision-making under conditions of risk, the anterior insula, a key region of the brain related to emotional processing, arousal, and mapping of internal body states, is quite clearly activated. This demonstrates the link between affect, cognition, and somatic responses when individuals are faced with risky decisions that may involve loss. Internal body states, or somatic responses to risk, serve as cues to the emotions that are processed in the anterior insula. In this way, feelings have been defined as "mental representations of physiological changes" emerging from the cognitive processing of emotion-eliciting stimuli (Dolan, 2002). Mohr and colleagues (2010) suggest that individuals then use the resulting activity in the anterior insula as an estimate of the degree to which a risky stimulus will likely result in an unwanted outcome. That is, the individual believes that experienced physiological arousal and heighted anxiety are valid indicators that the risk of a negative outcome is high (figure 7.1).

FIGURE 7.1 The influence of somatic and emotional responses on risk decision-making

Source: Modified from Mohr, Biele, & Heekeren, 2010.

One formulation regarding the association between somatic response, affect, and decision-making has been advanced by Slovic and colleagues through what they refer to as the "affect heuristic" (Slovic, Finucane, Peters, & MacGregor, 2004). In this formulation, thought is understood to be largely constructed from a series of images from previous life experiences, some of which are marked as emotionally positive, and some as emotionally negative. Each of these emotional markers is linked to a particular physical or somatic reaction. Each of us can tune in to our own personal experiences of this phenomenon. As we imagine a pleasurable time with loved ones, we smile; our body straightens or relaxes; we may perhaps experience a sense of relaxation and calm, or elation and excitement. Conversely, if we recall a highly conflictual interaction, our stomach tenses, our face may show strain or anger, and we feel unsettled.

These somatic markers are important contributors to decision-making and indeed have been viewed to increase its accuracy and efficiency (Domasio in Slovic, et al., 2004, p. 314). Slovic and colleagues suggest that using an overall, readily available affective impression can be easier and more economical than weighing all the pros and cons in a deliberative manner. For instance, a social worker assessing an individual who is at risk of harming another may experience a feeling that they have previously encountered when interviewing similar clients, contributing helpfully to their overall evaluation of the client. However, as the evocation of past feeling states biases the decision-making process toward or away from a particular option (Dolan, 2002), it can also negatively influence risk assessment. In reviewing a series of experiments, Slovic and colleagues (2004) demonstrate that immediate feelings override logical decision-making in a wide range of fields, such as toxicology, finance, as well as forensic psychiatry and psychology. When individuals feel favorably toward an activity, issue, or person, they view the risks to be low and the benefits to be high. In this model, affect precedes and guides experiences of risk.

Slovic and colleagues suggest that there are two ways that experiential thinking can misguide decision-making. First, past experiences may increase one's vulnerability to deliberate manipulation of feelings by those who wish to control behaviors. Advertising and marketing are examples of this type of deliberate manipulation, for instance when a product such as soup is linked with motherly nurturing. In the clinical example of risk assessment, clients who are charming and likable or evoke sympathy may be judged as less likely to be a risk to others, which may or may not be justified. Second, the experiential system has limitations. For instance, an individual may be deeply moved by the death of one person, but then appear unaffected by the death of thousands of people in a catastrophic event. The second event defies experience and comprehension. Similarly, the experiential system fails those who begin smoking early in life because the immediate experiences take precedence over future risk. This occurs because illness and death are not represented in the individual's experiential repertoire (Slovic et al., 2004).

Researchers in other fields have observed that people's interpretation of the world around them tends to reflect their current emotional state. For example, anxiety is associated with an increased likelihood of interpreting ambiguous stimuli, such as facial expressions (Richards et al., 2002), or ambiguous words such as homophones (*tear* versus *tier*) or homographs (*arms* as limbs or *arms* as weapons), as threatening (Blanchette & Richards, 2003). Anxious individuals not only interpret neutral stimuli more negatively, but also perceive themselves as being at greater risk and believe the personal costs of negative events to be higher, ultimately leading to more risk-averse decision-making (Blanchette & Richards, 2010a). People in an angry state are more likely to make judgments based on heuristics, rely on stereotypes, and show automatic prejudice to members of other groups than individuals who are sad or neutral.

Interestingly, however, angry individuals are equally likely as happy individuals to predict a higher probability of positive rather than negative events (Angie, Connelly, Waples, & Kligyte, 2011). Individuals experiencing positive emotions are more likely to take risks than those experiencing negative emotions, particularly when under time pressure (Hu, Wang, Pang, Xu, & Guo, 2015). Overall, however, a meta-analysis of studies conducted by Angie and colleagues (2011) revealed that sadness, disgust, and guilt are some of the most influential emotions in decision-making.

Blanchette and Richards (2010a) propose four processes that explain the impact of emotion on decision-making: attentional effects, priming of concepts and knowledge structure, computational capacity, and reflective processes. Attentional effects refer to biases in information that is preferentially processed. That is, individuals demonstrate a more rapid detection of, and a preference toward, information that is congruent with their current mood (Dolan, 2002). For instance, Nabi (2003) discovered that when faced with scenarios about a drunk driver, individuals in an angry state were more likely to seek and attune to information consistent with a retribution model, while those in a fearful state sought information about solutions that would enhance general public protection.

Priming effects proposed by Blanchette and Richards refer to the process by which certain elements of semantic or autobiographical knowledge are more strongly activated when an individual is in a particular emotional state. Thus a fearful individual will retrieve memories of other threatening situations. These threatening memories become the basis on which the present situation is judged. This is an example of how the availability heuristic can be applied. While other experiences exist, the emotional state privileges certain memories, making these particular frames of reference more available to aid in rapid decision-making. Added to this is the fact that computational capacity may be limited by heightened emotional states, and thus individuals rely more heavily on heuristics because deliberative cognitive processing and decision-making capacity are not readily available.

Reflective processes refer to the manner in which information is used strategically in decision-making. That is, emotional states determine what material individuals deem to be relevant to the decision at hand. Neurobiological research has demonstrated that the prefrontal amygdala is highly influential when an individual is processing information in a state of anxiety (Blanchette & Richards, 2010a). The amygdala decodes emotions and processes stimuli that serve as warnings of danger or threat; it is the brain's alarm center. Thus, anxious individuals continue to focus attention on a threatening interpretation of stimuli once such an interpretation has been generated. This results in a risk of confirmation bias, as discussed in chapter 6, in which information that confirms the initial impression is incorporated while information that is disconfirming is ignored.

Emotions thus serve as frames of reference and affect the manner in which information is gathered, stored, recalled, and used to make judgments (Nabi, 2003). Interestingly, emotions can also override beliefs in decision-making. In neutral conditions, participants perform more accurately on tasks when the logical conclusion is consistent with their beliefs. However, Goel and Vartanian (2011) demonstrate that negative emotional content can cause a person to override their beliefs, causing them to accept solutions that are inconsistent with their views. This is of particular relevance to social workers whose values, such as fundamental issues of equity, may become compromised when they experience fear, anger, or threat.

Finally, emotions also influence people's risk-taking tendencies. For example, depressed individuals are significantly more conservative in taking risks than are individuals in neutral or positive moods and indeed appear to assess the risks in a particular situation as being higher. It would seem, therefore, that child welfare workers who are depressed may be more likely to view a child to be at risk of abuse from a parent. On the other hand, those with positive moods did not differ significantly from those in neutral moods (Yuen & Lee, 2003).

DECISION-MAKING AND PERFORMANCE UNDER STRESS

A specific examination of the relationship between emotions and decision-making relates to experiences of stress. Stress response is generally considered to have two dimensions: state anxiety (anxiety related to the immediate situation) and trait anxiety (anxiety that is a pervasive and continuing feature of the individual's experience). Both state and trait anxiety have an influence on decision-making and performance. For instance, both are associated with an increased likelihood of interpreting ambiguous stimuli, such as facial expressions, as threatening (Blanchette & Richards, 2003). Nevertheless, this section will focus on anxiety that is evoked by the situation.

One aspect of the stress literature focuses on the way in which the appraisal of stress impacts the interpretation of physical response. As was discussed in chapters 2 and 4, Lazarus and Folkman (1984) have suggested that when faced with a stressful situation, the individual begins with an appraisal of the situation. This appraisal is comprised of two processes: primary appraisal, which involves consideration of whether the event carries the risk of harm, threat, or loss versus potentially positive outcomes; and secondary appraisal, which involves the individual's sense of whether he or she has the ability to deal with the challenge and its potential outcomes. According to this theory, when the resources are perceived as sufficient to meet the demands, the situation is interpreted as a challenge, leading the individual to experience positive stress (motivation) and rise to the task of meeting the challenge. When the demands are perceived as likely to tax or exceed resources, the individual interprets the situation as a threat and experiences anxiety or negative stress that can impair performance (Tomaka, Blascovich, Kibler, & Ernst, 1997). Interestingly, it is not the anticipated outcome of the event alone that influences this interpretation, but also the larger social implications. That is, when individuals believe that they will be evaluated on their performance in a stressful situation, their anxiety and perception of risk increase (Tomaka et al., 1997). Thus, in applying this to life-and-death decisions in social work, media attention and the possibility of public inquiries would be important elements of the cognitive appraisal of risk to the individual worker.

Further, individuals' appraisal of their own ability to meet the stressor is dependent on their previous experiences with success. If their sense of self (or self-schema) includes a belief that their expertise is sufficient to manage the situation, they will be less likely to experience negative stress. This was reflected in the studies presented in chapter 6 on confidence in social workers and students assessing the risk of child abuse and the risk of suicide. Those with low confidence in their ability reported feeling flustered, out of control, and uncomfortable. High-confidence workers were able to remain calm despite the client's emotional state and the danger of their situation. These workers could also focus on the facts of the case in evaluating risk.

Earlier I discussed the manner in which somatic responses can trigger emotion and influence cognition. Stress theories, however, begin with the other side of the equation, suggesting that the cognitive appraisal of a challenging event or task shapes both an individual's psychological responses and also their physiological responses to a stressor. When a threat is perceived, the sympathetic nervous system is activated, resulting in an increase in involuntary processes such as increased heart rate and respiration required to respond to the threat. Specifically, the sympathetic nervous system rapidly releases norepinephrine and epinephrine into the bloodstream from the adrenal gland, resulting in what is experienced as an adrenaline rush. Simultaneously, the hypothalamic-pituitary-adrenal (HPA) axis is activated, resulting in the increased release of the hormone cortisol in the blood. This occurs less rapidly than the adrenaline process, peaking at twenty to forty minutes after activation and returning to normal forty to sixty minutes after an event (Kemeny, 2003). However, the increase in cortisol levels also influences areas of the brain that are involved with cognitive processes (LeBlanc, 2009). Thus we can quickly see an interactive process between perception, emotion, and physiology in stress appraisal and response. For instance, in a meta-analytic review of 208 studies on acute psychological stressors, Dickerson and Kemeny (2004) demonstrated that stressors that are uncontrollable and contain a socio-evaluative component are associated with the largest cortisol responses and the longest time to recovery (figure 7.2).

The intersection between appraisal, psychological distress, and physiological stress response has important implications for professional decision-making under conditions of acute stress. One aspect of this, as noted earlier, is selective attention. This was evident in a qualitative study that colleagues and I conducted with police officers that had been involved in shooting events. In describing the experience of being in a life-threatening situation, one officer said,

> I saw . . . the gun barrel pointed about three feet from my face, and [it was] a very small weapon, but it looked pretty big at the time. . . . My first inclination was to get the hell out of there, but

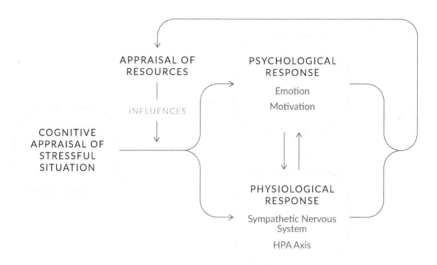

FIGURE 7.2 Physiological feedback loop and risk appraisal
Source: Modified from Kemeny, 2003.

you know that you can't, you just can't, that's your job . . . and the physical, your physical environment, all those kinds of things become blurred, all you look at is here's this guy, and here's the threat which is the weapon, and afterwards I could tell, well, I think he may have been a bit older, he may have been a bit younger, maybe he had a mustache, and I think he had close-cropped hair . . . but I could describe the gun to you.
(C. Regehr, Johanis, Dimitropoulos, Bartram, & Hope, 2003, p. 387)

LeBlanc (2009) notes that this selective attention has an adaptive purpose, allowing individuals to focus on the relevant information and preventing cognitive processes from becoming overloaded. Alternatively, however, research has demonstrated that anxious individuals have an attentional bias toward threat stimuli, assessing the risks in a particular situation as higher and responding faster to threat than individuals in neutral or positive moods (Bishop, 2007; Yuen & Lee, 2003). In this way, risk appraisal influences judgment regarding the likelihood of future events (i.e., the risk will lead to a negative outcome) (Blanchette & Richards, 2010b) and subsequently the behavior of the individual. For instance, police officers experiencing anxiety are more easily distracted by task-irrelevant threat-related information and show a response bias toward shooting (Nieuwenhuys, Savelsbergh, & Oudejans, 2012). Similarly, a study investigating the impact of anxiety on police officers' arrest and self-defense skills demonstrated that high anxiety was associated with greater avoidance behavior and decreased effective performance (Renden et al., 2014). Individuals under threat stress are often unable to overcome their first autonomic responses and make a controlled, rational adjustment to the threat, leading to less-than-optimal performance (Starcke & Brand, 2012).

Acute stress also has an impact on memory. LeBlanc (2009) summarizes the literature on three components of memory impacted by stress responses and cortisol increases: working memory, or the ability to store and manipulate information in the immediate situation; memory consolidation, or the manner in which information is translated into longer-term memory; and information retrieval. Laboratory-based studies have shown that when individuals are required to perform under acutely stressful conditions that lead to increases in cortisol levels, both their ability to remember previously learned information (memory recall) and their ability to store and process information in current use (working memory) are impaired. Further, anxious individuals demonstrate impairments in verbal reasoning, especially on high-demand tasks, when compared to individuals with low levels of anxiety (Blanchette & Richards, 2010b).

Research conducted to identify the effects of stress on performance across groups of individuals has provided equivocal findings (C. Regehr, LeBlanc, Jelley, & Barath, 2008). For example, one study examined military recruits in Navy SEAL training. Nicknamed "Hell Week," the training consists of constant physical, psychological, and environmental challenges under conditions of total or extreme sleep deprivation. Not surprisingly, perhaps, the participants showed marked impairments on tasks of memory, visual reaction time, and motor learning after seventy-two hours of stressful exposure. However, these effects were largely mitigated by the administration of caffeine (Lieberman, Tharion, Shukitt-Hale, Speckman, & Tulley, 2002), which most people would agree is not an ideal coping strategy.

Similarly, a study reported in the *Journal of Human Performance in Extreme Environments* looked at Army trainees who were led to believe that they were under personal threat via artillery attack or the crash landing of an airplane. This study found that performance diminished under conditions of high stress related to personal threat (Berkun, 2000). On the other hand, another study, conducted with forty-four soldiers at a U.S. Army survival school in a realistic captivity experience that challenged participants with unavoidable physical and mental stress, found that while exposure resulted in increased cortisol levels across all participants, those with higher levels of cortisol release had higher performance scores. Many of the individual differences existed *before* the stress exposure, leading to speculation about individual differences in hardiness (Morgan et al., 2001).

Overall, stress appears to impair the performance of some individuals in some circumstances but to enhance it for others (LeBlanc, McConnell, & Monteiro, 2014). For instance, in a study of paramedics, significant individual variations were found in anxiety responses and in performance changes when paramedics were exposed to a stressful simulated scenario (LeBlanc et al., 2005). After working through challenging simulated scenarios, 60 percent of the paramedics demonstrated impairment in their ability to perform drug dosage calculations, 20 percent showed no change in performance, and the remaining 20 percent showed an increase in performance. In a study of emergency medicine and surgery residents, Harvey and colleagues further demonstrated that those who cognitively appraised a stressful event as a challenge rather than a threat were able to perform despite heightened state anxiety and cortisol elevations (Harvey, Nathens, Bandiera, & LeBlanc, 2010). That is, some individuals appraise the same situation as a challenge rather than a threat because of their assessment of the resources they have to bring to the situation. While these individuals may also experience heightened physiological reactions, in some circumstances they are able to use these heightened senses to address the challenge.

POSTTRAUMATIC STRESS, PERFORMANCE, AND DECISION-MAKING

Society relies on professionals in social work, health care, and emergency service occupations to make sound judgments and perform effectively in the face of highly stressful, life-threatening events. Yet as a result of working in such environments, individuals in these professions are prone to high rates of stress-related problems themselves (Johnson et al., 2005), including posttraumatic stress disorder (Berger et al., 2012). Studies of paramedics report trauma symptoms in a range consistent with PTSD in 20 to 30 percent of respondents (Alexander & Klein, 2001; Clohessy & Ehlers, 1999; C. Regehr, Goldberg, & Hughes, 2002). Our study of police communicators found that 31 percent reported symptoms at a level consistent with a diagnosis of PTSD (C. Regehr, LeBlanc, Barath, Balch, & Birze, 2012). Following a critical event, such as a police shooting, trauma symptoms in the high or severe range can affect as many as 46 percent of those involved (Carlier, Lamberts, & Gersons, 2000). As noted in chapter 2, social workers in a variety of fields experience burnout, vicarious trauma, and posttraumatic stress. A study by Bride (2007) of social workers in the southern United States reported that over 15 percent met the criteria for PTSD. Child protection workers, charged with assessing children at risk of future abuse, report high levels of posttraumatic symptoms related not only to exposure to the trauma of others, but also to personal threats and assaults (C. Regehr, Hemsworth, Leslie, Howe, & Chau, 2004). In our studies, 19 percent of child welfare workers (C. Regehr, LeBlanc, Shlonsky, & Bogo, 2010) and 22.5 percent of mental health social workers (C. Regehr, LeBlanc, Bogo, Paterson, & Birze, 2015) reported symptoms at a level consistent with a diagnosis of PTSD.

The association between emergency service work and posttraumatic stress has been recognized by organizations that provide disability insurance, such as through the U.S. Federal Employees' Compensation Act (FECA) (U.S. Department of State, 2013). Section 24.2(2) of the Alberta (Canada) Workers' Compensation Act that came into effect in December 2012 states, "If a worker who is or has been an emergency medical technician, firefighter, peace officer or police officer is diagnosed with posttraumatic stress disorder by a physician or psychologist, the posttraumatic stress disorder shall be presumed, unless the contrary is proven, to be an injury that arose out of and occurred during the course of the worker's employment in response to a traumatic event or series of traumatic events to which the worker was exposed in carrying out the worker's duties" (Alberta, 2012). More recent legislation in some jurisdictions has been more expansive and includes a wider range of high-risk professions, including social work. This legislative approach suggests an underlying assumption that PTSD, impairment of functioning, and disability are linked.

Perhaps in part due to confounds of comorbid psychiatric disorders (Horner & Hamner, 2002) and motivational factors, such as the fear of losing disability benefits, that may contribute to exaggeration of symptoms (Frueh, Hamner, Cahill, Gold, & Hamlin, 2000), research on the specific deficits that are attributable to PTSD has been somewhat contradictory (Brewin, Kleiner, Vasterling, & Field, 2007). PTSD has been associated with mild impairments in memory, attention, and learning in individuals who are seeking treatment and who manifest a high incidence of comorbid psychiatric illnesses (Bremner et al., 1993; Jelinek et al., 2006; Yehuda, Colier, Tischler, Stavitsky, & Harvey, 1995). More recently, Horner and colleagues found that patients with PTSD had deficits in attentional functioning compared to those without a diagnosis on a measure of focused attention and digit span memory (Horner, Mintzer, Turner, Edmiston, & Brawman-Mintzer, 2013). However, other researchers reported an absence of neuropsychological deficits associated with PTSD and trauma exposure in non-patient populations (Twamley, Hami, & Stein, 2004). Furthermore, individuals with PTSD largely perform within the normal range of standardized tests of neuropsychological functioning, suggesting that where deficits exist, they are not at the level of clinical impairment (Dalton, Pederson, & Ryam, 1989; Gilbertson et al., 2006; Horner & Hamner, 2002).

To better assess apparently contradictory research findings, Brewin and colleagues (2007) conducted a meta-analysis and found a mild to moderate relationship between PTSD and memory impairment related to emotionally neutral information in both civilian and military samples. This relationship was stronger for verbal memory than for visual memory. More recently, in a meta-analysis of sixty studies, Scott and colleagues (2015) revealed significant neurocognitive effects associated with PTSD, particularly in the areas of verbal learning, speed of information processing, attentional working memory, and verbal memory. Effect sizes, however, were significantly larger in people with PTSD who sought treatment than those in the community who did not. This suggests that attentional impairment in people with PTSD may be selective and that a more nuanced approach to assessing the effects of PTSD on performance is required.

EVALUATING THE IMPACT OF ACUTE STRESS AND PTSD ON PROFESSIONAL DECISION-MAKING

Given my previous work in determining the levels of traumatic stress and other symptoms experienced by emergency service workers and factors associated with acquiring these symptoms, the obvious question was "How do these levels of symptoms affect the performance of those required to work and make decisions in highly charged and urgent environments?" Thus, Vicki LeBlanc and I designed a series of studies investigating the impact of acute stress and PTSD in professional decision-making with five different samples: child welfare workers assessing risk of child abuse; police officers responding to a 911 call regarding domestic violence; paramedics responding to a cardiac arrest; police emergency dispatchers responding to distress calls; and mental health social workers assessing suicide risk. In each of five studies, participants completed a series of questionnaires before participating in a simulated stressful scenario. In each of the studies, we collected information through short questionnaires to determine age, gender, and years of service. Trauma exposure in the workplace was assessed in three studies (child protection, mental health social workers, and police communicators) using a specially designed instrument. In a fourth study, with police recruits, the Critical Incident History Questionnaire (CIHQ) (Brunet et al., 1998) was used to assess police duty–related trauma history by measuring the frequency of exposure to each of thirty-four critical incidents (for example, being shot at).

Traumatic stress symptoms were elicited by the Impact of Event Scale—Revised (IES-R) (Weiss & Marmar, 1997), which assesses posttraumatic stress symptoms for any specific life event. The stress responses of the workers were assessed with a subjective anxiety measure (the State-Trait Anxiety Inventory, or STAI) and a physiological measure (salivary cortisol). Baseline measurements were taken at the start of the study sessions, and response measures were obtained at specific times following each simulation. The STAI is a commonly used assessment that has been shown to be sensitive to acute stress manipulations (Spielberger, 1983). Activation of the hypothalamic-pituitary-adrenal axis, which occurs during acute stress responses, was measured using salivary cortisol levels. Salivary cortisol levels are closely associated with plasma cortisol levels (Harris et al., 1990), yet are collected in a simple, noninvasive manner (Sanchez-Martin et al., 2001). The salivary cortisol analyses were conducted using an immunoassay technique (Dressendorfer, Kirschbaum, Rohde, Stahl, & Strasburger, 1992). Two baseline measures were obtained in the introduction phase (at one and ten minutes before each scenario), as well as twenty and thirty minutes after the onset of each event. To control for diurnal variations in baseline cortisol levels, data collection occurred between the hours of 11 A.M. and 5 P.M., when baseline cortisol levels are stable (Kemeny, 2003; Van Cauter & Turek, 1995).

Police Recruits

In the first study (LeBlanc, Regehr, Jelley, & Barath, 2007), police recruits participated in a scenario utilizing a FATS (Firearms Training Systems) simulator, which was described in chapter 4. The scenario constructed for this research involved a 911 call to a domestic dispute involving an aggressive male and an unresponsive female discovered lying on the floor. The recruits thus faced some personal risk as they were in a confined environment with an aggressive individual, as well as clear risk to a member of the public (the unconscious woman who had been assaulted). As shown in the figures in chapter 4, we successfully created a scenario that resulted in stress, as demonstrated by cardiac activity, cortisol response, and subjective ratings.

Of the eighty-four police recruit participants, 79.3 percent reported being exposed to at least one critical event, including being seriously injured or beaten, being threatened with a weapon, being present when another officer was severely injured, receiving threats against loved ones in retaliation for their police work, and/or seeing someone die or discovering human remains. With respect to trauma symptoms, 51 percent of the recruits scored in the no trauma to low trauma symptom range, 16 percent scored in the moderate range, 14 percent scored in the high range, and 19 percent scored in the severe range, which is consistent with a diagnosis of PTSD (C. Regehr, LeBlanc, Jelley, Barath, & Daciuk, 2007). Thus, although these individuals were relatively new to the job, they had already encountered a significant number of personal risk situations, and a significant number qualified for a diagnosis of PTSD. This in itself requires consideration.

Participants were videotaped during the simulations for the purpose of later evaluation. Three expert raters at the Ontario Police College independently assessed the videotaped performance of each participant on two measures: one focusing on specific behavioral competencies in the scenario, and a second ranking performance against peers. In this way, we added the component of evaluative stress to the simulation. The expert raters determined that there was a wide range of performance among the eighty-four participants, with some demonstrating high levels of skill in addressing the simulated situation and others demonstrating relatively low levels of skill. However, neither the participants' scores on the Critical Incident History Questionnaire nor their scores on the measure of posttraumatic stress symptoms (IES-R) correlated with their scores on the performance measures (LeBlanc et al., 2007). That is, neither the degree of exposure to traumatic events nor the resulting symptoms of traumatic stress resulted in performance deficits or enhancement during this highly stressful event. This is a positive finding given that society relies on police officers' ability to perform effectively in risky situations.

Acute stress, as measured by the STAI, the measure of subjective distress, was not correlated with performance at any time period. However, cortisol levels twenty minutes after the event were significantly correlated with both the comparative ranking of performance against peers and the performance checklist. Thus, while subjective distress was not associated with performance, *higher* cortisol levels were associated with *better* performance in this study (C. Regehr et al., 2008). This was an example of the finding discussed in previous research where increased cortisol release was associated with better performance in a high-risk situation.

Child Protection Workers

The child protection worker study investigated the degree to which the previous experiences of workers and their preexisting emotional state interact with variables encountered in a clinical situation, and whether these, in turn, influence professional judgment regarding the acute risk to a child (C. Regehr, LeBlanc, Shlonsky, & Bogo, 2010). As described in chapter 4, two fifteen-minute scenarios simulating acutely stressful clinical encounters were developed and pilot-tested with a cross-section of child protection workers to ensure that they were experienced as realistic client encounters. One scenario involved an interview with a mother ("Ms. Smith") of an infant following the reported observation of welts on the child by the child's day care provider. A second scenario involved an interview with the mother ("Ms. Samuels") of a latency-aged child following a school report that the child had reported physical abuse. Each scenario was presented in one of two forms: one with the parent being confrontational, and the other with the parent being non-confrontational. The order of interviews was varied and randomized to allow for examination of various order effects (confrontational vs nonconfrontational, mother of older child versus mother of younger child). Standardized patients (SPs) were utilized to portray the role of parents. SPs are healthy individuals trained to portray the personal history, physical symptoms, emotional characteristics, and everyday concerns of actual patients. At the end of each scenario, participants completed risk assessment measures: the Ontario Risk Assessment Measure (ORAM) and the Ontario Safety Assessment (OSA) (described in more detail in (C. Regehr et al., 2010). The workers were familiar with both tools and used them as a standard part of mandated practice.

Ninety-six child protection workers employed at twelve different child protection offices in a large urban center, smaller cities, and rural communities participated in the study. Eighty-five percent of respondents indicated that they had been exposed to at least one critical incident at work, including the death of a child, the death of an adult client, or assaults and threats against themselves. Scores on the Impact of Event Scale indicated that a sizable minority of participants currently experienced high levels of traumatic stress symptoms. Thirty individuals (32 percent) scored in the high or severe range of the scale. Of these, eighteen (19 percent of total participants) fell in the range that is considered consistent with a clinical picture of PTSD. These high rates of reported exposure to critical events and traumatic stress symptoms are consistent with our previous research on child protection workers (C. Regehr et al., 2004). Scores on the traumatic stress scale correlated positively with peak-state anxiety scores. That is, workers with higher preexisting levels of traumatic symptom scores experienced greater anxiety during the simulations (C. Regehr et al., 2010a).

Despite the association between PTSD and anxiety, however, these two manifestations of stress played out differently with respect to risk assessment. Workers that had *higher* levels of symptoms of traumatic stress were more likely to determine that a child was at *lower* risk of abuse or neglect. On the other hand, *higher* levels of acute emotional stress as measured by the self-report tool and *higher* levels of physiological stress as measured by cortisol response were significantly associated with identifying that a child was at *higher* risk, particularly in situations in which the parent was confrontational (C. Regehr et al., 2010a). Thus posttraumatic stress was inversely related to ratings of risk, while acute stress was directly related to ratings of risk.

Paramedics

In this study, LeBlanc and colleagues used a high-fidelity mannequin placed in an ambulance simulator. These remarkably realistic mannequins appear to breathe and have audible heart rates and palpable pulses; they come with a monitor that replicates the body activity one would see on an ICU monitor. The paramedics were required to attend to a patient complaining of chest pain. The patient's symptoms and the expectations for appropriate treatment were developed by the consensus of four experts. Several stressors were added to create a high-stress version of the scenario. Noise was created by setting the volume and alarms on monitors to the highest level and by having constant two-way radio communication noise. We knew from our previous studies that family members present at emergency scenes create a great deal of stress for paramedics. Thus we had an actor play the role of the patient's highly distressed partner and challenge the paramedic's actions and decisions. Clinical performance was videotaped, and experts scored the participants on a checklist of specific tasks and assigned a global rating of performance. The paramedics also completed patient care documentation following each scenario, which was scored for accuracy and completeness (LeBlanc et al., 2012).

Twenty-two advanced care paramedics, seventeen men and five women, from regional land and air ambulance services in Canada took part in the study. In this sample, 27.3 percent of the paramedics scored in the no-to-low trauma symptom range, 9.1 percent scored in the moderate symptom range, 13.6 percent scored in the high range, and 50 percent scored in the severe range. Posttraumatic stress was not significantly correlated with either the anxiety or the cortisol responses to the scenarios (LeBlanc et al., 2011). Thus the paramedic study had a significantly higher percentage of people who could qualify for a diagnosis of PTSD than the child welfare and police studies.

As expected, the paramedics reported greater anxiety and had higher cortisol responses to the high-stress scenario than they did to the low-stress scenario. This heighted emotional and physiological stress had an impact on performance. First, the overall rating of performance for the paramedics was significantly lower in high-stress scenarios than in low-stress scenarios. Second, paramedics demonstrated a higher number of commission errors (reporting information and/or procedures that were not part of the scenarios) following high-stress scenarios. That is, paramedics seemed to believe that they had gathered information that influenced their decision-making and behavior that they had not actually asked about or measured (LeBlanc et al., 2012).

While acute stress had significant impacts on performance in this study, the paramedics' posttraumatic symptom scores were not significantly associated with any of the performance measures. It is possible that the absence of association was related to the smaller size of our sample, as correlations were high ($r = 0.30$) but did not reach statistical significance.

Police Communicators

Police communicators answer the emergency phone lines and speak to often distraught members of the public, collect critical information, liaise with emergency personnel, and ensure that resources reach the emergency situation. Surprisingly, the experiences of psychological distress and physiological stress have been relatively unexamined in this group of emergency responders who remain behind the scenes, literally out of the public eye. In this study, communicators responded to simulated 911 calls from members of the public in a large computer room designed to resemble an active dispatch center with the sounds of other communicators in the background. The initial call was routine, followed by a call that contained strong emotional content. The high-stress call involved the severe injury of a police officer and the need to ensure that this colleague received assistance. The participants were required to document the information that was conveyed during each of the calls. Immediately after the scenario, they were required to complete a series of tests of cognitive ability. In what is referred to as a Stroop-like task, based on the pioneering method developed by Stroop in 1935, participants were required to read, as fast as possible without making errors, the words in a chart regardless of the visual appearance of the words (e.g., "LARGE large SMALL" would be reported as "large, large, small"). In a more complex version of the chart task, participants were required to report the words as fast as possible without making errors, but based on the visual appearance rather than the word itself (e.g., "LARGE large SMALL" would be reported as "large, small, large"). The participants also completed a spelling test of commonly used words in police communications and a test of the alpha-codes alphabet (e.g., when hearing the letter "a," the correct response is "alpha") (C. Regehr & LeBlanc, 2017).

One hundred and thirteen police communicators, employed by both provincial and municipal policing services, were recruited from both rural and urban areas. Using the conservative diagnostic cut-off of 33 for PTSD on the IES-R suggested by Creamer, Bell, and Failla (2003), 31 percent of the sample had symptoms of traumatic stress that met the criteria for PTSD. This is considerably above rates reported in the literature for both female and male police officers (Berger et al., 2012; Bowler et al., 2010).

Performance on the complex chart task was significantly worse following the high-stress scenario, and the time to complete the task was significantly longer than following the low-stress scenario. There were no differences in the simpler tasks, such as spelling, less complex chart naming, and alpha-code performance between the low-stress and high-stress scenarios. As the high-stress scenario followed the low-stress scenario, practice effects may have damped the effect size attributable to stress.

Higher levels of PTSD symptoms were significantly associated with greater errors in alpha codes following the high-stress scenario, but not following the low-stress scenario (C. Regehr & LeBlanc, 2017). They were not associated with other measures of performance. PTSD symptoms were associated with greater anxiety levels post-scenario, but not with cortisol levels.

Mental Health Social Workers

In the final study of this series, we examined mental health social workers conducting a suicide risk assessment (C. Regehr, LeBlanc, et al., 2015). Seventy-one people participated in this study: thirty-seven final-year MSW students at the University of Toronto who were specializing in mental health, and thirty-four experienced social workers primarily employed in inpatient and outpatient departments of large mental health facilities in three cities. Participants were asked to assess two simulated patients, portrayed by standardized patients, presenting with suicidal ideation. Through random assignment, half of the participants interviewed one client first and the other half interviewed the other client first to control for order effects. One client was an adolescent (Karolina) presenting with a situational crisis, and the second was a depressed middle-aged woman (Margaret) who was a victim of intimate partner violence. The scenarios were pilot-tested with a cross section of social workers to ensure that they were experienced as realistic client encounters. At the end of each fifteen-minute scenario, participants were asked to determine whether the client required hospitalization due to imminent risk of suicide. Participants then completed three standardized suicide risk assessment measures: the Beck Scale for Suicide Ideation (Beck & Steer, 1996), the Hamilton Rating Scale for Depression (Hamilton, 1960), and the Columbia Suicide Severity Rating Scale (Posner et al., 2011). The standardized measures were not used as clinical guides in this study but rather were used to assess factors that workers included in their judgment. In addition, in this study Maslach's Burnout Inventory was added to consider the impact of burnout on decision-making (Maslach & Jackson, 1981).

Thirty-one percent of participants indicated that they had worked with a patient who committed suicide (52.9 percent of experienced workers and 10.8 percent of students); 20 percent had been assaulted by a patient; 47.1 percent had been threatened with violence; 65.7 percent had colleagues that had been threaten by a patient; and 23.9 percent worked with patients who had inflicted severe injuries on others. A total of 73.2 percent of respondents indicated that they had experienced at least one work-related critical incident (82.4 percent of experienced workers and 64.9 percent of students). Twenty-five individuals (35.2 percent) scored in the high or severe range of the traumatic stress scale. Of these, sixteen (22.5 percent) fell in the severe range, which is considered consistent with a clinical picture of PTSD.

There was considerable variability in participants' assessment of suicidal risk for the two simulated patients. Seventy percent of participants believed that the adolescent patient in acute crisis (Karolina) did not require hospitalization as a result of suicide risk, while 30 percent believed that she should be hospitalized. Similarly, 62.9 percent of participants believed that the depressed middle-aged woman (Margaret) should be hospitalized, whereas 37.1 percent believed she did not require hospitalization. MSW students were significantly less likely to believe that Karolina required hospitalization. Participants that believed that Karolina required hospitalization were no more or less likely to think that Margaret required hospitalization. Further, having actually known a patient who committed suicide did not influence judgment regarding the need for hospitalization of the standardized patients in the study.

The professional judgment that Karolina should be hospitalized was associated with two factors in a logistic regression: the scores on the Beck Suicide Scale, which independently accounted for 47 percent of the variance; and the age of the study participant, which accounted for an additional 8 percent of the variance. That is, younger participants were less likely to assess that Karolina was in need of hospitalization. The professional judgment that Margaret should be hospitalized was associated with only one factor: scores on the Beck Suicide Scale, which accounted for 24 percent of the variance. Thus, scores on the standardized measures were the best predictors of professional judgment that the patient required hospitalization. At first glance, this is very positive. However, there was considerable variation in the manner in which participants completed the standardized measures. Posttraumatic stress symptoms were a significant predictor of the scores that workers gave patients on the Beck Suicide Scale and the Columbia Suicide Scale for Margaret, and with the Columbia scale for Karolina (figure 7.3). That is, just as in the child welfare study, workers with *higher* levels of posttraumatic stress symptoms rated patients as at *lower* risk of suicide.

FIGURE 7.3 The relationship between worker PTSD and judgments of client suicide risk

Source: Author's own data.

There was no significant association between measures of patient risk and worker scores on the burnout scale.

What Did We Learn About the Effects of Stress and Trauma on Decision-Making?

This series of five studies involved four different occupational groups: police recruits, paramedics, police communicators, and social workers in two different fields of practice. Consistent with the discussions thus far in this book, individuals in each of these studies reported high levels of exposure to potentially traumatizing events involving witnessing death and injury, hearing about human cruelty inflicted on others, and being exposed to direct threats and risk themselves. Correspondingly, participants in these studies reported high levels of posttraumatic stress symptoms relative to others in the general population. The percentages of individuals who reported symptoms at a level consistent with a diagnosis of PTSD were 19 percent for police recruits (C. Regehr et al., 2007); 19 percent for child protection social workers (C. Regehr et al., 2004); 50 percent for paramedics (LeBlanc et al., 2011); 31 percent for police communicators (C. Regehr, LeBlanc, et al., 2012); and 22.5 percent for mental health social workers (C. Regehr, LeBlanc, et al., 2015). Clearly, this is an issue of concern for workers, the organizations in which they are employed, and society as a whole. In addition to concern for the health and well-being of individual workers, there is concern with respect to performance and decision-making in the professional context. Incidents for which emergency workers are called to respond are characterized by heightened emotion, violence, and injury. In short, they are highly stressful. Thus, it is important to look at the association between stress, trauma, and decision-making.

Most previous research has involved laboratory studies in which variables and possible confounds can be controlled, but the degree to which performance in a lab is applicable to the real-world decision-making of professionals is not clear. Some studies have used immersion experiences such as "Hell Week" with military personnel. While realistic, this may go beyond the bounds of what we might reasonably or ethically do in research with emergency professionals and social workers. We have tried to find a balance, replicating work-like situations and creating some stress without endangering participants, and I believe that this approach has shed some light on the subject.

In the five studies, we used similar but slightly different methods. The police recruit study used one scenario for which the participants had recently been trained. The nature of training in this circumstance is repetitive and is aimed at producing more or less automatic responses to acute situations. For instance, in a 911 domestic violence call, the police officer must gain entry to the home. It is thus reassuring that acute anxiety and PTSD symptoms were not correlated with performance. Officers could perform tasks despite emotional symptoms. In addition, those that performed best had a greater cortisol response and seemed to get an adrenaline rush from the crisis situation. This is what we might wish for in police officers.

The studies involving child protection social workers, paramedics, and police communicators each had two levels of scenarios. One scenario that was closer to the normal course of business (albeit involving life-saving decisions), and one scenario involving higher emotional distress (an angry parent, a distressed family member, a colleague at risk). In each of these studies, performance and decision-making were affected in the high-stress scenario. Child protection workers who experienced higher stress were more likely to feel that the child was at risk. Paramedics had lower overall performance and made more errors in the high-risk scenario. Interestingly, the errors involved recording information about the case that they had not actually obtained. Communicators made more errors on complex tasks but not on simple tasks. Thus, in each of these cases, emotion interfered with or at least influenced performance and decision-making (table 7.1).

TABLE 7.1

The association between PTSD, acute stress, and performance

	Acute Stress	**Posttraumatic Stress**
Police recruits (one scenario)	• Subjective distress not correlated with performance • Cortisol positively correlated with performance	• No correlation between PTSD and performance
Child protection workers (two scenarios, one iteration higher stress)	• Acute stress associated with higher likelihood of determining a child is at risk when parent is confrontational	• PTSD associated with less likelihood of determining a child is at risk
Paramedics (two scenarios, one high-stress, one normal course of business)	• Global performance lower in high stress • More commission errors following high stress	• No correlation between PTSD and performance
Communicators (two scenarios, one high-stress, one normal course of business)	• More errors on complex tasks following high stress	• PTSD associated with decreased performance in high-acuity scenarios
Mental health social workers (two scenarios, equal stress)	• Acute stress not associated with risk assessment	• PTSD associated with less likelihood of determining client is at risk of suicide

(Regehr & LeBlanc, 2017)

The scenarios that the social workers faced, assessing the future risk of harm to a child and the future risk of suicide of a client, involved the most complex form of decision-making and judgment. Unlike the paramedics and the police personnel, there is no script that directs actions. Paramedics know that if certain symptoms are present, particular actions must be taken—intubate to assist breathing, defibrillate when the patient has a life-threatening dysrhythmia, give adrenaline to someone experiencing a severe allergic reaction. The risk is visible and present, the results of the remedy often immediate. Social work decision-making about risk is far more nebulous, and the results are not immediately (and perhaps never) known. Police communicators fall somewhere in the middle of these two extremes. In these studies, while PTSD was not associated with performance in police personnel or paramedics, in social workers it had an inverse relationship to risk assessment. Those with higher levels of trauma symptoms perceived the risk of both the children and the adult patients to be lower.

In addition, there was an interactional effect between stress and posttraumatic stress. Three of the studies (police recruits, child protection workers, and police communicators) demonstrated that those individuals who report higher levels of PTSD symptoms also report higher levels of subjective anxiety during high-acuity simulations. This is perhaps not surprising given that the high-acuity simulations are likely reminiscent of the events that led to the development of PTSD in the first place. In police communicators, PTSD was associated with performance deficits on a verbal memory task following the high-stress scenario but not the low-stress scenario. In summary, then, it seems that PTSD has a greater influence on performance in high-stress situations than in low-stress situations.

UNDERSTANDING THE IMPACT OF STRESS AND TRAUMA ON PROFESSIONAL DECISION-MAKING

As a result of exposure to stressful workplace environments and traumatic workplace encounters, social workers may suffer from a wide variety of physical, psychological, and emotional symptoms. These physical, psychological, and emotional reactions interact with one another and influence cognitive appraisal of situations and professional decision-making.

Acute stress reactions can result in selective attention and, in particular, an attentional bias toward information that would suggest that the threat is higher. This was demonstrated in our child welfare study in which social workers with higher levels of stress were more likely to determine a child was at risk of abuse when confronted with an angry parent compared to social workers who had lower levels of stress. We can surmise that these workers may have been using an affect heuristic—believing that their responses to parental anger reflected higher levels of risk to the child. In a sense, they may have been responding to a "gut feeling." This is not to say the feeling was wrong. Indeed, it is possible that the other workers were underestimating risk.

Acute stress responses also impact the ability to store and manipulate information in the immediate situation, the ability to consolidate information into long-term memory, and the ability to retrieve information from memory (LeBlanc, 2009). This was demonstrated in our studies with paramedics and police communicators. In high-stress situations, participants did not perform as well on complex cognitive tasks, had memory impairments, and reported information about the case that had not actually been gathered. Other studies conducted by colleagues have also shown that paramedics exposed to high-stress events show impairments in the ability to calculate drug dosages, to provide cardiac resuscitation, and to recall pertinent details from clinical scenarios (LeBlanc, MacDonald, McArthur, King, & Lepine, 2005; LeBlanc, Tavares, King, Scott, & Macdonald, 2010).

Posttraumatic stress disorder also has an influence on performance and decision-making when more complex clinical decision-making is required. Previous studies on the impact of PTSD on cognition has been variable, but in general PTSD is associated with deficits in verbal processing, attentional working memory, and verbal memory (Brewin et al., 2007). In our studies, we did not find evidence that PTSD has a direct impact on global performance on tasks for which emergency responders are highly trained. These might be understood to be overlearned tasks that emerge from repetition models of training. However, we did find an association between PTSD symptom levels in workers and their assessment of risk in two different clinical situations: suicide risk and risk of child abuse. In both cases, higher levels of symptoms in workers were associated with lower levels of perceived risk for clients.

Why might this finding have emerged in two different situations? Emotional arousal narrows and focuses attention, reducing the number of cues to which the individual attends (LeBlanc, McConnell, & Monterio, 2015). One possibility is that social workers with higher levels of traumatic stress symptoms were less likely to ask questions that would elicit information about suicidal thoughts from patients or were less likely to ask questions that would lead to the conclusion that a child was at risk. They may also have been less likely to attend to clinical cues and therefore made assumptions that risk was lower. Supporting this possibility are studies of clinical decision-making that have found that individuals in positive mood states are more thorough in their clinical investigations and consider a wider range of diagnoses and treatments than people in negative mood states. However, research also demonstrates that individuals in negative mood states are more likely to take risks (LeBlanc et al., 2015). This raises the possibility that those workers with PTSD have higher risk tolerance and are less likely to intervene and err on the side of safety. Thus, two processes may be interacting: the narrowing of information collected and a higher risk tolerance.

If stress and trauma affect professional performance and decision-making, it is critical that social workers who make high-stakes decisions include this consideration in their decision-making processes and have strategies for reducing both stress and trauma responses that may be interfering with clinical excellence. I will address these issues in the two next chapters.

CHAPTER EIGHT

Mitigating the Effects of Stress and Trauma on Decision-Making

The clients with whom social workers engage have histories of deprivation, violence, abuse, and exclusion. The systems in which social workers are employed are buffeted by financial constraints, changing government policies, and social attitudes that are characterized by conflicting demands. As a consequence, stress and trauma exposure are an inevitable part of social work practice. This exposure affects not only individual workers and their families, but also the decisions that social workers make and ultimately the quality of services that they provide to clients. As discussed in chapters 3 and 4, the factors that give rise to stress and trauma reactions are a complex interplay of the individual, the organization, and the larger societal environment. Approaches to mitigating the effects of stress and trauma on decision-making must therefore be multifaceted. This chapter addresses organizational considerations, approaches that individuals can take to managing workplace stress and trauma, and implications for social work education.

ORGANIZATIONAL AND SOCIAL POLICY APPROACHES TO MITIGATING STRESS AND TRAUMA

It is well established in the research literature that individuals in certain professions have high rates of exposure to situations and environments characterized by stress and trauma. Correspondingly, these professions have higher rates of symptoms and disorders related to stress and trauma. The association between high-risk professions and posttraumatic stress disorder is now recognized in the legislation of several jurisdictions, as evidenced by the recent inclusion of presumptive clauses. That is, if members of identified occupations have PTSD, they do not need to demonstrate that the cause was workplace exposure in order to qualify for disability benefits. This recognition of the work and workplace environment as primary contributors to the experience of stress and trauma symptoms requires organizations to take responsibility for reducing such exposure to the extent possible, mitigating the impacts of this exposure, and providing services when individual workers are suffering.

ATTENDING TO SAFETY

As noted in chapter 2, approximately one-quarter to one-third of social workers report being assaulted at some time in their careers, and approximately one-half to three-quarters have been threatened with physical harm (MacDonald & Sirotich, 2001, 2005; Newhill, 1996; C. Regehr, Leslie, Howe, & Chau, 2005; Rey, 1996). Social workers describe scenarios in which clients are verbally threatening or physically violent toward them, steal or destroy their property, and hurl verbal racial abuse at them (Kosny & Eakin, 2008). As a result of their exposures, Studies of social workers in various settings suggest that between 15 and 22 percent report symptoms on scales at the level consistent with a diagnosis of posttraumatic stress disorder (Bride, 2007; C. Regehr, LeBlanc, Bogo, Paterson, & Birze, 2015; C. Regehr, LeBlanc, Shlonsky, & Bogo, 2010).

While posttraumatic stress symptoms relate to a particular traumatic event or events, the existence of ongoing stressors related to workload, difficult clients, organizational change, and public scrutiny have a profound impact on the individual's experience of traumatic events and are directly related to higher posttraumatic stress disorder (PTSD) symptom scores (C. Regehr, Hemsworth, Leslie, Howe, & Chau, 2004). Social workers report high levels of ongoing stress when compared to other high-stress professions. In a large-scale study conducted in England, social workers scored first in terms of poor psychological well-being, third (after paramedics and teachers) in terms of poor physical health, and fifth in terms of poor job satisfaction (S. Johnson et al., 2005). Organizations employing social workers thus have obligations to ensure safety and to address issues of ongoing workload stresses.

Spencer and Munch (2003) discussed the role of management in addressing issues of violence toward social workers in community mental health programs. They recommended that agency supervisors and managers ensure that all personnel receive safety training during initial orientation, during periodic in-service training, and as a regular feature of staff meetings and supervision sessions. The recommended training includes three elements: (1) the assessment of risk of violence in clients, including acute symptoms, behavioral change, medication and drug use, and history of violence; (2) environmental assessments, including specific issues related to the worker's car, the community, the neighborhood geography, and the client residence; and (3) worker precautions, including communication protocols, self-defense and de-escalation skills, and awareness. Further, these authors and others point to the need for robust policies and procedures for reporting and responding to incidents of violence. This should include a clear philosophy of zero tolerance for violence as well as mechanisms for recording incidents of client violence in a database available to workers (MacDonald & Sirotich, 2001; Spencer & Munch, 2003).

The more recent NASW Guidelines for Social Work Safety in the Workplace acknowledge that there are practice settings (for example, child welfare, adult protective services, mental health, criminal justice, domestic violence shelters) where social workers may be at increased risk of violence (National Association of Social Workers, 2013). The guidelines clearly state, "Agencies that employ social workers should establish and maintain an organizational culture that promotes safety and security for their staff" (p. 9). Underpinning such a culture must be policies and procedures that address violence; the establishment of a safety committee; and the development of data management systems that document and track incidents of threat, violence, or property damage and allow for analysis and preventive planning. It also requires that physical environments be designed to minimize the possibility of violence (centrally located and visually open office spaces) and provide mechanisms for assistance should threats occur (alarm systems, easy exits). Technologies that enhance safety (GPS, mobile phones, security cameras) are now readily available and should be viewed as high-priority purchases. Home or other community visits should be preceded by planning, assessing potential risks, and sharing of information regarding travel plans with others. In summary, NASW guidelines for safety are founded on several principles:

- Social workers have the right to work in safe environments and to advocate for safe working conditions.
- Social workers who report concerns regarding safety should not fear retaliation, blame, or questioning of their competence.
- Agencies must develop systems that enhance safety.
- Social workers themselves have a responsibility to routinely practice universal safety precautions, including understanding environmental risks and internet-based risks related to personal information sharing.

BUILDING A CULTURE OF SUPPORT

Research on social workers, unlike research on many high-risk professions, has not found that higher levels of personal social support are associated with lower levels of symptoms related to trauma (C. Regehr, Hemsworth, et al., 2004), secondary traumatic stress (Dagan, Itzhaky, & Ben-Porat, 2015), or burnout (Shin et al., 2014). In each of these cases, social workers were found to have high levels of personal social supports compared to the general population, suggesting that social workers are effective in developing supportive networks in their personal lives. However, high levels of stress and trauma exposure on the job override the benefits provided by these supports. On the other hand, research has found an association between social support in the workplace, particularly from superiors, and levels of distress, and conversely levels of job satisfaction in social workers (Davis-Sacks, Jayaratne, & Chess, 1985; Elpers & Westhuis, 2008; McFadden, Campbell, & Taylor, 2015; C. Regehr, Hemsworth, et al., 2004). That is, higher levels of organizational support lead to lower levels of trauma symptoms and higher levels of job satisfaction. This parallels foundational research examining factors associated with distress level in emergency service workers following traumatic workplace events (Alexander & Wells, 1991; Burke, 1993; Fullerton, McCarroll, Ursano, & Wright, 1992; Weiss, Marmar, Metzler, & Ronfeldt, 1995).

Supervisors are seen to play a critical role in promoting the effectiveness of social work staff and ensuring quality service provision, particularly when clients are involuntary (Bibus, 1994). Supervisors are urged to debrief and support staff who perform emotionally taxing work (Anderson, 2000) and to further assist staff who are experiencing personal losses that are exacerbated by traumatic stimuli on the job (DiGiulio, 1995). Supervisors and managers have a responsibility to develop effective change management practices in response to rapidly changing public policies (Shields & Milks, 1994).

While recognizing the pivotal role of social work supervisors in supporting workers in a stressful and often traumatic work environment, it is important to note the impact that these same factors have on supervisors. A study that colleagues and I conducted involving forty-seven supervisors and managers in a child welfare agency (representing one-third of all managerial and supervisory staff in the agency) revealed tremendous dedication to both the work of serving families and children, as well as to the staff who provided the services. However, as would be expected, supervisors and managers were also exposed to traumatizing events. When compared to frontline staff, supervisors and managers were significantly more likely to have experienced the death of a child for whom they had service responsibility. They were also significantly more likely to have been questioned in internal reviews of child mortality, to have appeared in coroner's inquests, and to have had their actions questioned. They identified experiencing added accountability as a result of inexperienced staff, as well as increased scrutiny by the media, public, and government funders. In addition, they were concerned about the safety of clients and about the health and well-being of their staff as a result of these pressures. Consequently, they placed an increased onus on themselves (C. Regehr, Chau, Leslie, & Howe, 2002a).

Peer support has long been recognized as an important component of workplace resources for workers affected by stress and trauma. In large part, peer support may be informal in nature. However, models for formal institutional approaches to peer support as an adjunct to informal networks have received increased attention. Csiernik and colleagues report the impact of a peer-led social support group for new employees in a child welfare organization. The group aimed to offer the opportunity to connect workers with one another and build social supports; to provide a safe environment to explore the emotional impact of the work and consider the management of emotions; and to introduce the idea of mentoring relationships into the workplace. Not surprisingly, over the months that the group met, nearly two-thirds of those participating encountered some sort of workplace critical incident, including threats, harassment, and stalking. The group was then also able to provide support in light of these troubling encounters. Workers found the group to be a supportive environment that allowed for ongoing opportunities to discuss difficult encounters on the job. The main difficulty for workers, ironically but not surprisingly, was finding the time to attend (Csiernik, Smith, Dewar, Dromgole, & O'Neill, 2010).

Another model of peer support is the formalized peer support team (PST). Peer support teams have many advantages, such localized knowledge about issues faced by individual workers, an understanding of the culture and politics of the organization, and ready accessibility to workers. Key features of a PST include the credibility of those selected as peers; easy availability; voluntary access; confidentiality; a clear understanding that team members are providing emotional first aid and not therapy; and facilitated access to other supports, such as the employee assistance program (C. Regehr & Bober, 2005; Van Pelt, 2008). In establishing a team, careful consideration must be given to developing policies and procedures related to the mandate and operations of the team; team member selection; team member training on such issues as ethics and boundaries of team members; and continuous review and evaluation of services. For a full description, see *In the Line of Fire: Trauma in the Emergency Services* (C. Regehr & Bober, 2005).

Peer support teams now take various forms and can be found in many social work, emergency service, and health care organizations. In an interesting example, PSTs are advocated as a means for assisting health care professionals following adverse medical events—that is, events that cause harm in patients such as medication or surgical errors. Health care providers in these situations, known as *second victims*, feel symptoms of distress including guilt, anger, frustration, and fear (Seys et al., 2013). However, as adverse events are shrouded in a "veil of silence," the devastating emotional impact on health care providers is obscured (Van Pelt, 2008). In this instance, the PST can provide health care providers with a safe environment to share the emotional impact of adverse events, promote the renewal of commitment and compassion, and in the end improve service to the public (Van Pelt, 2008).

Critical incident stress debriefing is one application of peer support teams that arose in the 1980s and '90s as a model for managing traumatic workplace events (Mitchell, 1983). Initially developed as an early intervention strategy to mitigate posttraumatic reactions in firefighters and other emergency responders, critical incident stress debriefing quickly became popular and spread to many other sectors (Dyregrov, 1989; Raphael, 1986). This model involves a single-session group debriefing approach that encourages workers to describe trauma exposures, vent feelings, share symptoms, and provide mutual aid. It is premised on the assumption that professionals possess the internal resources to deal with most work-related events but can benefit from limited assistance in extreme situations. Early anecdotal and qualitative evidence demonstrated high levels of satisfaction among participants. However, subsequent controlled trials demonstrated that these debriefing sessions not only failed to reduce symptoms of PTSD, but may indeed have exacerbated them (Bisson et al., 2007; Rose, Bisson, Churchill, & Wessely, 2002; Van Emmerik, Kamphuis, Hulsbosch, & Emmelkamp, 2002).

A study that John Hill and I conducted demonstrated that these two findings occurred simultaneously in a sample of firefighters. While firefighters attending debriefings after a traumatic event did indeed feel supported by their organization and rated the group process as helpful, their subsequent levels of PTSD were higher than that of colleagues who did not attend debriefings (C. Regehr & Hill, 2001). This suggested that the original critical incident stress debriefing approach of sharing gruesome images and experiences in a highly charged emotional environment contributed to secondary trauma reactions. After considering the strengths and limitations of the original approach, a revised model is recommended in which (1) information is shared on the status of the event and of colleagues that have been injured; (2) individuals are allowed to discuss the impact of the experience; (3) strategies for coping are shared; and (4) social supports are mobilized (C. Regehr, 2001).

Peer supports must not only be directed at frontline staff. While supervisors and managers in our child welfare study described a strong structure of support within the management team, the evident overload of others prevented them from seeking assistance (C. Regehr, Chau, et al.,

2002a). If a peer support team specifically for supervisors and managers is not possible within the organization itself, a cross-sector support team for managers and supervisors may be necessary. The most senior managers in our child welfare study relied on supports from others with similar roles in sister organizations.

MANAGING LIABILITY

Social workers who must make high-stakes decisions as part of their daily practice face the risk that these decisions could have negative outcomes. Given that decisions are made in highly contested areas with conflicting societal demands, the risks are even greater. For instance, child welfare social workers must walk the line between intruding on the sanctity of the family and ensuring that a child is safe from harm (Kanani, Regehr, & Bernstein, 2002). Mental health social workers must consider the rights and freedoms of individual patients to determine the nature of treatment they will receive and whether they will receive treatment at all, with concerns that they may commit suicide (Mishna, Antle, & Regehr, 2002). A social worker providing care to elderly people in their homes must weigh their right to autonomy with concern that other family members are exposing them to neglect or harm (Donovan & Regehr, 2010). In each of these cases, a personal liability paradox is created. Workers may be damned if they do and damned if they don't. Risk, as discussed, is difficult to assess, and decisions must often be made based on incomplete, inadequate, or misleading information. Situations can deteriorate or change quickly and without warning. Social workers must predict the client's future conduct, but according to some authors, evidence suggests that prediction of dangerousness is at best an inexact science and at worst little better than chance (R. Rogers, 2000).

When negative outcomes occur, it is not uncommon for society to react with outrage. At a time of prosperity in the Western world, vulnerable members of our society continue to be victims of neglect, abuse, and murder. Nevertheless, it is overwhelming to address issues such as poverty and the societal structures that limit the choices and opportunities available to some. In this environment, public reviews become expedient ways to address public concern and guilt. The result can be public condemnation, professional discipline, civil litigation, or criminal charges against social workers. Chapter 3 reviewed studies that outlined factors that lead to stress and trauma responses in social workers, including re-exposure to traumatic stimuli related to the event; the prolonged and intense process of the review itself; the questioning of the worker's personal and professional integrity; and negative media attention that permeates all aspects of the worker's personal and professional life. This parallels recent research with health care providers following adverse events (Seys et al., 2013).

Two issues arise for the organization and society in this regard. First is an obligation owed to those professionals who assume risk in the interests of assisting others. Caring for others despite the risk is the foundation of practice for social workers, emergency responders, and health care professionals. There is a societal interest in maintaining these vital professionals. Second, when professionals begin making decisions to avoid liability, the best interests of individual clients suffer. Thus organizations that employ social workers must ensure that their workers can be confident in the knowledge that if they act in good faith and make the best judgments according to their expertise and the best available evidence, they will be supported. This means that the managerial team will continue to support them, legal and other expert advice will be provided to them, others will accompany them to hearings and critical meetings, and they will be afforded the time necessary to attend to the process. Further, while in the course of any career social workers will rarely be called to court to testify in their own defense, they will more commonly be asked to prepare court reports or testify on cases. Organizations should ensure that systems are in place to train and mentor social workers who are performing these functions. For instance, Glancy (2016) provides a model of simulation training for testimony in court using a mock trial approach. This provides opportunities for expert feedback and deliberate practice.

ESTABLISHING A MEDIA AND GOVERNMENT RELATIONS STRATEGY

In large part, media attention to social work occurs as a result of high-profile cases with negative outcomes. Studies of social workers reveal that they believe that this attention is primarily negative and beset with inaccuracies (Legood, McGrath, Searle, & Lee, 2016). The result of the media attention is reduced public confidence in social workers and the services they provide, damaged morale among individual social workers, a climate of fear and blame within social work organizations, and staff turnover and recruitment challenges (Ayre, 2001; Legood et al., 2016; Munro, 2011; C. Regehr, Chau, Leslie, & Howe, 2002b). Clearly, these factors have an impact on the quality of the services provided and the decisions made.

The media focuses on acute and exceptional manifestations that become the overall public view of the profession or field (Ayre, 2001). This focus provokes fear in not only the public, but also policy makers. On one hand, it may drive resource allocation, but on the other hand, it drives policy reform. Warner (2013) suggests that media campaigns that focus intensively on an individual case can be understood to be part of a wider social movement in which the press engages with others to manufacture dissent. In the end, a moral mandate is created for politicians to respond with emotion-driven actions. In this respect, Ayre (2001) identifies what he calls "an unholy trinity" that follows scandalous events: the aggressive public pillorying in the mass media of agencies deemed responsible for the tragic outcome; publication of ever more detailed recommendations to organizations resulting from public inquiries; and the issuing of increasingly intricately wrought practice guidelines intended to prevent recurrence (Ayre, 2001).

For instance, while child welfare systems in North America and Europe have been transformed as a result of public inquiries into child homicides, the cases that they review do not reflect the maltreatment and neglect cases that child welfare agencies generally see. Child homicides are both rare and random, and there is little evidence of a continuum of violence between child maltreatment and child homicide. Further, child fatalities do not appear to be influenced by increased child protection services (Lindsey & Trocmé, 1994). As a result, the changes to practice are not necessarily in the best interest of the larger client group. Prompted by scathing reviews, the past two decades have seen a shift in child protection work from treating families to surveillance, investigation, and collection of assessment evidence. As a result of recommendations for reform, child protection services have become more tightly structured and regulated.

In a report to the U.K. government on child welfare reform, Munro suggests that "the false hope of eliminating risk has contributed significantly to the repeated use of increasing prescription as the solution to perceived problems. Consequently, this has increased defensive practice by professionals so that children and young people's best interests are not always at the heart of decisions. It is a major challenge to all involved in child protection to make the system less risk averse and more risk sensible" (2011, pp. 134–135). Munro reports that the resulting increase in rules has a number of unintended consequences, including reduced sense of satisfaction, self-esteem, and personal responsibility; staff turnover and absenteeism; less time actually spent with families requiring services; and ultimately a lower quality of service.

Studies examining high-profile media attention to agency-related child maltreatment fatalities have confirmed that this attention has spurred substantive legislative change in the United States (Chenot, 2011; E. Douglas, 2009; Gainsborough, 2009). Douglas attributes this to rational decision-making theory being applied at a policy level. In light of cases where children die, policies focused on oversight and prevention make sense—certainly from a political standpoint. Gainsborough, however, demonstrates that while scandals and lawsuits provoke policy reform, they do not spur increased spending on child welfare services. She suggests that states engage in symbolic, rather than substantive, responses to crises of this sort.

In her review of child welfare services, Munro (2011) suggests that addressing media concerns be a shared responsibility involving the following parties:

- The national, provincial, or state regulatory body for social work as a common voice with broad-based expertise
- A senior government official responsible for social work (Munro's report recommended a chief social worker for the United Kingdom)
- Social work employers, who should prioritize positive stories for press release and ensure that the media are well informed about the complexities of cases encountered as well as the importance of social work for a healthy society
- Social workers, who must work closely with in-house communications and press teams to build relationships of trust

An automatic approach to media among most professionals is to avoid contact and keep their head low. This approach is generally reinforced by organizations that are attempting to manage the flow of information. However, as Ayre (2001) notes, when social workers and the agencies themselves do not provide information to fill gaps in the story, journalists will publish what they have. This reinforces workers' perceptions that news stories are half-truths. Ongoing media relationships should involve promoting successes and developing ongoing relationships with the press. Ayre notes that social work agencies can also learn from recent approaches used by police organizations, which involve engaging in breaking stories early on and making the people close to the issue available to the press.

ACKNOWLEDGING AND CELEBRATING SUCCESSES

Some years ago, colleagues and I conducted a study of operating room nurses who were members of a team responsible for the surgical removal of organs for transplantation (C. Regehr, Kjerulf, Popova, & Baker, 2004). Organ donation is a pressing need in society; at a time when success rates of organ transplantation are high, the number of individuals awaiting organs far outstrips the availability of donors. However, the process of cadaveric procurement was described as a highly stressful and disturbing task for nursing staff. Concern for the donor and his or her family was added to a fast-paced and long surgical procedure in which multiple transplant teams arrive from different hospitals to procure organs with little time in between. One respondent summed it up as follows: "It's almost like a sinking feeling. I get very saddened. . . . I think about the family or whoever gave permission. It's a wonderful thing. I've a lot of respect for it . . . but when I see the cases that I've done of relatively young people, there's a bit of emotion there. . . . The surgeons all appear, the science comes in. . . . It's a long procedure. If you take multiple organs, you're there all day, so it can be rough" (p. 432). Nurses used cognitive strategies for managing the emotion, including compartmentalizing the tasks to be performed, maintaining emotional distance, and focusing on the positive outcome of saving another life. However, nurses in this study indicated that the outcomes of procedures were rarely shared with them. Rather, the transplant teams at the hospitals receiving the organs witnessed the miracle transformations in the lives of the recipients. A simple approach to change and mitigating stress suggested by nurses in this study was to share not only general information on success rates in transplantation, but specific examples: what happened to the heart I was involved in saving?

Social work organizations can similarly consider how they share the outcomes of successful cases, families who are now doing well, children who left foster care to attend university, a client with mental health concerns that has secured meaningful employment. While many organizations have media campaigns that highlight specific individuals who have thrived after treatment, to what extent are more incremental successes of specific social workers and their clients celebrated and incorporated into models of decision-making?

INDIVIDUAL APPROACHES TO MITIGATING STRESS AND TRAUMA

The literature that discusses secondary trauma in social workers is replete with suggestions for reducing the impact of the work emanating primarily from qualitative interviews and the clinical reflections of experts. Suggestions have included developing personal supports and outside interests as a buffer against trauma, making adequate time for rest and relaxation, ensuring proper diet and exercise, and seeking personal therapy to address unresolved events from the past (Hesse, 2002; Pearlman & Saakvitne, 1995; Salston & Figley, 2003). Seeking peer consultation is also recommended (McCann & Pearlman, 1990a). Cerney asserts emphatically, "Much secondary trauma could be avoided or ameliorated if therapists seek regular supervision or consultation" (1995, p. 139). However, limited research supports these recommended methods for reducing trauma.

As noted in chapter 3, Ted Bober and I constructed the Coping Strategies Inventory with items derived from a comprehensive review of the literature on strategies for reducing symptoms of secondary trauma (Bober, Regehr, & Zhou, 2006). We then used the inventory to assess the impact of these strategies on 259 mental health professionals providing services to traumatized individuals, 48 percent of whom were social workers (Bober & Regehr, 2006). In this group, while participants generally believed in the usefulness of recommended coping strategies, including leisure activities, self-care activities, and supervision, there was no association between the time devoted to these activities and traumatic stress scores. That is, we found no evidence that the strategies were effective in mitigating the effects of trauma exposure. Rather, the key factor in predicting levels of traumatic stress symptoms was the number of hours per week that individuals spent counseling traumatized individuals. The primary importance of caseload mix, specifically the percentage of cases involving trauma, was recently confirmed in an Israeli study (Dagan et al., 2015) and a meta-analysis of studies on secondary traumatic stress (Hensel, Ruiz, Finney, & Dewa, 2015).

As a result of our findings, which have subsequently been confirmed by others, we raised the concern that while the mental health field recognizes that those who are abused or battered must not be blamed for their victimization and subsequent traumatic response, when addressing trauma experienced by colleagues, the focus has been on the use of individual strategies (Bober & Regehr, 2006), in effect suggesting that workers who feel traumatized may not be balancing life and work adequately and may not be making effective use of leisure, self-care, or supervision. We thus argued for the need for organizational interventions. While I continue to be committed to organizational responses, it is also important for individual social workers to exercise control over their own experiences. Thus this section will focus on individual approaches to addressing stress and trauma response.

Stress Reduction Techniques

In 2012, a Canadian newspaper reported survey results under a headline that read, "Mental Health Crisis on Campus: Canadian Students Feel Hopeless, Depressed, Even Suicidal" (Lunau, 2012). Various sources reported that half of university students felt hopeless and experienced overwhelming anxiety, and that over one-third reported feeling depressed (Craggs, 2012). Similar findings were reported in other parts of the world. Among the 5,689 American university students who participated in the 2007 Healthy Minds Survey, 50.7 percent tested positive for major depression, panic disorder, or generalized anxiety using the Patient Health Questionnaire (PHQ-9) (Keyes et al., 2012). In a random sample of 8,155 students from fifteen American universities, 6.75 percent reported suicidal ideation, and 0.5 percent reported an attempt in the past year (Downs & Eisenberg, 2012). A study of 1,616 Turkish university students revealed rates of moderate depression in 27.1 percent, anxiety in 47.1 percent, and stress in 27.1 percent of the sample (Bayran & Bilgel, 2008). Students with mental health problems report poorer relationships with other students and faculty members, lower levels of engagement in campus clubs and activities, lower grade averages, and lower rates of graduation than students not suffering from mental health problems (Byrd & McKinney, 2012; Keyes et al., 2012; Salzer, 2012; Storrie, Ahern, & Tuckett, 2010).

As a result of repeated findings that approximately half of the student body experiences significant levels of stress in the form of anxiety and depression, my research team conducted a meta-analysis on interventions used to reduce stress in university students. Twenty-four controlled trials examining stress interventions with 1,431 students in a wide range of disciplines including nursing, medical science, medicine, economics, social work, law, psychology, technology, and general arts and science were included in the analysis (C. Regehr, Glancy, & Pitts, 2013). All of the studies that met the inclusion criteria based on scientific rigor examined interventions that incorporated components of cognitive, behavioral, or mindfulness-based techniques. Hayes (2004) characterizes these techniques as representing three waves: the first wave focused on behavioral techniques, the second incorporated social learning and cognitive components, and the third included mindful awareness and acceptance of present experiences. Others argue that all these techniques share fundamental characteristics and should not be considered different waves but rather different forms of cognitive-behavioral therapy (CBT) (Hoffman, Sawyer, & Fang, 2010).

It is nevertheless useful to consider the relative contributions of cognitive, behavioral, and mindfulness interventions in addressing stress and anxiety responses. Behavioral stress reduction interventions often focus on control of physical stress reactions through controlled breathing or muscle relaxation. Cognitive-behavioral therapy incorporates cognitive, behavioral, and social learning theory components to explain functioning as a product of reciprocal interactions between personal and environmental variables. Cognitive therapy strategies aim to assist individuals to identify and modify dysfunctional beliefs that influence response to stimuli and subsequent physiological and psychological distress. These interventions can also involve modeling of effective communication techniques that are likely to result in lower levels of interpersonal stress in the workplace. Mindfulness-based interventions focus on lowering reactivity to challenging experiences through nonjudgmental self-awareness, particularly of physical sensations, cognitions, and emotions.

Five studies in the meta-analysis (Gaab et al., 2003; Gaab, Sonderegger, Scherrer, & Ehlert, 2006; Hammerfald et al., 2006; Kooken & Hayslip, 1984; Sheehy & Horan, 2004) examined interventions based on stress inoculation training (SIT). First developed by Meichenbaum in 1977, this model of intervention involves three interlocking and overlapping phases: (1) education regarding sources of stress, including irrational thinking, and ways to reduce psychological and physiological stress; (2) coping skills, including relaxation training and cognitive restructuring; and (3) application of new strategies for real or simulated situations (Meichenbaum, 1977, 1993; Meichenbaum & Deffenbacher, 1988). While originally developed for clinical populations, stress inoculation training has increasingly been used in a variety of populations to assist with the management of occupational stress and to enhance performance under stress (Saunders, Driskell, Johnston, & Salas, 1996).

Other studies in this review used a combination of techniques encompassed in stress inoculation training, including psycho-educational elements, relaxation training, and cognitive restructuring. One such approach was mindfulness-based stress reduction (MBSR), which was used in seven studies reviewed (Astin, 1997; Jain et al., 2007; Lynch, Gander, Kohls, Kudielka, & Walach, 2011; Oman, Shapiro, Thoresen, Plante, & Flinders, 2008; Shapiro, Brown, Thoresen, & Plante, 2011; Shapiro, Schwartz, & Bonner, 1998; Warnecke, Quinn, Ogden, Towle, & Nelson, 2011). Developed by Kabat-Zinn (1982), MBSR incorporates three mindfulness practices: (1) sweeping, or an awareness of the body focusing on breath awareness and relaxation; (2) mindfulness of breath; and (3) hatha yoga postures. Sessions generally cover mindfulness in stressful situations and social interactions, as well as acceptance of self and others. In this model, weekly MBSR sessions are augmented by audio recordings that lead practice at home. Originally designed as a behavioral

Anxiety in Cognitive/ Behavioral/ Mindfulness-Based Trials

Study name	Statistics for each study							Std diff in means and 95% CI
	Std diff in means	Standard error	Variance	Lower limit	Upper limit	Z-Value	p-Value	
Astin, 1997	-1.263	0.518	0.268	-2.278	-0.248	-2.439	0.015	
Charlesworth, 1981	-0.440	0.480	0.230	-1.381	0.500	-0.918	0.359	
Deckro et al, 2002	-0.663	0.217	0.047	-1.087	-0.238	-3.060	0.002	
Dehghan-Nayeri, 2011	-0.995	0.150	0.022	-1.289	-0.702	-6.639	0.000	
Enright, 2000	-0.841	0.353	0.124	-1.533	-0.150	-2.384	0.017	
Fehrang, 1983	-0.817	0.289	0.083	-1.382	-0.251	-2.829	0.005	
Gaab, 2003	-0.663	0.296	0.088	-1.244	-0.082	-2.235	0.025	
Gaab, 2006	-0.743	0.392	0.153	-1.510	0.025	-1.896	0.058	
Godbey, 1994	-0.195	0.477	0.227	-1.129	0.739	-0.409	0.683	
Hamdan-Mansour, 2009	-1.149	0.236	0.056	-1.611	-0.687	-4.872	0.000	
Heaman, 1995	-0.992	0.335	0.113	-1.649	-0.334	-2.957	0.003	
Jain et al, 2007	-0.734	0.274	0.075	-1.271	-0.197	-2.677	0.007	
Jones et al 2000	-1.481	0.272	0.074	-2.014	-0.948	-5.444	0.000	
Kooken, 1984	-0.272	0.452	0.204	-1.157	0.613	-0.602	0.547	
Lynch, 2007	-0.657	0.529	0.280	-1.695	0.380	-1.242	0.214	
Oman, 2008	-0.335	0.322	0.104	-0.966	0.296	-1.041	0.298	
Russler, 1991	-0.026	0.324	0.105	-0.662	0.610	-0.080	0.937	
Shapiro, 1998	-0.475	0.237	0.056	-0.940	-0.009	-1.999	0.046	
Shapiro, 2011	-0.532	0.372	0.138	-1.260	0.197	-1.431	0.153	
Sheehy, 2004	-1.302	0.469	0.220	-2.223	-0.382	-2.774	0.006	
Stephens, 1992	-0.343	0.207	0.043	-0.749	0.064	-1.653	0.098	
StLawrence, 1983	-0.814	0.455	0.207	-1.705	0.077	-1.790	0.073	
Warnecke, 2012	-0.758	0.279	0.078	-1.305	-0.210	-2.712	0.007	
	-0.733	0.077	0.006	-0.883	-0.583	-9.565	0.000	

-1.00   -0.50   0.00   0.50   1.00

Favours A   Favours B

Meta Analysis

FIGURE 8.1 Interventions to reduce anxiety in university students
Source: Regehr, Glancy, & Pitts, 2013.

medicine technique for patients with chronic pain (Kabat-Zinn, 1982), the model has subsequently been tested on people with a broad spectrum of issues, including anxiety disorders (Kabat-Zinn et al., 1991).

Given the overlap between SIT, MBSR, and other cognitive-behavioral interventions (for instance, see Segal, Teasdale, & Williams, 2002), these approaches were combined for analysis, the results of which are depicted in figure 8.1. The findings of the meta-analysis suggest that cognitive, behavioral, and mindfulness-based interventions focused on stress reduction significantly reduce symptoms of anxiety and depression. Further, despite variations in length of intervention, specific components of the intervention (including such aspects as cognitive restructuring, relaxation, and meditation), program of study, and country, these results are remarkably consistent.

In light of research findings suggesting that physicians face a wide variety of stressors that result in acute symptoms of stress, anxiety, and burnout and ultimately may affect patient care, my team conducted a second study involving a meta-analysis of interventions to reduce stress in physicians. This analysis included twelve studies involving 1,034 partici-

Stress in Physicians

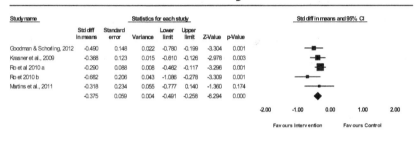

Study name	Std diff in means	Standard error	Variance	Lower limit	Upper limit	Z-Value	p-Value	Std diff in means and 95% CI
Justo, 2010	-1.435	0.364	0.132	-2.149	-0.722	-3.945	0.000	
McCue & Sachs, 1991	-0.966	0.280	0.078	-1.514	-0.418	-3.457	0.001	
Saadat et al., 2012	-0.735	0.335	0.112	-1.392	-0.078	-2.191	0.028	
Sood et al., 2011	-1.292	0.399	0.159	-2.074	-0.509	-3.235	0.001	
	-1.066	0.168	0.028	-1.394	-0.737	-6.350	0.000	

-4.00 -2.00 0.00 2.00 4.00

Favours Intervention   Favours Control

Meta-Analysis of Controlled Studies

FIGURE 8.2 Interventions to reduce stress in physicians
Source: Regehr, Glancy, Pitts, & LeBlanc, 2014.

Burnout in Physicians

Study name	Std diff in means	Standard error	Variance	Lower limit	Upper limit	Z-Value	p-Value	Std diff in means and 95% CI
Goodman & Schorling, 2012	-0.490	0.148	0.022	-0.780	-0.199	-3.304	0.001	
Krasner et al., 2009	-0.368	0.123	0.015	-0.610	-0.126	-2.978	0.003	
Ro et al 2010 a	-0.290	0.088	0.008	-0.462	-0.117	-3.296	0.001	
Ro et 2010 b	-0.682	0.206	0.043	-1.086	-0.278	-3.309	0.001	
Martins et al., 2011	-0.318	0.234	0.055	-0.777	0.140	-1.360	0.174	
	-0.375	0.059	0.004	-0.491	-0.258	-6.294	0.000	

-2.00 -1.00 0.00 1.00 2.00

Favours Intervention   Favours Control

Meta-Analysis of Single Group Design Studies

FIGURE 8.3 Interventions to reduce burnout in physicians
Source: Regehr et al., 2014.

pants. The results from this review and meta-analysis provide strong support that cognitive, behavioral, and mindfulness-based approaches are effective in reducing stress in physicians. The results also provide emerging evidence that these models may contribute to lower levels of burnout in physicians (C. Regehr, Glancy, Pitts, & LeBlanc, 2014). The results can be found in figures 8.2 and 8.3.

Moderating Empathy

Chapter 4 reviewed the critical role that empathy plays in the professional practice of social work. Indeed, clinician empathy has been linked to a wide range of patient outcomes, including satisfaction, engagement in treatment, and improved physical and mental health (Hojat, 2016). In chapter 4, I differentiated between two types of empathy: emotional empathy and cognitive empathy. Emotional empathy can be understood to be a vicarious emotional experience, or a sort of emotional contagion that has both biological and social roots. From a biological perspective, empathy can thus be understood as a simulation of the mental states of others through the activation of the neurological systems (Gallese, 2001; Iacoboni, 2009). This emotional transfer is more powerful for distressing emotions than for positive emotions (De Gelder, Snyder, Greve, Gerard, & Hadjikhani, 2004). Thus while empathic attunement may be a central aspect of working with traumatized others, it can lead to strain and other negative consequences for therapists and other professionals (C. Regehr, Goldberg, & Hughes, 2002; Wilson & Thomas, 2004).

Cognitive empathy is the ability to accurately imagine the plight of another without actually experiencing it (Kant, 1788/1949; C. Rogers, 1957). This process was observed and described by Fox (1959), who coined the term *detached concern*. Cognitive empathy is taught in programs for paramedics, who encounter highly distressing situations requiring cognitive and behavioral precision every day. Some scholars have focused on the detached side of this equation, suggesting that it socializes emotion out of the trainee (Underman & Hirshfield, 2016). Fox (2011), however, rebutted that remaining detached and expressing concern were not meant to be dichotomies, but rather coexisting states. In exploring detached concern with nurses, Cadge and Hammonds (2012) view these to be dual role obligations—providing care and managing one's own emotions. As discussed earlier in regard to social workers, these authors also point to the way in which nurses express their dedication and concern to individual patients. Cognitive empathy thus allows workers to focus on the task at hand rather than on their own emotional response.

In relating this to social work, King (2011) concurs that emotional and cognitive empathy do not need to be mutually exclusive. Rather, from an affective empathy perspective, social workers can be caring and develop an interpersonal connection with clients. In addition, they can be congruent, communicating to clients that they are open to and understand their unique situation. Nevertheless, King's formulation of emotional empathy is highly akin to his description of cognitive empathy, which involves intellectual flexibility, openness to understanding the client, and taking the perspective of another. Thus while *detached concern* may not be a term that seems congruent with social work practice, what is imagined in social work is a deliberate use of empathy, not a sense of becoming overcome through mirroring the emotions of another.

A related concept is emotional labor, or the effort to regulate emotions in the workplace (Hochschild, 1983). Emotional labor applies more to situations in which the social worker has negative feelings toward a client, such as a parent who abuses his or her child. Workers may manage emotions on the job by suppressing them or faking emotional responses—that is, expressing emotions that they do not actually feel (Hülsheger & Schewe, 2011). This may result in burnout and other negative outcomes (Pugliesi, 1999) and can be understood as an avoidant coping style.

Alternatively, the social worker can reframe the situation to truly understand the causes of client attitudes or behavior that conflicts with the social worker's own beliefs or values. Several authors speak to the importance of positive reappraisal in social work. For instance, painful and exhausting experiences of working with individuals who are dying can be reappraised as worthwhile and meaningful, and in doing so, maintain a sense of optimism (Collins, 2007). Interestingly, this reframing seems to have positive benefits even in light of posttraumatic symptoms. Both our studies (Cadell, Regehr, & Hemsworth, 2003; C. Regehr, Hemsworth, et al., 2004) and a recent meta-analysis (Hensel et al., 2015) demonstrated that higher levels of posttraumatic growth are associated with higher levels of posttraumatic stress in those caring for others.

Gerdes and Segal (2009) present a social work model of empathy that encompasses affect, cognition, and action. The first element, involving automatic *affective responses*, requires an awareness of automatic physiological reactions to another's emotions. The second element is *cognitive processing*, which uses voluntary and flexible thought processes to interpret the social worker's own affective response to another person and his or her ability to take the perspective of another. The third element is conscious decision-making leading to *empathic action.* That is, the social worker voluntary chooses action in response to cognitive understanding. The key to this model is therefore transforming empathy into action to create change. This change may involve assisting an individual to maximize their choices, creating new programs that address issues, or changing social policy. It is important to note, however, that empathic action requires courage.

Demonstrating Courage

A few years ago, I chaired a search committee for a faculty member in social work. A student representative sitting on the committee was my doctoral student Cindy Blackstock, the director of the First Nations Caring Society of Canada. As we were reviewing the standard questions we asked of all perspective faculty members, Cindy asked us to add one more. Her suggested question was "When in your career have you demonstrated courage? Give us an example of when you have demonstrated courage." This question has stuck with me and in some ways haunted me. Cindy was certainly a social work professional who had demonstrated courage herself. A member of the Gitksan First Nation, Cindy is renowned for her activism with respect to child protection and indigenous children's rights. Among her many initiatives, Cindy filed a complaint with the Canadian Human Rights Commission against the federal government. In it she argued that the government discriminates against Indigenous children on reserves by failing to provide the level of health and social services available to all other Canadian children. The finding of the Human Rights tribunal concurred and stated that the funding model "resulted in denials of services and created various adverse impacts for many First Nations children and families living in reserves" (CBC, 2016).

As indicated in chapter 4, role conflict is an organizational and social policy factor that impacts the development of stress and burnout responses in social workers. Researchers have reported that social workers experience moral distress when institutional structures and resources available (including time to adequately address the problem) create obstacles to pursuing what is judged to be the morally right course of action (Jameton, 1992) and when policies and rules cause them to be either ineffective, overly controlling, or punitive (Stanford, 2009). This effect is ameliorated to some degree when workers have a sense of job autonomy and when they perceive their work to be challenging (Acker, 2004; Kim & Stoner, 2008). That is, as work is experienced as more meaningful and challenging and as workers have the scope to address these challenges in a creative manner, chronic stress associated with the job is reduced.

There is no question that this type of conflict must be addressed by institutional and social policies that do not place social workers in situations where they must choose between what they believe to be morally right and what is required by policy. Further, as noted above, institutional structures must allow social workers to employ their professional skills and exercise professional judgement. In addition, however, social workers as professionals must identify where there is scope for judgment and social action and embrace these opportunities bravely.

Unlike Cindy Blackstock, most social workers do not work in an agency where there is scope to launch legal action against the federal government. However, other opportunities to exercise professional autonomy and judgment exist. Michael Lipsky famously coined the term *street-level bureaucracy* in 1980. In the preface to the thirtieth anniversary edition of his book, Lipsky explains that street-level bureaucrats are the "teachers, social workers, police officers and other public workers who regularly interact with . . . and have wide discretion over dispensation of benefits or the allocation of public sanctions . . . in the course of their jobs" (Lipsky, 2010, p. xi). This exercise of discretion in fact shapes the manner in which social policy was experienced at the ground level by clients of various social systems. He argued that "the decisions of street-level bureaucrats, the routines they establish, and the devices they invent to cope with uncertainties and work pressures, effectively become the public policies they carry out" (p. xiii). Lipsky rather critically suggested that the work could not be performed to the highest standards because these workers lacked the time, information, and resources to properly respond to each case. He concluded that, contrary to the high ideals of individuals entering these professions, cases were dealt with in a routine and rigid manner that ultimately resulted in poor standards of care and what appeared to be poor social policy.

Lipsky views discretion of professionals working directly with the public to be inherently problematic. Nevertheless, he does point to the power of individuals not only to affect the lives of their individual clients, but also to interpret and ultimately shape the policies that govern their work. More recent analysts have suggested that since Lipsky's original work, discretion has been increasingly curtailed by public accountability (including court systems, organizational supervisors and executives, colleagues, clients, and the media) (T. Evans, 2012; Hupe &

Hill, 2007), yet social work professionals do have considerable discretion in individual cases. For instance, in a case study by Evans, supervisors and managers stated that professional social workers did have the ability to "practice quite autonomously" on a day-to-day basis (2010, p. 378). Indeed, in this study Evans noted that procedure manuals were so elaborate that they created more discretion by allowing people to decide what to follow and what to ignore. Further, information systems that may be implemented to systematize and monitor activities may actually rely more on the expertise on the individual social worker, affording them a greater role and greater autonomy (Shaw, Morris, & Edwards, 2009). Thus at the level of the individual social worker, identifying the breadth of discretion and bravely making decisions based on knowledge, expertise, and values can afford a sense of power and accomplishment.

IMPLICATIONS FOR SOCIAL WORK EDUCATION

Spencer and Munch noted in 2003 that one of the roles of social work education, according to the Council on Social Work Education, is to prepare effective professionals. Yet they lamented that few schools included specific education about safety training either in their curriculum or in their practicum manual. They also noted that few social work textbooks addressed issues of personal safety for social workers or social work students. The National Association of Social Workers (NASW) (2013) guidelines on safety now assert that social work safety should be part of the curriculum and training for both field practice educators and for students. Further, they suggest that schools should have clear systems whereby students can express safety concerns. The role of the field-faculty liaison can be critical in this respect, ensuring that agencies have safety procedures in place and that the conversation about safety is alive within the organization for the benefit of all staff.

Safety education should also address issues of privacy. Today's students are entering the social worker profession with a long history of sharing personal information broadly through social media and other internet-based sites. This information makes them more vulnerable to intrusions into their personal lives and more open to threat. Social work students need to learn to protect their privacy and that of their families online.

As noted earlier, students in general report high levels of stress and distress while attending university. For social work students, engaging with clients and troubling material for the first time in their careers can be an additive factor. Social work educational programs are thus charged with the dual responsibility of supporting the mental health needs of students related to their education in a manner expected of all higher education, while also preparing them for the emotional demands of practice (Grant, Kinman, & Baker, 2014; Hen & Goroshit, 2011). Indeed, the *Professional Capabilities Framework* of the British Association of Social Workers explicitly states that prior to entering practicum, students must, among other things, describe and demonstrate the following: the importance of professional behavior, the importance of personal and professional boundaries, and the importance of emotional resilience (British Association of Social Workers, 2017).

Grant, Kinman, and Baker (2014) recommend an evidence-based emotional curriculum that integrates resilience into all elements of the program. Curricula should incorporate components that acknowledge stress and trauma responses (Spencer & Munch, 2003), providing information and modeling the sharing and managing of difficult reactions to practice situations. Techniques used by instructors in a study by Grant and colleagues (2014) included managing empathy, mindfulness, emotional literacy, peer coaching, reflective writing, reflective supervision, and exploring sources of support and work-life balance. Instructors in Australia described allowing space for exploration, building a resilience knowledge base, fostering peer support and reflective supervision, developing coping strategies, and demonstrating professionalism (Beddoe, Davys, & Adamson, 2013).

Hen and Goroshit (2011) describe a model for teaching emotional intelligence in social work programs. In this context, emotional intelligence was described as the ability to perceive, assimilate, express, and manage emotions. A specially designed course encouraged students to explore emotional situations and reflect on their own and others' responses. During classes, instructors modeled emotional regulation, introspection, and empathy. Additional learning opportunities included exposure to emotional-intelligence theories and journaling of experiences. At the University of Toronto, we have had graduate students adopt the role of mentors and teach stress management techniques to others. In this model, graduate students trained in mindfulness-based stress reduction were employed as seminar leaders for undergraduate students who were in a course that incorporated MBSR. This allowed the graduate students to master and demonstrate skills for the benefit of others, reinforce their own learning, and practice the techniques for themselves.

Leadership development has been largely ignored in social work (Elpers & Westhuis, 2008; Rank & Hutchison, 2000). The intensive relationship between schools of social work and social agencies through the field faculty liaison role provides an opportunity for leadership training of social work staff as they perform the role of student supervisors. In addition, strong partnerships between universities and national organizations, such as that established between nine universities and the National Child Welfare Institute in the United States, provide opportunities for enhanced leadership training (Bernotavicz, McDaniel, Brittain, & Dickinson, 2013). The resulting leadership model focuses on building collaborations, workforce development, leading change through goal-setting, and leading for results through accountability frameworks.

A MULTIFACETED APPROACH TO MITIGATING THE EFFECTS OF STRESS AND TRAUMA ON DECISION-MAKING

As indicated, stress and trauma have significant impacts not only on the well-being of social workers and the agencies in which they work, but also on the professional judgments that social workers must make in the course of their practice. An obvious solution is to develop and implement approaches that reduce exposure to stress and trauma, that mitigate responses to stress and trauma when exposed, and that ameliorate the symptoms experienced. I suggest four main approaches that require concerted efforts by social work organizations, individual social workers, and schools of social work. These four approaches are depicted in figure 8.4.

- *Enhance safety.* To enhance safety, schools of social work and social work organizations must provide safety education. Organizations must provide physical spaces and technological solutions that enhance safety.

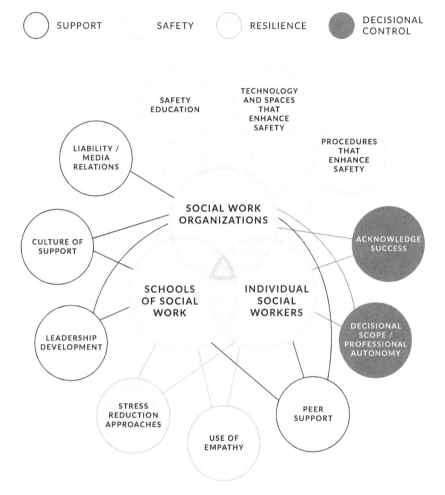

○ SUPPORT ○ SAFETY ○ RESILIENCE ● DECISIONAL CONTROL

SAFETY EDUCATION

TECHNOLOGY AND SPACES THAT ENHANCE SAFETY

PROCEDURES THAT ENHANCE SAFETY

LIABILITY / MEDIA RELATIONS

SOCIAL WORK ORGANIZATIONS

ACKNOWLEDGE SUCCESS

CULTURE OF SUPPORT

SCHOOLS OF SOCIAL WORK

INDIVIDUAL SOCIAL WORKERS

DECISIONAL SCOPE / PROFESSIONAL AUTONOMY

LEADERSHIP DEVELOPMENT

STRESS REDUCTION APPROACHES

USE OF EMPATHY

PEER SUPPORT

FIGURE 8.4 A multifaceted approach to mitigating the effects of stress and trauma on decision-making

Source: Author's own data.

Social workers must partner with their organizations to establish procedures that enhance safety and then follow those procedures, ensuring that they do not relegate their safety as secondary to client needs.

- *Enhance support.* Through educational programs, schools of social work begin the process of instilling cultures of organizational support and peer support as central values of social work. Schools of social work can partner with social work organizations to develop leadership that attends to issues of stress, trauma, and support. When adverse events occur, organizations must ensure that they support workers engaged in review processes and have robust approaches to managing media and governmental concerns.

- *Enhance resilience.* Social workers must take responsibility for developing and using strategies for enhancing resilience, such as practicing stress management techniques and using empathy in a deliberate manner. Schools of social work (and health science professions) are increasingly including resilience enhancement as a central component of the professional curriculum.
- *Enhance decisional control.* Policies and procedures that attempt to eliminate professional discretion are not only demoralizing but also doomed to fail given the multiplicity of factors that affect decision-making in complex cases. Social work organizations must acknowledge and support some level of individual autonomy in professional decision-making. In addition, social workers must identify where they have discretion and not hide behind policies and procedures. This requires courage. It also requires that we attend not only to the adverse consequences of high-risk decisions but also the successes as areas for learning.

This leads to the second key element of addressing the impact of stress and trauma on decision-making, which is to develop decision-making models that acknowledge and capitalize on emotional responses. That is the focus of the next chapter.

CHAPTER NINE

Improving Decision-Making in Situations of Uncertainty

It is now clear that stress and trauma exposure are significant aspects of social work practice. It is also clear that the natural reactions of social workers to stress and trauma can affect professional decision-making, particularly in situations of risk and uncertainty. For instance, stress and trauma can alter perceptions, impair cognitive processing, and affect memory. The first approach to improving social workers' decision-making and the services they provide is to address the stress and trauma side of the equation. As noted in chapter 8, this requires a multifaceted approach to reduce stress and trauma exposure and to address worker distress when exposure occurs.

On the other hand, emotional and physiological reactions can augment decision-making practices, providing additional sources of information to be considered. However, the influence of emotion on decision-making is largely unconscious, contributing to what are experienced as intuitive responses. To improve decision-making, social workers must better understand the impact of emotional factors on their professional judgment in order to evaluate whether these responses are helping or hindering the process of arriving at optimal decisions. This chapter describes a process by which social workers can assess and improve the professional decisions they must make in situations involving risk.

ASSESSING THE CURRENT LEVEL OF COMPETENCE AND EXPERTISE

A first step in improving decision-making is assessing one's current level of competence and expertise. This appraisal can assist social workers and social work students to moderate possible overconfidence that they have in their decisions, consider the degree to which they should rely on actuarial tools and structured professional judgments, and know when they should seek the advice of others.

Research has demonstrated that professionals can arrive at very different conclusions when assessing the same cases (Arad-Davidzon & Benbenishty, 2008; Paterson et al., 2008; C. Regehr, LeBlanc, Bogo, Paterson, & Birze, 2015; Schuerman, Rossi, & Budde, 1999). More surprisingly, individual professionals can also arrive at different conclusions when they assess the same case at different times (Paterson et al., 2008). Despite these divergent opinions, assessors may express great confidence in their ultimate decisions. That is, some practitioners can be highly confident that the risk of a negative outcome is high, while others can be equally confident that the risk of a negative outcome is low (Hendryx & Rohland, 1997; C. Regehr et al., 2016; C. Regehr, Bogo, Shlonsky, & LeBlanc, 2010).

In general, confidence in professional decision-making increases with practice experience (Hay et al., 2008). However, in some cases, novices with relatively little experience, such as social work students and physician trainees, are found to be more confident in their judgments of risk than are workers with considerably more experience (Hodges, Regehr, & Martin, 2001; Mendel et al., 2011; C. Regehr et al., 2016). This pattern is reflected in other research that reports that student confidence actually decreases as their knowledge base increases (Ge & Hardré, 2010). Kruger and Dunning (1999) referred to this phenomenon as "unskilled and unaware." In clinical practice environments, it has been called "overconfidence" (Baumann, Deber, & Thompson, 1991). In part, those with lower levels of experience and knowledge have not developed the metacognitive ability to reflect on their own abilities and practice (Kruger & Dunning, 1999). Also contributing to overconfidence is the tendency of individuals to base predictions on abstract models and to underestimate the importance of context variables (Trope & Liberman, 2003). As students and practicing professionals progress in the development of competence and ultimately expertise, they become more aware of the complexities inherent in clinical situations and the importance of context. This increased awareness allows individuals to become more realistic about their abilities, and the risk of overconfidence is reduced.

While confidence in professional decisions may well be justified, overconfidence can contribute to errors in judgment (Berner & Graber, 2008; Smith & Dumont, 2002). This may occur when professionals reach a conclusion prematurely and do not fully consider information that conflicts with the initial judgment (Croskerry, Singhal, & Mamede, 2013). It may also occur when the individual's level of expertise does not justify the level of confidence. As indicated in chapter 5, the acquisition of expertise is a stepwise process that involves (1) learning the rules for practice and following them regardless of context (novice); (2) applying knowledge to real situations and beginning to recognize additional elements to be considered (advanced beginner); (3) having an awareness of the vast range of factors to be considered and possessing the ability to select relevant factors (competence); (4) assimilating experience developing intuitive responses (proficiency); and (5) extending knowledge by operating at the boundaries of competence and comfort, resisting familiar routines, and mastering novel situations (expertise) (Dreyfus & Dreyfus, 2005; Scardamalia & Bereiter, 1991). To improve decision-making, it is important to determine one's own stage in the development of expertise.

Marion Bogo and I worked with colleagues to investigate field practice educators' views regarding the characteristics of struggling, competent, and exemplary students. We determined that the skills and abilities described by field educators fell into two broad categories: procedural competencies and meta-competencies. Procedural competencies include assessment skills, intervention skills, and professional communication. Meta-competencies include the ability to understand and manage interpersonal interactions; a strong sense of the professional role, including social work values and ethics; an awareness of the need to continue to develop learning; and the cognitive capacity to conceptualize practice (Bogo, 2010; Bogo et al., 2006). Hardré, Ge, and Thomas (2006) arrived at a similar model when describing the development of expertise in instructional design. They identified three layers: knowledge of domain-specific facts and principles; skill in applying and adapting knowledge; and metacognition, or self-awareness and self-regulation. The competencies identified by our team in some ways parallel Thorndike's earlier formulation of three types of intelligence: (1) *mechanical intelligence*, such as knowing which questions to ask in an assessment and how to write a report; (2) *social intelligence* related to interactions with others; and (3) *abstract intelligence*, or the ability to reflect on and integrate concepts (Thorndike, 1920). We suggested that not all competencies are equal, and instead that procedural and meta-competencies were hierarchical. Further, whereas procedural competencies are developed in the first few stages of expertise development defined above, meta-competencies are required to reach the proficient and expert stages.

A challenge, however, is that meta-competencies are more difficult to quantify and thus do not easily fit into scales for assessing competence. Our research has further suggested that it is these very areas, the ones that are most important in the development of expertise, that are the most difficult for individuals to assess in themselves (C. Regehr, Regehr, Leeson, & Fusco, 2002). They are also the most challenging areas in which to receive corrective or negative feedback from others. In a study exploring field practice educators' experiences in providing feedback to students, participants reported that upon hearing negative feedback, some students became fearful, and their struggles with learning were intensified (Bogo, Regehr, Power, & Regehr, 2007). This dissuaded instructors from sharing difficult information with students and exacerbated the students' lack of awareness regarding their own deficits in competence. We thus engaged in a multiyear process for developing two new online practice-based evaluation tools for use in social work education: one focused on clinical practice (C. Regehr, Bogo, & Regehr, 2011) and one for use in community and organizational practice (C. Regehr, Bogo, Donovan, Lim, & Regehr, 2012). In these scales, we addressed concerns about previous methods of student evaluation in the practicum by hiding numerical rating scales; using the language of expert field educators; and having students and instructors complete the instruments independently before comparing their appraisals with one another. These tools are available for use in other social work programs and can be found in *Achieving Competence in Social Work Through Field Education* (Bogo, 2010).

In addition, we suggested that the assessment of practice competence should not be entirely delegated to the field practicum. Rather, schools of social work also bear a responsibility for ensuring the competence of their students. Consequently, we embarked on a program of study led by Marion Bogo to adapt for social work an evaluation model that was already used in medicine and other health professions. The model, the *Objective Structured Clinical Examination* (or OSCE), requires students to perform clinical assessments of standardized patients, who are actors playing the role of clients. Students are observed and rated on a tool designed specifically for that purpose. Feedback is then provided to the students, and they are encouraged to share it with their field practice educator. The model's success in measuring competence and student satisfaction has resulted in its becoming a regular component of the lab-based course, which students are required to complete before entering the practicum at the University of Toronto (Bogo et al., 2012).

While evaluation of the student competence is an important gate-keeping function of schools of social work and the field practicum, once a social worker enters practice there are few organizations that require evaluation of continuing competencies. In addition, there are few tools available for this purpose, although some excellent domain-specific tools are available, such as the Hartford Geriatric Social Work Competency Scale (Bonifas & Simons, 2014) and the Hospital Social Work Self-Efficacy Scale (Holden et al., 1997). We used the OSCE model to examine and compare the practice of experienced social workers to that of students. However, we were quick to acknowledge that this approach is certainly not practical as a standard expectation in the profession. Organizations employing social workers often have yearly performance evaluations, but I am not aware of an organization that regularly and systematically evaluates competence or growing levels of expertise. In addition, harkening back to the finding that students have difficulty receiving feedback on performance deficits, particularly those related to meta-competencies, and the finding that field supervisors have difficulty providing the feedback, we can expect that this dynamic is intensified in the case of evaluating practicing social workers. Thus, modification of the model that we developed of relative ranking of competencies for students may be a solution.

As described in chapter 5, the relative ranking model instructs the evaluator and the individual being evaluated to rank-order competencies from the skill that requires the most attention to the one that requires little or no attention. Thus, rather than having each skill rated on a scale from 1 to 5, in which each individual expects at least a 4.5 on each item, everyone has areas where they are most or least proficient (C. Regehr et al., 2002). In table 9.1, I selected competence items from our previously validated Practice-Based Education Tool and placed them in a sample tool format. The evaluation tool is completed independently by the social worker and by a colleague or supervisor. The results are then compared as the basis for discussions about expertise. This allows for recognition of areas of greatest strength and areas requiring attention. It also provides a basis for future supervision or peer mentoring sessions. Such an approach addresses one element for reducing the potential for errors in judgement, that is, deliberately increasing knowledge and experience in areas in which the individual possesses lower levels of competence and expertise (Graber et al., 2012).

EXAMINING THE COGNITIVE ASPECTS OF DECISION-MAKING

The art and skill of the expert are characterized by intuitive or automatic decision-making. Although this may appear somewhat magical, in actuality intuition is a process of rapidly linking pieces of information together (Dane & Pratt, 2007). Information from the current situation is compared to deeply held yet unconscious models or schemas for organizing information. In this way, rapid and holistic judgments are made based on complex patterns or maps of how various factors relate to one another (Salas, Rosen, & DiazGranados, 2009). These have been referred to in other contexts as illness scripts (Schmidt & Boshuizen, 1993). That is, patients or clients are seen to present with characteristic patterns involving enabling conditions (biological predeterminants, lifestyle choices, social conditions), causal factors (job loss, death of a family member), and consequences (arrest, suicidal ideation). New clinical encounters are fit into existing scripts, allowing for rapid assessment and decision-making. Social workers will easily identify with the experience of feeling they have encountered this situation or this type of client

TABLE 9.1
Relative ranking of competencies

Expertise Evaluation	
Skill	**Rank**
Demonstrates confidence in taking risks and challenging self appropriately	
Flexible and adaptable with colleagues	
Capable of clear, concise and comprehensive assessment that lead to goal-directed interventions	
Able to sustain effective, genuine and creative relationships with a broad array of clients	
Able to understand and draw from personal experiences to understand clients and this life situation	
Possesses strong critical thinking skills	
Flexibly uses a variety of theories in practice	
Possess comprehensive written and verbal skills	
Maintain ethical practice without being overly rigid	
Understands and carries out agency mandate while remaining sensitive to client situations and needs	
Communicates effectively with other team members	

Instructions:

Consider your skills at this point in time, and indicate which areas need more work and which need less work.

a) Select the skill that needs the *most* work (the skill that you would work on if you could only work on one). *Write "1" beside that skill.*

b) Select the skill that needs the *least* work (the skill that you could ignore if you did not have the time to work on everything). *Write "10" beside that skill.*

c) Select the skill that represents your middle level of ability (the skill that you would work on if you had the time but would be in the middle of your priority list). *Write "5" beside that skill.*

d) With these anchors in mind, now place the remaining numbers next to the remaining skills, until you have used them all up. Try to compare each skill to those you have used as anchors. Half your skills should fall above the middle and half below.

(Regehr, Regehr, Leeson, & Fusco, 2002)

before. In a recent study on decision-making, social workers described this as "getting a snapshot" or "building a picture" of the case (Saltiel, 2016).

While this process has the benefits of providing quick and generally correct answers to complex problems, it also carries risk of bias and error. For instance, the clinician can be subject to an anchoring effect, or confirmation bias. Anchoring is the process by which people are overly swayed by their first impression and subsequently attend to information that confirms this earlier impression (De Bortoli & Dolan, 2015; Tversky & Kahneman, 1985). Similarly, a clinician may overestimate the degree to which a client represents a classic case, thereby neglecting to search for unique characteristics that may influence outcome. There may also be an overemphasis on the individual's disposition and an underemphasis on situational variables that are influencing the presentation of symptoms or problems (Arkes, 1981; Baumann, Deber, & Thompson, 1991; Glascoe & Dworkin, 1993; Smith & Dumant, 2008).

As intuitive expertise occurs outside the realm of conscious deliberation, people cannot articulate the steps, inductive thinking, or incremental decisions that lead to their final conclusion or actions. It is knowing without knowledge of the process by which the decision was made (Salas et al., 2009). Thus improving decision-making involves understanding how decisions were made and what information was taken into account. It is a process of making the implicit, explicit. This can be practiced in a wide range of domains.

One day, a family member and I stopped at a drive-through Tim Horton's coffee shop at a service center on the side of the highway. As I held the paper cup filled with liquid, I announced that I would not hand the tea to the driver yet. I then reflected on what was involved in my decision. I noticed that I was holding the paper cup by the bottom rim because the exterior of the cup was too hot to hold around the middle. As I brought the cup close to my face, I could feel steam emitting from the small air hole in the lid. I observed that liquid was oozing out of the air hole, indicating that the cup had been overfilled. I surmised that if I opened the drinking hole, hot tea would spill out over my hand and lap. I noted that the access road back to the highway was not smoothly paved, and I anticipated that the car would bump up and down, sloshing the liquid. I recalled other times when drinks had spilled when driving, and recalled the experience of having hot drinks spill on me. I considered the danger of a driver entering the highway while distracted by pain, surprise, or discomfort. I thus determined it was a safety risk to pass the cup to the driver.

We all make these types of decisions every day—selecting one piece of fruit in the store rather than another; deciding whether to walk across the street now or wait until the traffic light changes; and deciding whether to allow our adolescent child to go swimming in the lake with friends. These are areas in which we have developed expertise. As we make the decision, we take into consideration observations and other sensory input (the smell of the fruit, wind that may cause waves in the lake); past experiences (how quickly fruit will ripen, what it feels like to be stuck in the middle of a busy street with traffic whizzing by in both directions); possible outcomes (arriving at an appointment on time versus getting hit by a car, the adolescent experiencing independence versus getting injured); and the relative risk of these outcomes. Social workers can ask themselves: What patterns am I seeing? What information am I considering? What is influencing my decision? In this way, social workers can shed light on their automatic processes and the schemas by which they organize information.

In addition to unconscious processes, professional decisions are influenced by non-patient or non-client-related factors. Leung and colleagues (2012) explored surgeon's perceptions of factors that influenced decision-making. What emerged were three sets of factors that her team named avowed factors, unavowed factors, and disavowed factors. Avowed factors were those that were aligned with the ideals of the profession and included professional values (such as acting in the best interest of the patient) and best practices (avoiding scarring). The second set of factors, those that were unavowed, related to organizational pressures, such as letting trainees operate on patients to further their learning, or rushing a case to ensure that the operating room is ready for the next surgical team. These factors can be understood to consider the greater good although they may not be strictly in the best interest of the individual patient. The final factors were those that were disavowed; these included risk to the personal reputation of the clinician (if I undertake this risky procedure my patient survival rate could be affected) or personal financial gain (this procedure pays more than that one). These were factors that would be publicly denied but could nonetheless be subtle, or not so subtle, influences on the decisions made in any given case (Leung et al., 2012). Munro pointed to the manner in which public inquiries into deaths of children due to child abuse or neglect resulted in "defensive practice by professionals so that children's and young people's best interests are not always at the heart of the decisions" (Munro, 2011, p. 134). This suggests that fear of public shame, litigation, or liability may similarly be disavowed factors in decision-making for social workers. We need to acknowledge these factors at least to ourselves and determine the degree to which they are influencing our decision-making process.

ASSESSING THE GENERAL LEVEL OF STRESS AND TRAUMA

In addition to cognitive elements, decision-making involves affective elements. This includes preexisting emotional states and emotional states evoked by the current situation. First I will examine the more pervasive experiences of stress and trauma response. It is important to recall that stress is not in and of itself a negative thing. A certain level of stress is required to motivate individuals to act in positive ways. For instance, stress motivates students to study for exams, and stress provokes most of us to prepare prior to giving a speech or public lecture. At certain levels, stress enhances performance. On the other hand, as discussed extensively in this book, excessive stress can lead to negative health, psychological, and social outcomes. The degree of stress required to helpfully motivate someone rather than impair functioning varies from one individual to another (LeBlanc, McConnell, & Monteiro, 2014). Some individuals function best and produce most when stress levels are particularly high, whereas others show impairment in cognitive and other functioning even at lower levels of stress. In part this is due to whether the individual perceives the situation to be a challenge or a threat.

In addition, emotional state colors the way in which individuals interpret that world. For instance, anxiety is associated with interpretations of information as threatening and perceptions that risk is higher. Angry individuals rely more heavily on stereotypes, demonstrate greater prejudice (Blanchette & Richards, 2010), and lean toward retribution and punishment as approaches to addressing problems (Nabi, 2003). Positive emotions are associated with greater willingness to take risks (Hu, Wang, Pang, Xu, & Guo, 2015). Thus emotional states are important for professional decision-making. If a professional enters an assessment in a state of anger regarding some unrelated event (such as a conflict with a coworker) or in a state of generalized anxiety, this can color the manner in which the professional perceives the client and acquires and processes information.

A number of scales can be used to assess ongoing levels of stress. For instance, the Perceived Stress Scale is a brief ten-item scale that addresses the degree to which situations in an individual's life are perceived to be stressful. Originally developed (as a fourteen-item scale) by Cohen and colleagues in 1983, the current version is available online, and norms are provided based on gender, race, and age (Cohen, Kamarck, & Mermelstein, 1983, 1994). Regardless of scores on standardized scales, however, all social workers must assess the degree to which stress is an impairment in their life. In the workplace, they may be aware that they are unable to concentrate on certain tasks, are making more mistakes, or are taking much longer to complete tasks. They may also note that stress is affecting their interpersonal relationships. For instance, they may become aware that they are more easily irritated or angry with clients or coworkers.

Although symptoms of traumatic stress are not similarly motivating, the intensity of symptoms that individuals can tolerate also differs. Scales such as the well-validated and easily accessible Post-Traumatic Scale (Foa, Cashman, Jaycox, & Perry, 1997) can be of assistance. A new version of the scale that parallels *DSM-5* criteria (American Psychological

Association, 2013) is now available online (https://adaa.org/sites/default/files/Yusko%20_210.pdf). Again, however, social workers must assess the degree to which the symptoms are interfering with their work. They should ask themselves: Am I avoiding situations, such as new intake assessments? Do I experience heightened levels of fear when anticipating going to certain places or facing certain types of clients? If this is the case, the strategies for managing stress that are described in chapter 8 may be helpful.

EXAMINING RESPONSES IN ACUTE SITUATIONS

A wide range of neuroscience and psychology research has led to the conclusion that emotion plays a significant role in making decisions in situations of risk or uncertainty (Vartanian & Mandel, 2011). Emotions interact with cognitive evaluation in situations of risk, and this interaction ultimately guides behavior (Mohr, Biele, & Heekeren, 2010). Indeed, Slovic and colleagues demonstrated that in situations of risk, emotion overrides cognition (Slovic, Finucane, Peters, & MacGregor, 2004). In making decisions, emotion determines what information we attend to; what schemas or illness scripts we evoke to frame the current situation; and how much risk we are willing to take (Blanchette & Richards, 2010; Goel & Vartanian, 2011; Nabi, 2003). These emotions are driven by somatic responses, as demonstrated in figure 7.1 in chapter 7. That is, internal body states such as a racing heart or sweating, trigger emotional responses. In this way, feelings have been defined as "mental representations of physiological changes" emerging from the cognitive processing of emotion-eliciting stimuli (Dolan, 2002).

The cognitive frameworks or schemas that underlie expert decision-making are influenced by emotionally significant experiences. Affective responses evoked by current situations trigger relevant schemas and contribute to intuitive responses. They can be understood as experiential information processing, or gut feelings (Dane, Rockmann, & Pratt, 2012; Gigerenzer, 2007). As depicted in figures 7.1 and 7.2, somatic response, emotion, and cognition interact to direct decision-making in situations of risk. Not only may emotions inform cognition, but they can also override logic in the decision-making process. Slovic and colleagues (2004) refer to this as the *affect heuristic*.

Gut feelings can be triggered by images of previous encounters, or experiences that have contributed to the development of schemas. They can also be triggered by the emotional reactions of others. For instance, when one imagines, hears about, or observes pain in others, the brain activity stimulated is similar to the activation that occurs when pain and injury are directly inflicted (Shirtcliff et al., 2009). Consequently, the individual experiences emotion-driven body-related changes "as if" the person had experienced the pain directly themselves (Damasio, 2001). Physiological and emotional reactions thus become cues to information that is gathered and processed at an unconscious level. Identifying these reactions and their influence can help us more fully understand and ultimately improve decision-making. The three examples of emotional and physiological experiences follow and are described and charted in table 9.2.

I asked an internationally known forensic psychiatrist to describe a situation in which his own emotional and physiological reactions informed an assessment of risk. Assessment of future dangerousness is a standard element of his practice, and it is not uncommon for individuals who are being assessed to be angry about the criminal justice process they have been thrust into, or the accusations leveled against them. Sometimes this anger is dispositional and reflects many of their interpersonal interactions. Sometimes the anger is exacerbated by situational factors. Sometimes it is almost entirely situational. In this case, the psychiatrist recounted a situation in which an individual was being assessed to determine if he presented a threat to his wife and child. During the interview, the individual became aggressive and hostile, raising his voice, standing up, and banging the desk. In response, the psychiatrist became uncharacteristically anxious about his own personal safety. His heart rate accelerated and his muscles tensed as he prepared to defend himself or flee. The psychiatrist thus determined that if this person could not manage his anger and aggression in this high-stakes situation, it was unlikely he would be able to do so when he feels angry at family members. Further, if the psychiatrist, who had a black belt in karate, felt threatened, he extrapolated that others must feel so to a much greater extent.

In our child welfare study, experienced child protection workers interviewed a standardized patient acting as a mother suspected of injuring her young child. As described in chapter 6, workers in the study were highly variable as to their determination of future risk to the child. Participants were interviewed to identify the factors they considered in their assessment of risk. One worker described the way in which she relied on her own emotional response as part of her decision that the child was not at high risk. She indicated that she felt she was able to develop a relationship with the mother and that this demonstrated that the mother had the capacity to form relationships. The social worker thus determined that the mother had the capacity to emphasize with her child and was unlikely be violent toward the child if the proper emotional supports and resources were put in place.

A social worker with extensive mental health experience assessed the risk of suicide in a depressed woman in an emergency room environment. The client answered in the affirmative to many factors included on the Beck Suicide Scale, suggesting that she may present as a risk. As part of the assessment, the social worker learned that the woman had a teenage daughter. She asked how the daughter might manage if her mother were not there. The client teared up and talked about her concern for her daughter's well-being. The social worker's emotion shifted from clinical detachment to sadness. Her face changed and mirrored the mother's expression, she leaned forward, and felt a bit of a lump in her throat. She determined that the mother's love for her daughter was a significant protective factor reducing the risk of suicide.

UNDERSTANDING AND DEVELOPING DECISION-MAKING TOOLS

Tools have been developed to assist or direct professional decision-making in a wide range of domains. One type of tool is developed via actuarial methods, that is, through statistical algorithms or linear models that incorporate factors elicited from large data sets. Common features of the population in question (such as people who suffer cardiac arrest or people who have committed violent sex crimes) are extracted from the data set, weighted on the basis of statistical probability, and combined to produce a general probability score (B. Brown & Rakow, 2016; De Bortoli & Dolan, 2015). Actuarial tools are clear and straightforward, and they include easy-to-assess items such as age at first offense and prior convictions for sexual offenses (Hanson & Thornton, 1999).

TABLE 9.2

Charting responses regarding decision-making—Examples

Factors in Decision-Making

Situation	Physical Response of Professional	Emotional Response of Professional	Cognitions of Professional
Client has made a threat to kill his partner—presents as angry, aggressive	Adrenaline rush Racing heart Tensing muscles	Sense of threat	Person cannot manage anger and aggression even in high stakes situation
Daycare reports that a young child has welts on her bottom, assessing mother for risk of future abuse	Calm	Warmth towards mother Sense of emotional connection	Mother has the capacity to connect with others, will be able to understand needs of her child
Woman presents with many symptoms and signs that suggest that she may be at risk of suicide	Face mirrors the client Lump forms in throat Body leans forward Shoulders slumped	Sadness Concern	Relationship and commitment to daughter is a significant protective factor

(Author's own data)

Several authors assert the superiority of actuarial measures over clinical judgment (Graber et al., 2012). For instance, Wedding and Faust, in proclaiming that actuarial tools surpass clinical models of decision-making in neuropsychology, wrote, "Virtually no conflicting evidence has appeared in either neuropsychology or in other areas of clinical decision-making" (1989, p. 263). Nevertheless, others have pointed out that such tools do not take into account contextual, dynamic, and unique variables of the individual client. Hart (2016), in discussing the use of violence risk assessment measures with Indigenous peoples, notes that these tools ignore social, economic, and structural issues and thus result in cultural bias. As a world-renowned tool developer, he acknowledges that the tools have not demonstrated cross-cultural validity. Dawes described the development of robust linear models of prediction and prophetically stated:

> But people are important. The statistical model may integrate the information in an optimal manner, but it is always the individual (judge, clinician, subjects) who chooses the variables. Moreover, it is the human judge who knows the directional relationship between the predictor variables and the criterion of interest, or who can code the variables in such a way that they have clear directional relationships. . . . The linear model cannot replace the expert in "what to look for," but it is precisely this knowledge of what to look for in reaching the decision that is the special expertise that people have.
> (Dawes, 1979, p. 573)

Critiques about mechanistic, inflexible tools led to the development of structured professional judgment (SPJ) tools. These tools provide evidence-based guidelines or frameworks that incorporate systemization and consistency, while at the same time allowing for flexibility in incorporating case-specific and contextual factors. Based on the recognition that risk is dynamic and sensitive to changing conditions, SPJ tools allow social workers to override actuarial factors when justified (Doyle & Dolan, 2002; Webster, Haque, & Hucker, 2013). SPJ tools serve as aide-mémoire, providing lists of empirical items over which the practitioner exercises judgment with respect to their relevance and weight in any given case (B. Brown & Rakow, 2016; De Bortoli & Dolan, 2015). These tools allow for the integration of actuarial factors with expertise.

In many social work settings, actuarial tools are provided for the assessment of risk. However, as I demonstrated in chapter 6, the use of any tool does not guarantee uniformity of response. Rather, social workers complete even the most standardized of measures in nonstandard ways, arriving at different conclusions. Bosk (2018) investigated situations in which social workers' assessments diverged from actuarial tools in child protection cases. She discovered that most divergence occurred in two circumstances: when workers perceived that the risk assessment tool overestimated risk and when workers perceived the consequences of the risk score to be too punitive. In other words, situations in which the social worker believed that the use of the tool resulted in an answer that was in some way unfair to the client or conflicted with social work values. This suggests that the tool was not taking into account the range of factors that the social workers were considering and may in fact have introduced the types of bias cautioned by Hart. Bosk identified the costs in terms of family life, organizational functioning, and worker morale when there is no mechanism to override perceived false positives.

Munro noted that "risk assessment instruments can be invaluable aids, but they cannot provide a satisfactory replacement for professional judgment" (1999, p. 754). Thus social workers must not use tools blindly. Rather, they must understand the nature of items included in the tools, why they were included, and the populations from which they were derived. This allows social workers to determine how much weight to place on any item, or combination of items, included in the tool and to determine when items should be overridden due to other considerations. It also provides social workers with the knowledge that can empower them to articulate how indiscriminate use of the tool contributes to unjust elements of organizational practice that disadvantage some recipients of service.

Fast and frugal decision trees are another method of organizing information and guiding decision-making. Fast and frugal trees are most effective in commonly encountered situations that require quick

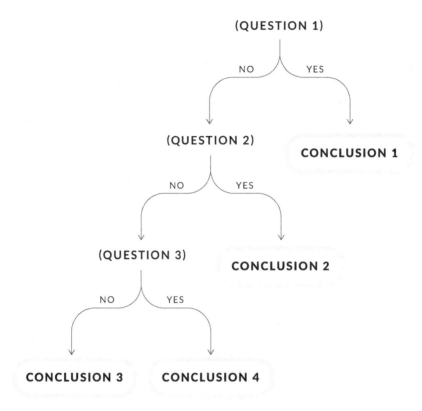

FIGURE 9.1 Fast and frugal decision tree template
Source: Author's own data.

decision-making, such as emergency room situations. Decision trees involve yes/no questions that clearly identify what information is most critical to the current situation, what information is sufficient for making an immediate decision, and what decision should be made (Gigerenzer, 2007). Research has demonstrated that in a wide range of situations involving high-stakes decisions (such as emergency medical care, violence risk prediction, or releasing an accused offender to the community), factors considered by expert decision-makers are often limited to three to five hierarchical questions (B. Brown & Rakow, 2016; Dhami, 2005; Green & Mehr, 1997). Fast and frugal decision trees explicate the factors considered and the manner in which they contribute to the final decision. While not appropriate for complex assessments, they can be developed for such purposes as telephone intake inquiries. A template can be found in figure 9.1.

IDENTIFYING AND MANAGING NOVEL SITUATIONS

All social workers, regardless of their experience or level of expertise, at times encounter novel situations. Novel situations are fundamental to the development of expertise, allowing individuals to work at the boundaries of their knowledge, experience, and comfort (Zilbert, Murnaghan, Gallinger, Regehr, & Moulton, 2015) adding to their repertoire of skills and to the richness and complexity of their decision-making frameworks. Novel situations also carry risk and are more likely to lead to adverse events or negative client outcomes than commonly encountered situations (Croskerry, 2003), especially if practitioners approach them in rigid, customary ways. Instead, practitioners must take advantage of the novel situation as an opportunity for reflection and professional growth.

Metacognition is the process of stepping back from the immediate situation, seeing the problem from a wider perspective, and consciously invoking strategies to improve the decision at hand (Croskerry, 2003). In novel situations, this requires the professional to consciously transition from automatic, nonanalytic decision-making to effortful, analytic forms of processing (Moulton, Regehr, Lingard, Merritt, & MacRae, 2010b). Yorke, Grant, and Csiernik (2016) describe a process using what they call "the third eye." In their formulation, the first eye is objective and theoretically informed; the second eye is attuned to the professional's own anxieties, reactions, and responses; and the third eye has the ability to disconnect and appraise the situation from a suspended vantage point. Several authors have suggested approaches to addressing novel situations in order to arrive at the optimal decision and achieve the best outcome (Croskerry, 2009; Croskerry et al., 2013; Graber et al., 2012; Moulton, Regehr, Lingard, Merritt, & MacRae, 2010a; Moulton, Regehr, Mylopoulos, & MacRae, 2007; Saltiel, 2016; Wedding & Faust, 1989). Some of these suggestions are as follows:

- *Slow down and reduce time pressures.* Find ways to reduce the pressure on the immediate decision by canceling your next appointment in order to extend the time allotted for this one, or put temporary strategies in place that take the urgency off the decision. In the emergency room, we would often have a client stay overnight in the waiting room or an examination room, reassessing them after they had slept and had breakfast.

- *Remove distractions.* When time pressures cannot be alleviated, work to remove other distractions, such as text messages or e-mails on unrelated matters. Remove background noise in the workplace and TV sounds during a home visit.
- *Tune in to your own emotional and physiological arousal.* Use your customary approaches to reduce your anxiety if it is interfering with your decision-making. This may include taking a break, getting some food if you are hungry, doing breathing exercises, or practicing self-talk.
- *Rule out the worst-case scenario.* This may not be possible in social work, where risk is harder to quantify, but providing temporary shelter so that a spouse is not injured or killed may allow the social worker to rule out the worst case for the time being.
- *Get more information, revise hypotheses, and consider alternatives.* This approach is referred to as the Bayesian method of problem-solving in which hypotheses are updated as new information becomes available. It involves consciously working to avoid the tendency to bolster initial impressions.
- *Assess whether decision tools may help.* Consider whether this is a situation in which standardized tools may assist with broadening your information search or structuring your line of inquiry.
- *Ask for help.* In novel situations, asking for advice, mentorship, or collegial support is always a good strategy. The situation may be new to you but not to others, and even if it is, a greater number of perspectives can potentially lead to better outcomes.
- *Know when you have enough information or input.* In the end, you will have to make a decision, so ensure that the process you undertake is not overwhelming or immobilizing. Know when you have enough information, document, and decide.
- *Modify existing models or schema.* Once you have successfully tackled a novel situation, ensure that this new information is used to modify existing schemas so that it can inform the next situation or encounter.

EXAMINING THE OUTCOMES OF DECISIONS
AND MODIFYING DECISION-MAKING MODELS

Social workers have legal and ethical duties to practice within their areas of competence and develop and enhance their professional expertise (National Association of Social Workers, 2008). In addition, social workers should analyze and evaluate the quality and outcomes of policies and practices (British Association of Social Workers, 2011; National Association of Social Workers, 2008). Principles of evidence-based practice also include a central role for monitoring and evaluating the outcome of interventions (Gibbs & Gambrill, 2002; M. Wilson et al., 1995). Thus, social workers must create a feedback loop to monitor the aftermath of their decisions and reflect on the implications of these consequences for future decision-making. This process has been referred to as metacognition, or reflective practice.

Individuals who are able to employ metacognition to modify existing knowledge schemas (Ge & Hardré, 2010; Schon, 1987) can continually develop their knowledge and abilities, thereby achieving greater levels of expertise. Conversely, those who fail to be aware of discrepant information—for instance when they receive information that the outcomes they predicted did not occur—will continue to rely on decision-making strategies that may or may not apply in a given situation. Croskerry and colleagues (2013) caution that the human tendency to bolster existing beliefs rather than search for new approaches impairs the ability of health care professionals to change their current practices. Thus it is important not to explain away outcomes that do not match predictions, thereby engaging in confirmation bias.

This analysis itself carries risk as it requires following up on cases in which one has made a decision and possibly exposing the fact that the decision was wrong and had adverse effects. Similar concerns have been noted in both aviation and in medicine, and consequently procedures have been implemented to allow for the analysis of risk factors in order to improve practice without punishing the professionals engaged in the analysis (Carson-Stevens et al., 2016; Helmreich, 2000; Weingart, Callanan, Ship, & Aronson, 2001). Nevertheless, Munro notes that "reviewing judgments critically is a hard task not only intellectually, but also emotionally." (1999, p. 755). Thus a supportive environment must be developed that allows for exploration and acknowledges that in working with high-risk populations and managing complex cases, practitioners' predictions will not always be correct.

In aviation and health care, the reporting and review of adverse events or "near misses" have been implemented at the system level. The Aviation Safety Reporting System (ASRS) is a voluntary reporting system established in the United States in 1976. Funded by the Federal Aviation Administration, the agency is responsible for the regulation and oversight of civil aviation, and is administered by the National Aeronautics and Space Administration (NASA). All employees in the airline industry can make confidential reports of situations or conditions that they believe will compromise, or have compromised, public safety. As ASRS has an immunity policy, it is able to gather information that would otherwise be hidden, enhancing the ability of the aviation community to improve equipment, procedures, and practices (NASA, 2016).

Following on this model, incident reporting systems have been developed in health care in various countries, including Australia, the United Kingdom, and the United States. By reducing barriers to reporting, these systems increase the breadth of information available regarding situations that endanger patient safety. They allow for quantitative analysis of large databases. As a result of the data and the concurrent rising culture of accountability and safety, they have the potential to improve health care services (Barach & Small, 2000). Nevertheless, several authors suggest that the use of these systems in health care has a number of limitations with respect to improving decision-making. For example, these systems collect too many reports, do not generate in-depth analyses, and do not result in strong interventions to reduce risk (Pham, Girard, & Pronovost, 2013). Most of the reports to health care incident reporting systems focus on highly technical issues, such as errors in the calculation of medications, and not on more complex professional judgments. In all, given the complexity of human factors in health care, the link between error and learning has often not been made despite the implementation of national systems (Kapur et al., 2015).

For many reasons, therefore, large-scale solutions from other industries do not provide easy answers for improving decision-making for social work organizations as a whole, and they certainly do not assist with improving decision-making for individual social workers. Individual social workers must therefore continue to find ways to examine the outcomes of their own decisions. On a practical level, it is often not easy for social workers to ascertain the outcomes of their cases, as risk-related decisions are frequently made in situations in which the social worker does not have ongoing responsibility, such as in emergency rooms or intake departments. Feedback information thus often comes sporadically and is solely focused on negative outcomes (not unlike reporting systems for adverse events). For instance, the media may report that an offender has been rearrested, or a coworker may report that a patient in a mental health facility has committed suicide. In such cases, social workers search their memory to determine when they last saw the client and the nature of that interaction. If we are to evaluate the outcomes of our decisions, we need a more systematic method, acknowledging that any approach will have limitations in terms of obtaining full information. A possible model for individual social workers working in organizations is as follows:

- Take note of cases in which risk decisions were required.
- At specified time periods (for instance, one week and six months), review the clients' case records to determine if they remained in care, were readmitted to hospital, and so on.
- Compare outcomes with written notes taken at the time of the decision (Wedding & Faust, 1989).
- Individually, and with supervisors and colleagues where appropriate, reflect on the implications of these outcomes for future decisions.

The model originally designed by Bogo and Vayda (1998) and later modified by Bogo (2010) can be used in both personal reflection and supervisory sessions. This model involves a feedback loop comprised of four stages: (1) retrieving and recalling salient facts related to the situation; (2) reflecting on subjective associations and reactions; (3) linking the facts and personal reactions to conceptual models; and (4) reconsidering the situation and planning for the next encounter.

EXPERTISE Assess level of competence and expertise
Address areas for development

COGNITIVE FRAMEWORKS Explicate cognitive processes and factors considered in decisions

GENERAL LEVEL OF STRESS / TRAUMA Assess levels of stress and trauma
Examine influences on decision-making

AFFECT HEURISTICS Identify sitation specific responses
Examine impact on decisions

DECISION-MAKING TOOLS Understand elements of acturarial and SPJ tools
Develop fast and frugal approaches

NOVEL SITUATIONS Identify situations on the boundaries of expertise
Develop strategies for managing / learning

EVALUATE OUTCOMES Develop a feedback loop and reflect
Modify decision-making practices

FIGURE 9.2 A comprehensive approach to improving decision-making in social work
Source: Author's own data.

A COMPREHENSIVE APPROACH TO IMPROVING
DECISION-MAKING IN SOCIAL WORK

Stress and trauma do have significant impacts on decision-making in social work. The first step for improving decision-making is to address stress and trauma and to ensure that social workers are in optimal condition to handle the high-stakes issues with which they are presented. Improving decision-making requires more than simply addressing stress and trauma, however. It also requires a multi-targeted approach (figure 9.2). First, expert decision-making relies on domain-specific expertise. Thus it is critical to assess practitioners' competence and expertise and identify areas of weakness. Second, expert decision-making relies on the ability to identify patterns of information that lead to particular outcomes. These patterns can be understood as schemas, developed from previous experiences. However, the nature of the schemas and the seemingly effortless way they are applied are often outside conscious thought, making them appear intuitive. An important aspect of improving expertise is explicating decision-making processes and identifying the factors considered. In addition, emotional responses can be important components of effective decision-making, contributing to intuitive processes by acting as additional sources of information. Another aspect of improving decision-making, therefore, is identifying and using emotional responses as an explicit part of implicit decision-making.

Decision tools, including actuarial tools, structured professional judgment tools, and fast and frugal decision trees, can serve as aids to decision-making. However, these tools are based on statistical models of common features. They cannot consider all the contextual variables that influence a given situation about which a decision must be made. Thus, social workers must become familiar with the tools and the factors included in the tools in order to decide when professional judgment should override the tool to ensure the best outcome in any given circumstance.

Social workers must also be able to identify when a situation is novel, sitting at the boundaries of their expertise. In these cases, social workers must take appropriate measures to slow down, seek assistance, and reflect on how the situation may call for a different approach. This new approach should then be integrated into the practitioner's decision-making repertoire. In addition, social workers must continuously evaluate decision-making processes, considering outcome information and modifying decision-making models and practices in response. Decision-making, in the complex environments in which social workers practice, will never be perfect. But through deliberate efforts, it can be optimized.

References

Acker, G. M. (2003). Role conflict and ambiguity: Do they predict burnout among mental health service providers? *Social Work in Mental Health, 1*(3), 63–80.

———. (2004). The effect of organizational conditions (role conflict, role ambiguity, opportunities for professional development, and social support) on job satisfaction and intention to leave among social workers in mental health care. *Community Mental Health Journal, 40*(1), 65–73.

Acker, G. M., & Lawrence, D. (2009). Social work in managed care: Measuring competence, burnout, and role stress of workers providing mental health services in the managed care era. *Journal of Social Work, 9*(3), 269–283.

Adams, R. E., Boscarino, J. A., & Figley, C. R. (2006). Compassion fatigue and psychological distress among social workers: A validation study. *American Journal of Orthopsychiatry, 76*(1), 103–108.

Adriaenssens, J., De Gucht, V., & Maes, S. (2015). Determinants and prevalence of burnout in emergency nurses: A systematic review of 25 years of research. *International Journal of Nursing Studies, 52*(2), 649–661.

Afifi, T. O., Asmundson, G. J., Taylor, S., & Jang, K. L. (2010). The role of genes and environment on trauma exposure and posttraumatic stress disorder symptoms: A review of twin studies. *Clinical Psychology Review, 30*(1), 101–112.

Alberta. (2012). Workers' Compensation Amendment Act, 2012, The Legislative Assembly of Alberta. http://www.assembly.ab.ca/ISYS/LADDAR_files/docs/bills/bill/legislature_28/session_1/20120523_bill-001.pdf

Alexander, D., & Klein, S. (2001). Ambulance personnel and critical incidents. *British Journal of Psychiatry, 178*, 76–81.

Alexander, D., & Wells, A. (1991). Reactions of police officers to body-handling after a major disaster: A before-and-after comparison. *British Journal of Psychiatry, 159*, 547–555.

American Psychological Association. (2013). *Diagnostic and statistical manual of mental disorders* (5th ed.). Washington, DC: APA Press.

Anderson, D. G. (2000). Coping strategies and burnout among veteran child protection workers. *Child Abuse and Neglect, 24*(6), 839–848.

Andersson, U., & Drury, F. (2016, May 23). Blood-smeared floors and walls of the child migrant centre where Swedish social worker was stabbed to death. *Mail Online.* Retrieved from http://www.dailymail.co.uk/news/article-3604936/PICTURED -Blood-smeared-floors-walls-child-migrant-centre-Swedish-social-worker-22 -stabbed-death-frenzied-attack-Somali-boy-TWENTY-ONE.html

Angie, A. D., Connelly, S., Waples, E. P., & Kligyte, V. (2011). The influence of discrete emotions on judgement and decision-making: A meta-analytic review. *Cognition and Emotion, 25*(8), 1393–1422.

Ansseau, M., Sulon, J., Doumont, A., Certfontaine, J., Legros, J., Sodoyaz, J., & Demey-Ponsart, E. (1984). Use of saliva cortisol in dexamethasone suppression test. *Psychiatry Research, 13*, 203–211.

Antai-Otong, D. (2007). Pharmacologic management of posttraumatic stress disorder. *Perspectives in Psychiatric Care, 43*(1), 55–59.

Arad-Davidzon, B., & Benbenishty, R. (2008). The role of workers' attitudes and parent and child wishes in child protection workers' assessments and recommendation regarding removal and reunification. *Children and Youth Services Review, 30*(1), 107–121.

Arkes, H. (1981). Impediments to accurate clinical judgment and possible ways to minimize their impact. *Journal of Consulting and Clinical Psychology, 49*(3), 323–330.

Arnold, D., Calhoun, L. G., Tedeschi, R., & Cann, A. (2005). Vicarious posttraumatic growth in psychotherapy. *Journal of Humanistic Psychology, 45*(2), 239–263. doi:10.1177/0022167805274729

Arvay, M., & Uhlemann, M. (1996). Counsellor stress and impairment in the field of trauma. *Canadian Journal of Counselling, 30*(3), 193–210.

Astin, J. (1997). Stress reduction through mindfulness meditation: Effects on psychological symptomatology, sense of control, and spiritual experiences. *Psychotherapy and Psychosomatics, 66*, 97–106.

Atkeson, B. M., Calhoun, K. S., Resick, P. A., & Ellis, E. M. (1982). Victims of rape: Repeated assessment of depressive symptoms. *Journal of Consulting and Clinical Psychology, 50*(1), 96–102.

Ayre, P. (2001). Child protection and the media: Lessons from the last three decades. *British Journal of Social Work, 31*(6), 887–901.

Baines, D. (2006). Staying with people who slap us around: Gender, juggling responsibilities and violence in paid (and unpaid) care work. *Gender, Work and Organization, 13*(2), 129–151.

Baines, D., & Cunningham, I. (2011). "White knuckle care work": Violence, gender and new public management in the voluntary sector. *Work, Employment and Society, 25*(4), 760–776.

Baird, C., & Wagner, D. (2000). The relative validity of actuarial- and consensus-based risk assessment systems. *Children and Youth Services Review, 22*(11), 839–871.

Baird, C., Wagner, D., Healy, T., & Johnson, K. (1999). Risk assessment in child protective services: Consensus and actuarial model reliability. *Child Welfare, 78*(6), 723–748.

Barach, P., & Small, S. D. (2000). Reporting and preventing medical mishaps: Lessons from non-medical near miss reporting systems. *BMJ, 320*(7237), 759–763.

Baumann, A. O., Deber, R. B., & Thompson, G. G. (1991). Overconfidence among physicians and nurses: The "micro-certainty, macro-uncertainty" phenomenon. *Social Science and Medicine, 32*(2), 167–174.

Bayran, N., & Bilgel, N. (2008). The prevalence and socio-demographic correlations of depression, anxiety and stress among a group of university students. *Social Psychiatry and Psychiatric Epidemiology, 43*(8), 667–672.

BBC. (2004). Britain's worst stalker jailed. *BBC News.* Retrieved from http://news.bbc .co.uk/2/hi/uk_news/england/london/3880293.stm

Beaton, R., Murphy, S., Johnson, C., Pike, K., & Corneil, W. (1999). Coping responses and posttraumatic stress symptomatology in urban fire service personnel. *Journal of Traumatic Stress, 12*(2), 293–308.

Beck, A., Emery, G., & Greenberg, R. (1985). *Anxiety disorders and phobias: A cognitive perspective.* New York, NY: Basic Books.

Beck, A., & Steer, R. (1996). *Manual for the Beck Depression Inventory.* San Antonio, TX: Psychological Corporation.

Beddoe, L., Davys, A., & Adamson, C. (2013). Educating resilient practitioners. *Social Work Education, 32*(1), 100–117.

Bell, H., Kulkarni, S., & Dalton, L. (2003). Organizational prevention of vicarious trauma. *Families in Society: The Journal of Contemporary Social Services, 84*(4), 463–470.

Ben-porat, A. (2015). Vicarious post-traumatic growth: Domestic violence therapists versus social service department therapists in Israel. *Journal of Family Violence, 30*(7), 923–933.

Ben-Zur, H., & Michael, K. (2007). Burnout, social support, and coping at work among social workers, psychologists, and nurses: The role of challenge/control appraisals. *Social Work in Health Care, 45*(4), 63–82.

Berg, K., Blatt, B., Lopreiato, J., Jung, J., Schaeffer, A., Heil, D., . . . Veloski, J. (2015). Standardized patient assessment of medical student empathy: Ethnicity and gender effects in a multi-institutional study. *Academic Medicine, 90*(1), 105–111.

Berg, K., Majdan, J. F., Berg, D., Veloski, J., & Hojat, M. (2011). Medical students' self-reported empathy and simulated patients' assessments of student empathy: An analysis by gender and ethnicity. *Academic Medicine, 86*(8), 984–988.

Berger, W., Coutinho, E., Figueira, I., Marqes-Portella, C., Luz, M., Neylan, C., . . . Mendlowicz, M. (2012). Rescuers at risk: A systematic review and meta-regression analysis of the worldwide current prevalence and correlates of PTSD in rescue workers. *Social Psychiatry and Psychiatric Epidemiology, 47*(6), 1001–1011.

Berkun, M. M. (2000). Performance decrement under psychological stress. *Journal of Human Performance in Extreme Environments, 5*(1), 92–97.

Berner, E. S., & Graber, M. L. (2008). Overconfidence as a cause of diagnostic error in medicine. *American Journal of Medicine, 121*(5), S2–S23.

Bernotavicz, F., McDaniel, N. C., Brittain, C., & Dickinson, N. S. (2013). Leadership in a changing environment: A leadership model for child welfare. *Administration in Social Work, 37*(4), 401–417.

Bibus, A. A., III. (1994). In pursuit of a missing link: The influence of supervision on social workers' practice with involuntary clients. *Clinical Supervisor, 11*(2), 7–22.

Billings, A. G., & Moos, R. H. (1981). The role of coping responses and social resources in attenuating the stress of life events. *Journal of behavioral medicine, 4*(2), 139–157.

Bishop, S. (2007). Neurocognitive mechanisms of anxiety: An integrative account. *Trends in Cognitive Science, 11*(7), 307–316.

Bisson, J. I., Ehlers, A., Matthews, R., Pilling, S., Richards, D., & Turner, S. (2007). Psychological treatments for chronic post-traumatic stress disorder. *British Journal of Psychiatry, 190*(2), 97–104.

Blanchard, E. B., Hickling, E. J., Mitnick, N., Taylor, A. E., Loos, W. R., & Buckley, T. C. (1995). The impact of severity of physical injury and perception of life threat in the development of post-traumatic stress disorder in motor vehicle accident victims. *Behaviour Research and Therapy, 33*(5), 529–534.

Blanchette, I., & Richards, A. (2003). Anxiety and the interpretation of ambiguous information: Beyond the emotion-congruent effect. *Journal of Experimental Psychology: General, 132*(2), 294–309.

——. (2010). The influence of affect on higher level cognition: A review of research on interpretation, judgement, decision making and reasoning. *Cognition and Emotion, 24*(4), 561–595.

Blatchford, C. (2001, April 12). She should be sterilized: My four extra recommendations to add to the jurors'. *National Post*, A1, A10.

Bleich, A., Gelkopf, M., & Solomon, Z. (2003). Exposure to terrorism, stress-related mental health symptoms, and coping behaviors among a nationally representative sample in Israel. *JAMA, 290*(5), 612–620.

Bober, T., & Regehr, C. (2006). Strategies for reducing secondary or vicarious trauma: Do they work? *Brief Treatment and Crisis Intervention, 6*(1), 1–9.

Bober, T., Regehr, C., & Zhou, Y. R. (2006). Development of the coping strategies inventory for trauma counselors. *Journal of Loss and Trauma, 11*(1), 71–83.

Bogo, M. (2010). *Achieving competence in social work through field education.* Toronto, Ontario, Canada: University of Toronto Press.

Bogo, M., Regehr, C., Hughes, J., Power, R., & Globerman, J. (2002). Evaluating a measure of student field performance in direct service: Testing reliability and validity of explicit criteria. *Journal of Social Work Education, 38*(3), 385–401.

Bogo, M., Regehr, C., Katz, E., Logie, C., Tufford, L., & Litvack, A. (2012). Evaluating an objective structured clinical examination (OSCE) adapted for social work. *Research on Social Work Practice, 22*(4), 428–436.

Bogo, M., Regehr, C., Power, R., & Regehr, G. (2007). When values collide: Field instructors' experiences of providing feedback and evaluating competence. *Clinical Supervisor, 26*(1–2), 99–117.

Bogo, M., Regehr, C., Woodford, M., Hughes, J., Power, R., & Regehr, G. (2006). Beyond competencies: Field instructors' descriptions of student performance. *Journal of Social Work Education, 42*(3), 191–205.

Bogo, M., & Vayda, E. J. (1998). *The practice of field instruction in social work: Theory and process.* Toronto, Canada: University of Toronto Press.

Bonifas, R. P., & Simons, K. (2014). An examination of the factor structure of the Hartford Geriatric Social Work Competency Scale-II Assessment and Intervention subscales. *Educational Gerontology, 40*(9), 700–712.

Bonnano, G., Galea, S., Bucciarelli, A., & Vlahov, D. (2007). What predicts psychological resilience after disaster? The role of demographics, resources and life stress. *Journal of Consulting and Clinical Psychology, 75*(5), 671–682.

Boscarino, J. A., Figley, C. R., & Adams, R. E. (2004). Compassion fatigue following the September 11 terrorist attacks: A study of secondary trauma among New York City social workers. *International Journal of Emergency Mental Health, 6*(2), 57–66.

Bosk, E. A. (2018). What counts? Quantification, worker judgment, and divergence in child welfare decision-making. *Human Service Organizations: Management, Leadership & Governance*, (just-accepted).

Bouch, J., & Marshall, J. J. (2005). Suicide risk: Structured professional judgement. *Advances in Psychiatric Treatment, 11*(2), 84–91.

Bowlby, J. (1979). *The making and breaking of affectional bonds.* London, England: Tavistock.

Bowler, R., Han, H., Gocheva, V., Nakagawa, S., Alper, H., DiGrande, L., & Cone, J. (2010). Gender differences in probable posttraumatic stress disorder in police responders to the 2001 World Trade Center terrorist attack. *American Journal of Industrial Medicine, 53*, 1186–1196.

Brady, J., Guy, J., Poelstra, P., & Brokaw, B. (1999). Vicarious traumatization, spirituality, and the treatment of sexual abuse survivors: A national survey of women psychotherapists. *Professional Psychology, 30*(4), 386–393.

Bramsen, I., Dirkzwager, A., & van der Ploeg, H. (2000). Predeployment personality traits and exposure to trauma as predictors of posttraumatic stress symptoms: A prospective study of former peacekeepers. *American Journal of Psychiatry, 157*, 1115–1119.

Bremner, J., Scott, T., Delaney, R., Southwick, S., Mason, J., Johnson, D., . . . Charney, D. (1993). Deficits in short-term memory in posttraumatic stress disorder. *American Journal of Psychiatry, 150*, 1015–1019.

Brewin, C., Kleiner, J., Vasterling, J., & Field, A. (2007). Memory for emotionally neutral information in posttraumatic stress disorder: A meta-analytic investigation. *Journal of Abnormal Psychology, 116*(3), 448–463.

Bride, B. E. (2007). Prevalence of secondary traumatic stress among social workers. *Social Work, 52*(1), 63–70.

British Association of Social Workers. (2011). *Code of ethics.* Retrieved from https://www.basw.co.uk/codeofethics

——. (2017). *Professional capabilities framework: Readiness for direct practice.* Retrieved from https://www.basw.co.uk/pcf/capabilities/?level=9

Brotheridge, C., & Grandey, A. (2002). Emotional labor and burnout: Comparing two perspectives of "people work." *Journal of Vocational Behavior, 60*(1), 17–39.

Brotheridge, C., & Lee, R. (2002). Testing a conservation of resources model of the dynamics of emotional labor. *Journal of Occupational Health Psychology, 7*(1), 57–67.

Brown, B., & Rakow, T. (2016). Understanding clinicians' use of cues when assessing the future risk of violence: A clinical judgement analysis in the psychiatric setting. *Clinical Psychology and Psychotherapy, 23*(2), 125–141. doi:10.1002/cpp.1941

Brown, J., Mulhern, G., & Joseph, S. (2002). Incident-related stressors, locus of control, coping, and psychological distress among firefighters in Northern Ireland. *Journal of Traumatic Stress, 15*(2), 161–168.

Brunet, A., Weiss, D., Best, S., Liberman, A., Fagan, J., & Marmar, C. (1998). Assessing recurring traumatic exposure: The Critical Incident History Questionnaire. In *Proceedings of the International Society for Traumatic Stress Studies, 49.* Washington, DC: International Society for Traumatic Stress Studies.

Bryant, R., & Harvey, A. (1996). Posttraumatic stress reactions in volunteer firefighters. *Journal of Traumatic Stress, 9*, 51–62.

Burgess, A., & Holmstrom, L. (1974). Rape trauma syndrome. *American Journal of Psychiatry, 131*(9), 981–986.

Burke, R. (1993). Work-family stress, conflict, coping, and burnout in police officers. *Stress Medicine, 9,* 171–180.

Burton, R. (1850). *The anatomy of melancholy.* New York, NY: John Wiley. (Original work published 1651)

Byrd, D., & McKinney, K. (2012). Individual, interpersonal, and institutional level factors associated with the mental health of college students. *Journal of American College Health, 60*(3), 185–193.

Cadell, S., Regehr, C., & Hemsworth, D. (2003). Factors contributing to posttraumatic growth: A proposed structural equation model. *American Journal of Orthopsychiatry, 73*(3), 279–287.

Cadge, W., & Hammonds, C. (2012). Reconsidering detached concern: The case of intensive-care nurses. *Perspectives in Biology and Medicine, 55*(2), 266–282.

Camasso, M. J., & Jagannathan, R. (2000). Modeling the reliability and predictive validity of risk assessment in child welfare. *Children and Youth Services Review, 22*(11–12), 873–896.

——. (2013). Decision making in child protective services: A risky business? *Risk Analysis, 33*(9), 1636–1649.

Caplan, G. (1964). *Principles of preventative psychiatry.* New York, NY: Basic Books.

Carlier, I., Lamberts, R., & Gersons, B. (2000). The dimensionality of trauma: A multidimensional comparison of police officers with and without posttraumatic stress disorder. *Psychiatric Research, 97,* 29–39.

Carpenter, J., Webb, C. M., & Bostock, L. (2013). The surprisingly weak evidence base for supervision: Findings from a systematic review of research in child welfare practice (2000–2012). *Children and Youth Services Review, 35*(11), 1843–1853.

Carson-Stevens, A., Hibbert, P., Williams, H., Evans, H. P., Cooper, A., Rees, P., . . . Butlin, A. (2016). Characterising the nature of primary care patient safety incident reports in the England and Wales National Reporting and Learning System: A mixed-methods agenda-setting study for general practice. *Health Services and Delivery Research, 4*(27). Retrieved from https://www.ncbi.nlm.nih.gov/books/NBK385186/ doi: 10.3310/hsdr04270

CBC. (2016). First Nations child welfare advocate Cindy Blackstock receives honorary degree. *CBC News.* Retrieved from http://www.cbc.ca/news/indigenous/cindy-blackstock-indigenous-child-welfare-honorary-degree-1.4161884

Cerney, M. S. (1995). Heroic treaters. In C. Figley (Ed.), *Compassion fatigue: Coping with secondary traumatic stress disorder in those who treat the traumatized* (pp. 131–149). New York, NY: Routledge.

Chambers, R., & Belcher, J. (1994). Predicting mental health problems in general practitioners. *Occupational Medicine, 44,* 212–216.

Chase, W. G., & Simon, H. A. (1973). Perception in chess. *Cognitive psychology, 4*(1), 55–81.

Cheetham, G., & Chivers, G. (1996). Towards a holistic model of professional competence. *Journal of European Industrial Training, 20*(5), 20–30.

Chenot, D. (2011). The vicious cycle: Recurrent interactions among the media, politicians, the public, and child welfare services organizations. *Journal of Public Child Welfare, 5*(2–3), 167–184.

Chi, M. T., Glaser, R., & Farr, M. J. (2014). *The nature of expertise*. New York, NY: Psychology Press.

Children's Research Center, National Council on Crime and Delinquency. (2015). *The structured decision making system for child protection services: The policy and procedures manual: Saskatchewan*. Retrieved from http://cwrp.ca/sites/default /files/publications/en/the-structured-decision-making-system-for-child -protective-services.pdf

Clohessy, S., & Ehlers, A. (1999). PTSD symptoms, response to intrusive memories and coping in ambulance service workers. *British Journal of Clinical Psychology, 38*(3), 251–265.

Cochrane-Brink, K. A., Lofchy, J. S., & Sakinofsky, I. (2000). Clinical rating scales in suicide risk assessment. *General Hospital Psychiatry, 22*(6), 445–451.

Cohen, M., Gagin, R., & Peled-Avram, M. (2006). Multiple terrorist attacks: Compassion fatigue in Israeli social workers. *Traumatology, 12*(4), 293–301.

Cohen, S., Kamarck, T., & Mermelstein, R. (1983). A global measure of perceived stress. *Journal of Health and Social Behavior, 24*, 385–396.

——. (1994). Perceived stress scale. *Measuring stress: A guide for health and social scientists*. Mindgarden.com http://mindgarden.com/documents/PerceivedStress Scale.pdf

Collings, J., & Murray, P. (1996). Predictors of stress amongst social workers: An empirical study. *British Journal of Social Work, 26*, 375–387.

Collins, S. (2007). Social workers, resilience, positive emotions and optimism. *Practice, 19*(4), 255–269.

Conrad, D., & Kellar-Guenther, Y. (2006). Compassion fatigue, burnout, and compassion satisfaction among Colorado child protection workers. *Child Abuse and Neglect, 30*(10), 1071–1080.

Cook, H., Harris, B., Walker, R., Hailwood, R., Jones, E., John, S., & Riad-Fahmy, D. (1986). Clinical utility of the dexamethasone suppression test assessed by plasma and salivary cortisol determinations. *Psychiatry Research, 182*, 143–150.

Cooper, L., Kirkcaldy, B., & Brown, J. (1994). A model of job stress and physical health: The role of individual differences. *Personality and Individual Differences, 164*(4), 653–655.

Coté, S. (2005). A social interaction model of the effects of emotion regulation on work strain. *Academy of Management Review, 30*(3), 509–530.

Cottingham, M. D., Erickson, R. J., & Diefendorff, J. M. (2015). Examining men's status shield and status bonus: How gender frames the emotional labor and job satisfaction of nurses. *Sex Roles, 72*(7–8), 377–389.

Coyne, J., & DeLongis, A. (1986). Going beyond social support: The role of social relationships in adaption. *Journal of Consulting and Clinical Psychology, 54*, 454–460.

Craggs, S. (2012, October 2). One-third of McMaster students battle depression: Survey. *CBC News.* Retrieved from http://www.cbc.ca/hamilton/news/story/2012/10/02/hamilton-mental-illness-awareness-week.html

Creamer, M., Bell, R., & Failla, S. (2003). Psychometric properties of the Impact of Event Scale-Revised. *Behavioral Research and Therapy, 41*, 1489–1496.

Croskerry, P. (2003). The importance of cognitive errors in diagnosis and strategies to minimize them. *Academic Medicine, 78*(8), 775–780.

——. (2009). A universal model of diagnostic reasoning. *Academic Medicine, 84*(8), 1022–1028.

Croskerry, P., Singhal, G., & Mamede, S. (2013). Cognitive debiasing 2: Impediments to and strategies for change. *BMJ Quality and Safety, 22*(Suppl 2), ii65–ii72.

Csiernik, R., Smith, C., Dewar, J., Dromgole, L., & O'Neill, A. (2010). A peer led social support group for new employees: Findings of a pilot study. *Ontario Association of Children's Aid Societies, 55*(4). Retrieved from http://www.oacas.org/pubs/oacas/journal/2010Fall/study.html

Cunningham, M. (1982). Admissions variables and the prediction of success in an undergraduate fieldwork program. *Journal of Education for Social Work, 18*(2), 27–34.

Dagan, K., Itzhaky, H., & Ben-Porat, A. (2015). Therapists working with trauma victims: The contribution of personal, environmental, and professional-organizational resources to secondary traumatization. *Journal of Trauma and Dissociation, 16*(5), 592–606.

Dalton, J., Pederson, S., & Ryam, J. (1989). Effects of post-traumatic stress disorder on neuropsychological test performance. *International Journal of Clinical Neuropsychology, 11*, 121–124.

Damasio, A. R. (2001). Emotion and the human brain. *Annals of the New York Academy of Sciences, 935*(1), 101–106.

Dane, E., & Pratt, M. G. (2007). Exploring intuition and its role in managerial decision making. *Academy of Management Review, 32*(1), 33–54.

Dane, E., Rockmann, K. W., & Pratt, M. G. (2012). When should I trust my gut? Linking domain expertise to intuitive decision-making effectiveness. *Organizational Behavior and Human Decision Processes, 119*(2), 187–194.

Davis, M. H. (1983). Measuring individual differences in empathy: Evidence for a multidimensional approach. *Journal of personality and social psychology, 44*(1), 113–126.

———. (1994). *Empathy: A social psychological approach.* Boulder, CO: Westview Press.

Davis-Sacks, M., Jayaratne, S., & Chess, W. (1985). A comparison of the effects of social support on the incidence of burnout. *Social Work, 30*(3), 240–244.

Dawes, R. M. (1979). The robust beauty of improper linear models in decision making. *American Psychologist, 34*(7), 571.

De Bortoli, L., & Dolan, M. (2015). Decision making in social work with families and children: Developing decision-aids compatible with cognition. *British Journal of Social Work, 7*(1) 2142–2160.

Decision Science News. (2012). Benjamin Franklin's rule for decision making. Retrieved from http://www.decisionsciencenews.com/2012/08/18/benjamin-franklins-rule -for-decision-making/.

De Gelder, B., Snyder, J., Greve, D., Gerard, G., & Hadjikhani, N. (2004). Fear fosters flight: A mechanism for fear contagion when perceiving emotion expressed by a whole body. *Proceedings of the National Academy of Sciences of the United States of America, 101*(47), 16701–16706.

De Groot, A. D. (1965). *Thought and choice in chess.* The Hague, Netherlands: Mouton.

DePanfilis, D., & Zuravin, S. J. (2002). The effect of services on the recurrence of child maltreatment. *Child Abuse and Neglect, 26*(2), 187–205.

Despart, Z. (2015, August 12). Police: Woman laughed after killing social worker. *Burlington (VT) Free Press.* Retrieved from http://www.usatoday.com/story/news /nation/2015/08/10/vermont-aid-worker-killed/31419713

Dewa, C. S., Loong, D., Bonato, S., Thanh, N. X., & Jacobs, P. (2014). How does burnout affect physician productivity? A systematic literature review. *BMC Health Services Research, 14*, 1–10.

Dhami, M. K. (2003). Psychological models of professional decision making. *Psychological Science, 14*(2), 175–180.

———. (2005). From discretion to disagreement: Explaining disparities in judges' pretrial decisions. *Behavioral Sciences and the Law, 23*(3), 367–386.

Dhami, M. K., Mandel, D. R., & Garcia-Retamero, R. (2011). Canadian and Spanish youths' risk perceptions of drinking and driving, and riding with a drunk driver. *International Journal of Psychology, 46*(2), 81–90.

Dickerson, S., & Kemeny, M. (2004). Acute stressors and cortisol responses: A theoretical integration and synthesis of laboratory research. *Psychological Bulletin, 130*, 355–391.

DiGiulio, J. F. (1995). A more humane workplace: Responding to child welfare workers' personal losses. *Child Welfare, 74*(4), 877–888.

Dolan, R. J. (2002). Emotion, cognition, and behavior. *Science, 298*(5596), 1191–1194.

Donovan, K., & Regehr, C. (2010). Elder abuse: Clinical, ethical, and legal considerations in social work practice. *Clinical Social Work Journal, 38*(2), 174–182.

Douglas, E. M. (2009). Media coverage of agency-related child maltreatment fatalities: Does it result in state legislative change intended to prevent future fatalities? *Journal of Policy Practice, 8*(3), 224–239.

Douglas, K. S., Ogloff, J. R., & Hart, S. D. (2003). Evaluation of a model of violence risk assessment among forensic psychiatric patients. *Psychiatric Services, 54*(10), 1372–1379.

Downs, M., & Eisenberg, D. (2012). Help seeking and treatment use among suicidal college students. *Journal of American College Health, 60*(2), 104–114.

Doyle, M., & Dolan, M. (2002). Violence risk assessment: Combining actuarial and clinical information to structure clinical judgements for the formulation and management of risk. *Journal of Psychiatric and Mental Health Nursing, 9*(6), 649–657.

Dressendorfer, R. A., Kirschbaum, C., Rohde, W., Stahl, F., & Strasburger, C. J. (1992). Synthesis of a cortisol-biotin conjugate and evaluation as a tracer in an immunoassay for salivary cortisol measurement. *Journal of Steroid Biochemistry and Molecular Biology, 43*(7), 683–692.

Dreyfus, H., & Dreyfus, S. E., (2000). *Mind over machine: The power of human intuition and expertise in the era of the computer.* New York, NY: The Free Press.

Dreyfus, H. L. (2005, November). Overcoming the myth of the mental: How philosophers can profit from the phenomenology of everyday expertise. *Proceedings and Addresses of the American Philosophical Association,* Vol. 79, No. 2, pp. 47–65.

Dreyfus, H. L., & Dreyfus, S. E. (2005). Peripheral vision expertise in real world contexts. *Organization Studies, 26*(5), 779–792. Retrieved from https://www.jstor.org/stable/30046213?seq=1 page_scan_tab_contents

Dückers, M. L., Alisic, E., & Brewin, C. R. (2016). A vulnerability paradox in the cross-national prevalence of post-traumatic stress disorder. *British Journal of Psychiatry, 209*(4), 300–305.

Duckworth, A. L., Peterson, C., Matthews, M. D., & Kelly, D. R. (2007). Grit: Perseverance and passion for long-term goals. *Journal of Personality and Social Psychology, 92*(6), 1087.

Duder, S., & Aronson, J. (1978). Values in the admission process: An application of multidimensional scaling. *Canadian Journal of Social Work Education/Revue canadienne d'éducation en service social, 4*(1), 56–75.

Duttweiler, P. (1984). The Internal Control Index: A newly developed measure of locus of control. *Education and Psychological Measurement, 44*(2), 209–221.

Dyrbye, L., Thomas, M., Huntington, J., Lawson, K., Novotny, P., Sloan, J., & Shanafelt, T. (2006). Personal life events and medical student burnout: A multicenter study. *Academic Medicine, 81*(4), 374–384.

Dyregrov, A. (1989). Caring for helpers in disaster situations: Psychological debriefing. *Disaster Management, 2*(1), 25–30.

Earvolino-Ramirez, M. (2007). Resilience: A concept analysis. *Nursing Forum, 42*(2) 73–82.

Eisenman, D., Gelberg, L., Liu, H., & Shapiro, M. (2003). Mental health and health-related quality of life among adult latino primary care patients living in the United States with previous exposure to political violence. *JAMA, 290*(5), 627–634.

Elpers, K., & Westhuis, D. J. (2008). Organizational leadership and its impact on social workers' job satisfaction: A national study. *Administration in Social Work, 32*(3), 26–43.

Endler, N., & Parker, J. (1994). Assessment of multidimensional coping: Task, emotion, and avoidance strategies. *Psychological Assessment, 6*, 50–60.

English, D. J., & Pecora, P. J. (1994). Risk assessment as a practice method in child protective services. *Child Welfare, 73*(5), 451–473.

Enosh, G., & Tzafrir, S. S. (2015). The scope of client aggression toward social workers in Israel. *Journal of Aggression, Maltreatment and Trauma, 24*(9), 971–985.

Eraut, M. (2004). Informal learning in the workplace. *Studies in Continuing Education, 26*(2), 247–273.

——. (2007). Learning from other people in the workplace. *Oxford Review of Education, 33*(4), 403–422.

Eres, R., Decety, J., Louis, W. R., & Molenberghs, P. (2015). Individual differences in local gray matter density are associated with differences in affective and cognitive empathy. *Neuroimage, 117*, 305–310.

Ericsson, K. A., Krampe, R. T., & Tesch-Römer, C. (1993). The role of deliberate practice in the acquisition of expert performance. *Psychological Review, 100*(3), 363–406.

Ericsson, K. A., & Smith, J. (1991). *Toward a general theory of expertise: Prospects and limits.* Cambridge, UK: Cambridge University Press.

Evans, S., Huxley, P., Gately, C., Webber, M., Mears, A., Pajak, S., . . . Katona, C. (2006). Mental health, burnout and job satisfaction among mental health social workers in England and Wales. *British Journal of Psychiatry, 188*(1), 75–80.

Evans, T. (2010). Professionals, managers and discretion: Critiquing street-level bureaucracy. *British Journal of Social Work, 41*(2), 368–386.

——. (2012). Organisational rules and discretion in adult social work. *British Journal of Social Work, 43*(4), 739–758.

Fan, Y., Duncan, N. W., de Greck, M., & Northoff, G. (2011). Is there a core neural network in empathy? An fMRI based quantitative meta-analysis. *Neuroscience & Biobehavioral Reviews, 35*(3), 903–911.

Fazel, S., Singh, J. P., Doll, H., & Grann, M. (2012). Use of risk assessment instruments to predict violence and antisocial behaviour in 73 samples involving 24 827 people: Systematic review and meta-analysis. *BMJ, 345*, e4692.

Figley, C. R. (1988). Reaction: Victimization, trauma, and traumatic stress. *Counseling Psychologist, 16*, 635–641.

——. (1995). Compassion fatigue: Toward a new understanding of the costs of caring. In B. H. Stamm (Ed.), *Secondary traumatic stress: Self-care issues for clinicians, researchers, and educators* (pp. 3–28). Baltimore, MD: Sidran Press.

——. (1999). Compassion fatigue: Toward a new understanding of the costs of caring. In H. Stamm (Ed.), *Secondary traumatic stress* (2nd ed., pp. 3–28). Lutherville, MD: Sidran.

——. (2002). Compassion fatigue: Psychotherapists' chronic lack of self care. *Journal of Clinical Psychology, 58*(11), 1433–1441.

Fluke, J., Baumann, D., England, P., Kern, H., Law, R., McFadden, T., & Schultz, F. (1995). Emerging critical conceptual issues in risk assessment research and practice. In *Eighth National Roundtable on CPS Risk Assessment* (pp. 239–250).

Fluttert, F., van Meijel, B., Nijman, H., Bjørkly, S., & Grypdonck, M. (2010). Detached concern of forensic mental health nurses in therapeutic relationships with patients: The application of the early recognition method related to detached concern. *Archives of Psychiatric Nursing, 24*(4), 266–274.

Foa, E. B., Cashman, L., Jaycox, L., & Perry, K. (1997). The validation of a self-report measure of posttraumatic stress disorder: The Posttraumatic Diagnostic Scale. *Psychological Assessment, 9*(4), 445–451.

Folkman, S. (1997). Positive psychological states and coping with severe stress. *Social Science and Medicine, 45*(8) 1207–1221.

Folkman, S., Lazarus, R. S., Gruen, R. J., & DeLongis, A. (1986). Appraisal, coping, health status, and psychological symptoms. *Journal of Personality and Social Psychology, 50*(3), 571–579.

Folkman, S., & Moskowitz, J. (2004). Coping: Pitfalls and promise. *Annual Review of Psychology, 55*, 745–774.

Fook, J., Ryan, M., & Hawkins, L. (1997). Towards a theory of social work expertise. *British Journal of Social Work, 27*(3), 399–417.

Fortes-Ferreira, L., Peiro, J., Gonzalez-Morales, G., & Martin, I. (2006). Work-related stress and well-being: The roles of direct action coping and palliative coping. *Scandinavian Journal of Psychiatry, 47*, 293–302.

Fox, R. (1959). *Experiment perilous: Physicians and patients facing the unknown.* Glencoe, IL: Free Press.

——. (2011). *In the field: A sociologist's journey.* London, UK: Transaction.

Frankel, R. M., & Levinson, W. (2014). Back to the future: Can conversation analysis be used to judge physicians' malpractice history? *Communication and Medicine, 11*(1), 27–39.

Frankl, V. E. (1985). *Man's search for meaning.* New York, NY: Simon and Schuster.

Franklin, B., & Parton, N. (2014). *Social work, the media and public relations.* Abindon, NY: Routledge.

Frueh, B., Hamner, M., Cahill, S., Gold, P., & Hamlin, K. (2000). Apparent symptom overreporting in combat veterans evaluated for PTSD. *Clinical Psychology Review, 20,* 853–885.

Fullerton, C., McCarroll, J., Ursano, R., & Wright, K. (1992). Psychological responses of rescue workers: Firefighters and trauma. *American Journal of Orthopsychiatry, 62*(3), 371–378.

Gaab, J., Blättler, N., Menzi, T., Pabst, B., Stoyer, S., & Ehlert, U. (2003). Randomized controlled evaluation of the effects of cognitive–behavioral stress management on cortisol responses to acute stress in healthy subjects. *Psychoneuroendocrinology, 28,* 767–779.

Gaab, J., Sonderegger, L., Scherrer, S., & Ehlert, U. (2006). Psychoneuroendocrine effects of cognitive behavioral stress management in a naturalistic setting: A randomized controlled trial. *Psychoneuroendocrinology, 31,* 428–438.

Gaffney, P., Russell, V., Collins, K., Bergin, A., Halligan, P., Carey, C., & Coyle, S. (2009). Impact of patient suicide on front-line staff in Ireland. *Death Studies, 33*(7), 639–656.

Gainsborough, J. F. (2009). Scandals, lawsuits, and politics: Child welfare policy in the US states. *State Politics and Policy Quarterly, 9*(3), 325–355.

Gallese, V. (2001). The "shared manifold" hypothesis: From mirror neurons to empathy. *Journal of consciousness studies, 8*(5–6), 33–50.

Galton, F. (1869). *Hereditary genius: An inquiry into its laws and consequences.* London, UK: Macmillan.

Gambrill, E. (2006). *Critical thinking in clinical practice: Improving the quality of judgments and decisions.* Hoboken, NJ: John Wiley & Sons.

——. (2008). Decision making in child welfare: Constraints and potentials. In D. Lindsey and A. Schlonsky (Eds.), *Child welfare research: Advances for practice and policy* (pp. 175–193). New York, NY: Oxford University Press.

Gambrill, E., & Shlonsky, A. (2000). Risk assessment in context. *Children and Youth Services Review, 22*(11–12), 813–837.

Ganzel, B. L., & Morris, P. A. (2011). Allostasis and the developing human brain: Explicit consideration of implicit models. *Development and Psychopathology, 23*(4), 955–974. doi:10.1017/S0954579411000447

Gates, D. M., & Gillespie, G. L. (2008). Secondary traumatic stress in nurses who care for traumatized women. *Journal of Obstetrical and Gynecological Neonatal Nursing, 37*(2), 243–249.

Ge, X., & Hardré, P. (2010). Self-processes and learning environment as influences in the development of expertise in instructional design. *Learning Environments Research, 13*(1), 23–41.

Gellis, Z. D. (2002). Coping with occupational stress in healthcare: A comparison of social workers and nurses. *Administration in Social Work, 26*(3), 37–52.

Gerdes, K. E., & Segal, E. A. (2009). A social work model of empathy. *Advances in Social Work, 10*(2), 114–127.

Gibbs, L., & Gambrill, E. (2002). Evidence-based practice: Counterarguments to objections. *Research on Social Work Practice, 12*(3), 452–476.

Gibbs, M. (1989). Factors in the victim that mediate between disaster and psychopathology: A review. *Journal of Traumatic Stress, 2*, 489–514.

Gibson, M. (2014a). Social worker shame in child and family social work: Inadequacy, failure, and the struggle to practise humanely. *Journal of Social Work Practice, 28*(4), 417–431.

——. (2014b). Social worker shame: A scoping review. *British Journal of Social Work, 46*, 549–565.

Gigerenzer, G. (2007). *Gut feelings: The intelligence of the unconscious.* New York, NY: Penguin.

Gigerenzer, G., & Gaissmaier, W. (2011). Heuristic decision making. *Annual Review of Psychology, 62*, 451–482.

Gigerenzer, G., & Goldstein, D. G. (1996). Reasoning the fast and frugal way: Models of bounded rationality. *Psychological Review, 103*(4), 650–669.

Gilbertson, M., Paulus, L., Williston, S., Gurvits, T., Lasko, N., Pitman, R., & Orr, S. (2006). Neurocognitive function in monozygotic twins discordant for combat exposure: Relationship to posttraumatic stress disorder. *Journal of Abnormal Psychology, 115*(3), 484–495.

Gladwell, M. (2008). *Outliers: The story of success.* London, UK: Penguin.

Glancy, G., & Regehr, C. (2004). Assessment measures for sexual predators. In A. Roberts & K. Yeager (Eds.), *Evidence based practice manual: Research and outcome measures in health and human sciences.* New York, NY: Oxford University Press.

Glancy, G. D. (2016). The mock trial: Revisiting a valuable training strategy. *Journal of the American Academy of Psychiatry and the Law, 44*(1), 19–27.

Glancy, G. D., Regehr, C., & Bradford, J. (2001). Sexual predator laws in Canada. *Journal of the American Academy of Psychiatry and the Law, 29*(2), 232–237.

Glascoe, F. P., & Dworkin, P. H. (1993). Obstacles to effective developmental surveillance: Errors in clinical reasoning. *Journal of developmental and behavioral pediatrics: JDBP, 14*(5), 344–349.

Goehring, C., Gallacchi, M., Kunzi, B., & Bovier, P. (2005). Psychosocial and professional characteristics of burnout in Swiss primary care practitioners: A cross-sectional survey. *Swiss Medical Weekly, 135*(7–8), 101–108.

Goel, V., & Vartanian, O. (2011). Negative emotions can attenuate the influence of beliefs on logical reasoning. *Cognition and Emotion, 25*(1), 121–131.

Goldbloom, D., & Bryden, P. (2016). *How can I help? A week in my life as a psychiatrist.* Toronto, Ontario, Canada: Simon and Schuster.

Graber, M. L., Kissam, S., Payne, V. L., Meyer, A. N., Sorensen, A., Lenfestey, N., . . . Singh, H. (2012). Cognitive interventions to reduce diagnostic error: A narrative review. *BMJ Quality and Safety, 27*(7) 535–557.

Grant, L., & Kinman, G. (2012). Enhancing wellbeing in social work students: Building resilience in the next generation. *Social Work Education, 31*(5), 605–621.

Grant, L., Kinman, G., & Baker, S. (2014). "Put on your own oxygen mask before assisting others": Social work educators' perspectives on an "emotional curriculum." *British Journal of Social Work, 45*(8), 2351–2367.

Green, L., & Mehr, D. R. (1997). What alters physicians' decisions to admit to the coronary care unit? *Journal of Family Practice, 45*(3), 219–226.

Greenhaus, J. H., & Beutell, N. J. (1985). Sources of conflict between work and family roles. *Academy of Management Review, 10*(1), 76–88.

Grigsby, D., & McKnew, M. (1988). Work-stress burnout among paramedics. *Psychological Reports, 63*, 55–64.

Grove, W. M., & Meehl, P. E. (1996). Comparative efficiency of informal (subjective, impressionistic) and formal (mechanical, algorithmic) prediction procedures: The clinical–statistical controversy. *Psychology, Public Policy, and Law, 2*(2), 293–323.

Gunaratnam, Y., & Lewis, G. (2001). Racialising emotional labour and emotionalising racialised labour: Anger, fear and shame in social welfare. *Journal of Social Work Practice, 15*(2), 131–148.

Guterman, N., & Jayaratne, S. (1994). "Responsibility at-risk": Perceptions of stress, control and professional effectiveness in child welfare direct practitioners. *Journal of Social Service Research, 20*(1/2), 99–120.

Gutierrez, L., Helmus, L. M., & Hanson, R. K. (2016). What we know and don't know about risk assessment with offenders of indigenous heritage. *Journal of Threat Assessment and Management, 3*(2), 97.

Guy, L. S., Packer, I. K., & Warnken, W. (2012). Assessing risk of violence using structured professional judgment guidelines. *Journal of Forensic Psychology Practice, 12*(3), 270–283.

Guy, M. E., Newman, M. A., Mastracci, S. H., & Maynard-Moody, S. (2010). Emotional labor in the human service organization. In Y. Hasenfeld (Ed.), *Human services as complex organizations* (pp. 291–310). Los Angeles, CA: Sage.

Haag, A. M., Boyes, A., Cheng, J., MacNeil, A., & Wirove, R. (2016). An introduction to the issues of cross-cultural assessment inspired by Ewert v. Canada. *Journal of Threat Assessment and Management, 3*(2), 65–75.

Hadley, J., Holloway, E., & Mallinckrodt, B. (1993). Common aspects of object relations and self representations in offspring from disparate dysfunctional families. *Journal of Counselling Psychology, 40*, 348–356.

Halpern, J. (2003). What is clinical empathy? *Journal of General Internal Medicine, 18*(8), 670–674.

Hamilton, M. (1960). A rating scale for depression. *Journal of Neurology and Neurosurgery, 23*, 56–61.

Hammerfald, K., Eberle, C., Grau, M., Kinsperger, A., Zimmermann, A., Ehlert, U., & Gaab, J. (2006). Persistent effects of cognitive-behavioral stress management on cortisol responses to acute stress in healthy subjects: A randomized controlled trial. *Psychoneuroendocrinology, 31*, 333–339.

Hanson, R. K., & Thornton, D. (1999). *Static 99: Improving actuarial risk assessments for sex offenders* (Vol. 2). Ottawa, Ontario, Canada: Solicitor General Canada.

Hardré, P. L., Ge, X., & Thomas, M. K. (2006). An investigation of development toward instructional design expertise. *Performance Improvement Quarterly, 19*(4), 63–90.

Harris, B., & Leather, P. (2011). Levels and consequences of exposure to service user violence: Evidence from a sample of UK social care staff. *British Journal of Social Work, 42*, 851–869.

Harris, B., Watkins, S., Cook, N., Walker, R. F., Read, G. F., & Riad-Fahmy, D. (1990). Comparisons of plasma and salivary cortisol determinations for the diagnostic efficacy of the dexamethasone suppression test. *Biological Psychiatry, 27*(8), 897–904. doi:0006-3223(90)90471-D [pii]

Harriss, L., & Hawton, K. (2005). Suicidal intent in deliberate self-harm and the risk of suicide: The predictive power of the Suicide Intent Scale. *Journal of Affective Disorders, 86*(2–3), 225–233.

Hart, S. D. (2016). Culture and violence risk assessment: The case of Ewert v. Canada. *Journal of Threat Assessment and Management, 3*(2), 76–96.

Harvey, A., Nathens, A. B., Bandiera, G., & LeBlanc, V. R. (2010). Threat and challenge: Cognitive appraisal and stress responses in simulated trauma resuscitations. *Medical Education, 44*(6), 587–594.

Hay, M. C., Weisner, T. S., Subramanian, S., Duan, N., Niedzinski, E. J., & Kravitz, R. L. (2008). Harnessing experience: Exploring the gap between evidence-based medicine and clinical practice. *Journal of Evaluation in Clinical Practice, 14*(5), 707–713.

Hayes, S. (2004). Acceptance and commitment therapy, relational frame theory and the third wave of behavioral and cognitive therapies. *Behavioral Therapy, 35*, 639–665.

Helgeson, V. S., Reynolds, K. A., & Tomich, P. L. (2006). A meta-analytic review of benefit finding and growth. *Journal of Consulting and Clinical Psychology, 74*(5), 797–816.

Helmreich, R. L. (2000). On error management: Lessons from aviation. *British Medical Journal, 320*(7237), 781.

Hen, M., & Goroshit, M. (2011). Emotional competencies in the education of mental health professionals. *Social Work Education, 30*(7), 811–829.

Hendryx, M., & Rohland, B. (1997). Psychiatric hospitalization decision making by CMHC staff. *Community Mental Health Journal, 33*(1), 63–73.

Hensel, J. M., Ruiz, C., Finney, C., & Dewa, C. S. (2015). Meta-analysis of risk factors for secondary traumatic stress in therapeutic work with trauma victims. *Journal of Traumatic Stress, 28*(2), 83–91.

Hesse, A. R. (2002). Secondary trauma: How working with trauma survivors affects therapists. *Clinical Social Work Journal, 30*(3), 293–309.

Hilton, N. Z., & Simmons, J. L. (2001). The influence of actuarial risk assessment in clinical judgments and tribunal decisions about mentally disordered offenders in maximum security. *Law and Human Behavior, 25*(4), 393–408.

Himle, D. P., Jayaratne, S., & Thyness, P. (1986). Predictors of job satisfaction, burnout and turnover among social workers in Norway and the USA: A cross-cultural study. *International Social Work, 29*(4), 323–334.

Hochschild, A. R. (1983). *The managed heart.* Berkeley: University of California Press.

Hodges, B., Regehr, G., & Martin, D. (2001). Difficulties in recognizing one's own incompetence: Novice physicians who are unskilled and unaware of it. *Academic Medicine, 76*(10), S87–S89.

Hoffman, S., Sawyer, A., & Fang, A. (2010). The empirical status of the "new wave" of CBT. *Psychiatric Clinics of North America, 33*(3), 701–710.

Hogan, R. (1969). Development of an empathy scale. *Journal of Consulting and Clinical Psychology, 33*, 307–316.

Hojat, M. (2016). Empathy and patient outcomes. In M. Hojat (Ed.), *Empathy in health professions education and patient care* (pp. 189–201). New York, NY: Springer.

Hojat, M., Louis, D. Z., Markham, F. W., Wender, R., Rabinowitz, C., & Gonnella, J. S. (2011). Physicians' empathy and clinical outcomes for diabetic patients. *Academic Medicine, 86*(3), 359–364.

Holden, G., Cuzzi, L., Spitzer, W., Rutter, S., Chernack, P., & Rosenberg, G. (1997). The hospital social work self-efficacy scale: A partial replication and extension. *Health and Social Work, 22*(4), 256–263.

Horner, M., & Hamner, M. (2002). Neurocognitive functioning in posttraumatic stress disorder. *Neuropsychology Review, 12*(1), 15–30.

Horner, M., Mintzer, J., Turner, T., Edmiston, K., & Brawman-Mintzer, O. (2013). Attentional functioning in patients with posttraumatic stress disorder: A preliminary study. *CNS Spectrums, 18,* 90–94.

Horowitz, M. (1991). *Person schemas and maladaptive interpersonal problems.* Chicago, IL: University of Chicago Press.

Horwath, J. (2007). The missing assessment domain: Personal, professional and organizational factors influencing professional judgements when identifying and referring child neglect. *British Journal of Social Work, 37*(8), 1285–1303.

Hu, Y., Wang, D., Pang, K., Xu, G., & Guo, J. (2015). The effect of emotion and time pressure on risk decision-making. *Journal of Risk Research, 18*(5), 637–650.

Hülsheger, U. R., & Schewe, A. F. (2011). On the costs and benefits of emotional labor: A meta-analysis of three decades of research. *Journal of Occupational Health Psychology, 16*(3), 361–389.

Hume, D. (1966). *Enquiries concerning the human understanding and concerning principles of morals.* Oxford, England: Clarenden Press. (Original work published 1777)

Hupe, P., & Hill, M. (2007). Street-level bureaucracy and public accountability. *Public Administration, 85*(2), 279–299.

Iacoboni, M. (2009). Imitation, empathy, and mirror neurons. *Annual Review of Psychology, 60,* 653–670.

In re Valdez, Smith et al., Judicial Circuit Florida.

Jaccard, J., & Wan, C. (1996). *Lisrel approaches to interaction effects in multiple regression.* New York, NY: Sage.

Jain, S., Shapiro, S., Swanick, S., Roesch, S., Mills, P., Bell, I., & Schwartz, G. (2007). A randomized controlled trial of mindfulness meditation versus relaxation training: Effects on distress, positive states of mind, rumination, and distraction. *Annals of Behavioral Medicine, 33*(1), 11–21.

Jameton, A. (1992). Dilemmas of moral distress: Moral responsibility and nursing practice. *AWHONN's Clinical Issues in Perinatal and Women's Health Nursing, 4*(4), 542–551.

Jayaratne, S., & Chess, W. A. (1984). Job satisfaction, burnout, and turnover: A national study. *Social Work, 29*(5), 448–453.

Jayaratne, S., Croxton, T., & Mattison, D. (2004). A national survey of violence in the practice of social work. *Families in Society: The Journal of Contemporary Social Services, 85*(4), 445–453.

Jayaratne, S., Himle, D., & Chess, W. A. (1988). Dealing with work stress and strain: Is the perception of support more important than its use? *Journal of Applied Behavioral Science, 24*(2), 191–202.

Jelinek, L., Jacobsen, D., Kellner, M., Larbig, F., Biesold, K., Barre, K., & Moritz, S. (2006). Verbal and nonverbal memory functioning in posttraumatic stress disorder (PTSD). *Journal of Clinical and Experimental Neuropsychology, 28*, 940–948.

Jenkins, S., & Baird, S. (2002). Secondary traumatic stress and vicarious trauma: A validation study. *Journal of Traumatic Stress, 15*(5), 423–432.

Johnson, K. (1999). Structural equation modeling in practice: Testing a theory for research use. *Journal of Social Service Research, 24*(3–4), 131–169.

Johnson, S. (2012). *Future perfect: The case for progress in a networked age.* New York, NY: Riverhead Books.

Johnson, S., Cooper, C., Cartwright, S., Donald, I., Taylor, P., & Millet, C. (2005). The experience of work-related stress across occupations. *Journal of Managerial Psychology, 20*(2), 178–187.

Joseph, S., & Linley, P. A. (2005). Positive adjustment to threatening events: An organismic valuing theory of growth through adversity. *Review of general psychology, 9*(3), 262–280.

Juster, R.-P., McEwen, B. S., & Lupien, S. J. (2010). Allostatic load biomarkers of chronic stress and impact on health and cognition. *Neuroscience and Biobehavioral Reviews, 35*(1), 2–16.

Kabat-Zinn, J. (1982). An outpatient program in behavioral medicine for chronic pain patients based on practice of mindfulness meditation: Theoretical considerations and preliminary results. *General Hospital Psychiatry, 4*, 33–47.

Kabat-Zinn, J., Massion, A., Kristeller, J., Peterson, L., Fletcher, K., Pbert, L., . . . Santorelli, S. (1991). Effectiveness of a meditation-based stress reduction program in the treatment of anxiety disorders. *American Journal of Psychiatry, 149*(7), 936–943.

Kanani, K., Regehr, C., & Bernstein, M. M. (2002). Liability considerations in child welfare: Lessons from Canada. *Child Abuse and Neglect, 26*(10), 1029–1043.

Kant, I. (1949). *Critique of practical reasoning* (L. Beck, Trans.). Chicago, IL: University of Chicago Press. (Original work published 1788)

Kapur, N., Parand, A., Soukup, T., Reader, T., & Sevdalis, N. (2015). Aviation and healthcare: A comparative review with implications for patient safety. *Journal of the Royal Society of Medicine Open, 7*(1), 1–10. doi: 10.1177/2054270415616548

Karasek, R. A., Jr. (1979). Job demands, job decision latitude, and mental strain: Implications for job redesign. *Administrative Science Quarterly, 24*(2), 285–308.

Kardiner, A. (1941). *Traumatic neuroses of war.* New York, NY: Hoeber.

Kassam-Adams, N. (1995). The risks of treating sexual trauma: Stress and secondary trauma in psychotherapists. In B. Stamm (Ed.), *Secondary traumatic stress: Self-care issues for clinicians, researchers, and educators* (pp. 37–50). Lutherville, MD: Sidran Press.

Keefe, T. (1976). Empathy: The critical skill. *Social Work, 21*, 10–14.

Kemeny, M. (2003). The psychobiology of stress. *Current Directions in Psychological Science, 12*(4), 124–129.

Kessler, R., Berglund, P., Demler, O., Jin, R., Merikangas, K., & Walters, E. (2005). Lifetime prevalence and age of onset distributions of DSM-IV disorders in the National Comorbidity Survey replication. *Archives of General Psychiatry, 62*, 593–602.

Keyes, C., Eisenberg, D., Perry, G., Dube, S., Kroenke, K., & Dhingra, S. (2012). The relationship of level of positive mental health with current mental disorders in predicting suicidal behavior and academic impairment in college students. *Journal of American College Health, 60*(2), 126–133.

Khvorostianov, N., & Elias, N. (2015). "Leave us alone!": Representation of social work in the Russian immigrant media in Israel. *International Social Work, 60*(2), 409–422.

Kim, H., & Stoner, M. (2008). Burnout and turnover intention among social workers: Effects of role stress, job autonomy and social support. *Administration in Social Work, 32*(3), 5–25.

King, S. H., Jr. (2011). The structure of empathy in social work practice. *Journal of Human Behavior in the Social Environment, 21*(6), 679–695.

Koenen, K. (2006). Developmental epidemiology of PTSD: Self-regulation as a central mechanism. *Annals of the New York Academy of Sciences, 1071*, 255–266.

Kooken, R., & Hayslip, B. (1984). The use of stress inoculation in the treatment of test anxiety in older students. *Educational Gerontology, 10*(1–2), 39–58.

Koritsas, S., Coles, J., & Boyle, M. (2010). Workplace violence towards social workers: The Australian experience. *British Journal of Social Work, 40*(1), 257–271.

Kosny, A. A., & Eakin, J. M. (2008). The hazards of helping: Work, mission and risk in non-profit social service organizations. *Health, Risk and Society, 10*(2), 149–166.

Kruger, J., & Dunning, D. (1999). Unskilled and unaware of it: How difficulties in recognizing one's own incompetence lead to inflated self-assessments. *Journal of Personality and Social Psychology, 77*(6), 1121–1134.

Långström, N. (2004). Accuracy of actuarial procedures for assessment of sexual offender recidivism risk may vary across ethnicity. *Sexual Abuse: A Journal of Research and Treatment, 16*(2), 107–120.

Lasalvia, A., Bonetto, C., Bertani, M., Bissoli, S., Cristofalo, D., Marrella, G., . . . Ruggeri, M. (2009). Influence of perceived organisational factors on job burnout: Survey of community mental health staff. *British Journal of Psychiatry, 195*(6), 537–544. doi:195/6/537 [pii]

Lazarus, R. S. (1993). Coping theory and research: Past, present, and future. *Psychosomatic medicine, 55*(3), 234–247.

——. (1998). *Fifty years of the research and theory of RS Lazarus: An analysis of historical and perennial issues.* Mahwah, NJ: Erlbaum.

Lazarus, R. S., & Folkman, S. (1984). *Stress, appraisal, and coping.* New York, NY: Springer.

LeBlanc, V. R. (2009). The effects of acute stress on performance: Implications for health professions education. *Academic Medicine, 84*(10), S25–S33.

LeBlanc, V. R., MacDonald, R., McArthur, B., King, K., & Lepine, T. (2005). Paramedic performance in calculating drug dosages following stressful scenarios in a human patient simulator. *Prehospital Emergency Care, 9*(4), 439–444.

LeBlanc, V. R., McConnell, M., & Monterio, S. (2015). Predictable chaos: A review of the effects of emotions on attention, memory and decision making. *Advances in Health Science Education, 20*(1), 265–282. doi:10.1007/s10459-014-9516-6

LeBlanc, V. R., McConnell, M. M., & Monteiro, S. D. (2014). Predictable chaos: A review of the effects of emotions on attention, memory and decision making. *Advances in Health Sciences Education, 20*(1), 265–282.

LeBlanc, V. R., Regehr, C., Birze, A., King, K., Scott, A., McDonald, R., & Tavares, W. (2011). The association between pre-existing trauma symptoms and acute stress responses in paramedics. *Traumatology, 17*(4), 10–16.

LeBlanc, V. R., Regehr, C., Jelley, R., & Barath, I. (2007). Does posttraumatic stress disorder (PTSD) affect performance? *Journal of Nervous and Mental Disease, 195*(8), 701–704.

LeBlanc, V. R., Regehr, C., Tavares, W., Scott, A., McDonald, R., & King, K. (2012). The impact of stress on paramedic performance during simulated critical events. *Prehospital and Disaster Medicine, 27*(4), 369–374.

LeBlanc, V. R., Tavares, W., King, K., Scott, A., & Macdonald, R. (2010). The impact of stress on paramedic performance during simulated critical events. *Simulation in Healthcare, 5*(6).

Leffler, C., & Dembert, M. (1998). Post traumatic stress symptoms among US Navy divers recovering TWA Flight 800. *Journal of Nervous and Mental Disorders, 186*, 574–577.

Legood, A., McGrath, M., Searle, R., & Lee, A. (2016). Exploring how social workers experience and cope with public perception of their profession. *British Journal of Social Work, 46*(7), 1872–1889.

Lent, J., & Schwartz, R. C. (2012). The impact of work setting, demographic characteristics, and personality factors related to burnout among professional counselors. *Journal of Mental Health Counseling, 34*(4), 355–372.

Leung, A., Luu, S., Regehr, G., Murnaghan, M. L., Gallinger, S., & Moulton, C.-A. (2012). "First, do no harm": Balancing competing priorities in surgical practice. *Academic Medicine, 87*(10), 1368–1374.

Levinson, W., Roter, D. L., Mullooly, J. P., Dull, V. T., & Frankel, R. M. (1997). Physician-patient communication: The relationship with malpractice claims among primary care physicians and surgeons. *JAMA, 277*(7), 553–559.

Lieberman, H. R., Tharion, W. J., Shukitt-Hale, B., Speckman, K. L., & Tulley, R. (2002). Effects of caffeine, sleep loss, and stress on cognitive performance and mood during US Navy SEAL training. *Psychopharmacology, 164*(3), 250–261.

Lindauer, R., Olff, M., van Meijel, E., Carlier, I., & Gersons, B. (2006). Cortisol, learning, memory and attention in relation to smaller hippocampal volume in police officers with posttraumatic stress disorder. *Biological Psychiatry, 59*(2), 171–177.

Lindsey, D. & Regehr, C. (1993). Protecting severely abused children: Clarifying the roles of criminal justice and child welfare. *American Journal of Orthopsychiatry, 63*(4), 509–517.

Lindsey, D., & Trocmé, N. (1994). Have child protection efforts reduced child homicides? An examination of data from Britain and North America. *British Journal of Social Work, 24*(6), 715–732.

Linke, S., Wojciak, J., & Day, S. (2002). The impact of suicide on community mental health teams: Findings and recommendations. *Psychiatric Bulletin, 26,* 50–52.

Linley, P. A., & Joseph, S. (2004). Positive change following trauma and adversity: A review. *Journal of Traumatic Stress, 17*(1), 11–21.

Lipman, T. (2004). The doctor, his patient, and the computerized evidence-based guideline. *Journal of Evaluation in Clinical Practice, 10*(2), 163–176.

Lipsky, M. (2010). *Street-level bureaucracy, 30th anniversary edition: Dilemmas of the individual in public service.* New York, NY: Russell Sage Foundation.

Lizano, E. L., & Barak, M. M. (2015). Job burnout and affective wellbeing: A longitudinal study of burnout and job satisfaction among public child welfare workers. *Children and Youth Services Review, 55,* 18–28.

Lunau, K. (2012, September 5). Mental health crisis on campus: Canadian students feel hopeless, depressed, even suicidal. *Macleans Magazine.* Retrieved from http://www.macleans.ca/education/uniandcollege/the-mental-health-crisis-on-campus/

Luthar, S., Cicchetti, D., & Becker, B. (2000). The construct of resilience: A critical evaluation and guidelines for future work. *Child Development, 71*(3), 543–562.

Lynch, S., Gander, M., Kohls, N., Kudielka, B., & Walach, H. (2011). Mindfulness based coping with university life: A non randomized waitlist controlled pilot evaluation. *Stress and Health, 27*(5), 365–375.

Lyons, P., Doueck, H. J., & Wodarski, J. S. (1996). Risk assessment for child protective services: A review of the empirical literature on instrument performance. *Social Work Research, 20*(3), 143–155.

MacDonald, G., & Sirotich, F. (2001). Reporting client violence. *Social Work, 46*(2), 107–114.

———. (2005). Violence in the social work workplace: The Canadian experience. *International Social Work, 48*(6), 772–781.

Mamassian, P. (2008). Overconfidence in an objective anticipatory motor task. *Psychological Science, 19*(6), 601–606.

Mann, S., & Cowburn, J. (2005). Emotional labour and stress within mental health nursing. *Journal of Psychiatric and Mental Health Nursing, 12*(2), 154–162.

Mänttäri-van der Kuip, M. (2015). Work-related well-being among Finnish frontline social workers in an age of austerity. *Akateeminen väitöskirja. Jyväskylä Studies in Education, Psychology and Social Research, 524.* https://jyx.jyu.fi/bitstream /handle/123456789/45924/978-951-39-6191-6_vaitos29052015.pdf?sequence=1

Marmar, C., McCaslin, S., Metzler, T., Best, S., Weiss, D., Fagan, J., . . . Neylan, C. (2006). Predictors of posttraumatic stress in police and other first responders. *Annals of the New York Academy of Sciences, 1071*(1), 1–18.

Marmar, C., Weiss, D., Metzler, T., Delucchi, K., Best, S., & Wentworth, K. (1999). Longitudinal course and predictors of continuing distress following critical incident exposure in emergency services personnel. *Journal of Nervous and Mental Disease, 187*(1), 15–22.

Maslach, C. (1976). Burned-out. *Human Behavior, 5*(9), 16–22.

——. (1978). The client role in staff burn-out. *Journal of Social Issues, 34*(4), 111–124.

Maslach, C., & Jackson, S. (1981). The measurement of experienced burnout. *Journal of Occupational Behavior, 2,* 99–113.

Maslach, C., Schaufeli, W. B., & Leiter, M. P. (2001). Job burnout. *Annual Review of Psychology, 52*(1), 397–422.

McCammon, S., Durham, T., Allison, E., & Williamson, J. (1988). Emergency worker's cognitive appraisal and coping with traumatic events. *Journal of Traumatic Stress, 1,* 353–372.

McCann, L., & Pearlman, L. (1990a). *Psychological trauma and the adult survivor: Theory, therapy, and transformation.* New York, NY: Brunner/Mazel.

——. (1990b). Vicarious traumatization: A framework for understanding the psychological effects of working with victims. *Journal of Traumatic Stress, 3*(1), 131–149.

McCann, L., Sakheim, D., & Abrahamson, D. (1988). Trauma and victimization: A model of psychological adaption. *Counselling Psychologist, 16*(4), 531–594.

McEwen, B. S. (1998). Protective and damaging effects of stress mediators. *New England Journal of Medicine, 338*(3), 171–179.

McEwen, B. S., & Stellar, E. (1993). Stress and the individual: Mechanisms leading to disease. *Archives of Internal Medicine, 153*(18), 2093–2101.

McFadden, P., Campbell, A., & Taylor, B. (2015). Resilience and burnout in child protection social work: Individual and organisational themes from a systematic literature review. *British Journal of Social Work, 45*(5), 1546–1563. doi:http://dx.doi .org/10.1093/bjsw/bct210

McFarlane, A., & Yehuda, R. (1996). Resilience, vulnerability and the course of posttraumatic reactions. In B. van der Kolk, A. McFarlane, & L. Weisaeth (Eds.),

Traumatic stress: The effects of overwhelming experience on mind, body and society (pp. 151–181). New York, NY: Guilford Press.

Mealer, M., Burnham, E. L., Goode, C. J., Rothbaum, B., & Moss, M. (2009). The prevalence and impact of post traumatic stress disorder and burnout syndrome in nurses. *Depression and anxiety, 26*(12), 1118–1126.

Meichenbaum, D. (1977). *Cognitive behavior modification: An integrative approach.* New York, NY: Plenum Press.

——. (1993). Stress inoculation training: A twenty year update. In L. Woolfolk & P. Lehrer (Eds.), *Principles and practice of stress management* (2nd ed., pp. 373–406). New York, NY: Guilford.

Meichenbaum, D., & Deffenbacher, J. (1988). Stress inoculation training. *Counseling Psychologist, 16*, 69–90.

Mendel, R., Traut-Mattausch, E., Jonas, E., Leucht, S., Kane, J., Maino, K., . . . Hamann, J. (2011). Confirmation bias: Why psychiatrists stick to wrong preliminary diagnoses. *Psychological Medicine, 41*, 2651–2659.

Mintowt-Czyz, L., & Edwards, R. (2004, June 21). Tale of Britain's worst serial stalker. *London Evening Standard.* Retrieved from https://www.standard.co.uk/news/tale-of-britains-worst-serial-stalker-6960657.html

Mishna, F., Antle, B. J., & Regehr, C. (2002). Social work with clients contemplating suicide: Complexity and ambiguity in the clinical, ethical, and legal considerations. *Clinical Social Work Journal, 30*(3), 265–280.

Mitchell, J. T. (1983). When disaster strikes: The critical incident stress debriefing process. *Journal of Emergency Medical Services, 8*(1), 36–39.

Mohr, P. N., Biele, G., & Heekeren, H. R. (2010). Neural processing of risk. *Journal of Neuroscience, 30*(19), 6613–6619.

Mollica, R., Brooks, R., Tor, S., Lopes-Cardozo, B., & Silove, D. (2014). The enduring mental health impact of mass violence: A community comparison study of Cambodian civilians living in Cambodia and Thailand. *International Journal of Social Psychiatry, 60*(1), 6–20.

Mollica, R., McInnes, K., Poole, C., & Tor, S. (1998). Dose-effect relationships of trauma to symptoms of depression and post-traumatic stress disorder among Cambodian survivors of mass violence. *British Journal of Psychiatry, 173*, 482–488.

Morgan, C., Wang, S., Rasmusson, A., Hazlett, G., Anderson, G., & Charney, D. (2001). Relationship among plasma cortisol, catecholamines, neuropeptide y, and human performance during exposure to uncontrollable stress. *Psychosomatic medicine, 63*, 412–422.

Mott, F. (1918). War psychoneurosis: Neurasthenia: The disorders and disabilities of fear. *Lancet, 1*, 127–129.

Moulton, C.-A., Regehr, G., Lingard, L., Merritt, C., & MacRae, H. (2010a). Slowing down to stay out of trouble in the operating room: Remaining attentive in automaticity. *Academic Medicine, 85*(10), 1571–1577.

——. (2010b). "Slowing down when you should": Initiators and influences of the transition from the routine to the effortful. *Journal of Gastrointestinal Surgery, 14*(6), 1019–1026.

Moulton, C.-A., Regehr, G., Mylopoulos, M., & MacRae, H. M. (2007). Slowing down when you should: A new model of expert judgment. *Academic Medicine, 82*(10), S109–S116.

Munro, E. (1996). Avoidable and unavoidable mistakes in child protection work. *British Journal of Social Work, 26*(6), 793–808.

——. (1999). Common errors of reasoning in child protection work. *Child Abuse and Neglect, 23*(8), 745–758.

——. (2011). *The Munro review of child protection: Final report: A child-centered system.* Stationary Office, UK. Retrieved from https://www.gov.uk/government /uploads/system/uploads/attachment_data/file/175391/Munro-Review.pdf

Muran, C., & Segal, Z. (1992). The development of an idiographic measure of self schemas: An illustration of the construction and use of self scenarios. *Psychotherapy and Psychosomatics, 4,* 524–535.

Nabi, R. L. (2003). Exploring the framing effects of emotion: Do discrete emotions differentially influence information accessibility, information seeking, and policy preference? *Communication Research, 30*(2), 224–247.

NASA. (2016). *Aviation safety reporting system.* Retrieved from https://asrs.arc.nasa .gov

National Association of Social Workers. (2008). *Code of ethics of the National Association of Social Workers.* Retrieved from https://www.socialworkers.org/About /Ethics/Code-of-Ethics/Code-of-Ethics-English

——. (2013). *Guidelines for social worker safety in the workplace.* Retrieved from http://www.socialworkers.org/practice/naswstandards/safetystandards2013.pdf

Naylor, C. D. (2001). Clinical decisions: From art to science and back again. *Lancet, 358*(9281), 523–524.

Nelson, T., Johnson, S., & Bebbington, P. (2009). Satisfaction and burnout among staff of crisis resolution, assertive outreach and community mental health teams: A multicentre cross sectional survey. *Social Psychiatry and Psychiatric Epidemiology, 44*(7), 541–549. doi:10.1007/s00127-008-0480-4

Newhill, C. (1996). Prevalence and risk factors for client violence toward social workers. *Families in Society: The Journal of Contemporary Social Services, 77*(8), 488–495.

Nieuwenhuys, A., Savelsbergh, G. J., & Oudejans, R. R. (2012). Shoot or don't shoot? Why police officers are more inclined to shoot when they are anxious. *Emotion, 12*(4), 827–833.

Nightingale, S. D., Yarnold, P. R., & Greenberg, M. S. (1991). Sympathy, empathy, and physician resource utilization. *Journal of General Internal Medicine, 6*(5), 420–423.

Olsson, A., Nearing, K. I., & Phelps, E. A. (2007). Learning fears by observing others: The neural systems of social fear transmission. *Social Cognitive and Affective Neuroscience, 2*(1) 3–11.

Oman, D., Shapiro, S., Thoresen, C., Plante, T., & Flinders, T. (2008). Meditation lowers stress and supports forgiveness among college students: A randomized controlled trial. *Journal of American College Health, 56*(5), 569–578.

Oppenheimer, B., & Rothschild, M. (1918). The psychoneurotic factor in the "irritable heart of soldiers." *British Medical Journal, 2*(3002), 29–31.

Orcutt, H. K., King, L. A., & King, D. W. (2003). Male-perpetrated violence among Vietnam veteran couples: Relationships with veteran's early life characteristics, trauma history, and PTSD symptomatology. *Journal of Traumatic Stress, 16*(4), 381–390.

Ortlepp, K., & Friedman, M. (2002). Prevalence and correlates of secondary traumatic stress in workplace lay trauma counselors. *Journal of Traumatic Stress, 15*(3), 213–222. doi:10.1023/A:1015203327767

Ozer, E., Best, S., Lipsey, T., & Weiss, D. (2003). Predictors of posttraumatic stress disorder and symptoms in adults: A meta-analysis. *Psychological Bulletin, 129*(1), 52–73.

Ozer, E., & Weiss, D. (2004). Who develops posttraumatic stress disorder? *Current Directions in Psychological Science, 13*(4), 169–172.

Page, H. (1883). *Injury of the spinal cord without apparent legion and nervous shock, in their surgical and medico-legal aspects.* London, England: J & A Church.

Palmieri, G., Forghieri, M., Ferrari, S., Pingani, L., Coppola, P., Colombini, N., . . . Neimeyer, R. A. (2008). Suicide intervention skills in health professionals: A multidisciplinary comparison. *Archives of Suicide Research, 12*(3), 232–237.

Panagopoulou, E., Montgomery, A., & Benos, A. (2006). Burnout in internal medicine physicians: Differences between residents and specialists. *European Journal of Internal Medicine, 17*(3), 195–200.

Paterson, B., Dowding, D., Harries, C., Cassells, C., Morrison, R., & Niven, C. (2008). Managing the risk of suicide in acute psychiatric inpatients: A clinical judgement analysis of staff predictions of imminent suicide risk. *Journal of Mental Health, 17*(4), 410–423.

Pearlman, L. A., & MacIan, P. (1995). Vicarious traumatization: An empirical study on the effects of trauma work on trauma therapists. *Professional Psychology, Research and Practice, 26,* 558–565.

Pearlman, L. A., & Saakvitne, K. W. (1995). Treating therapists with vicarious traumatization and secondary traumatic stress disorders. In C. Figley (Ed.), *Compassion fatigue: Coping with secondary traumatic stress disorder in those who treat the traumatized* (pp. 150–177). New York, NY: Brunner-Routledge.

Pecora, P. J. (1991). Investigating allegations of child maltreatment: The strengths and limitations of current risk assessment systems. *Child and Youth Services, 15*(2), 73–92.

Pedrini, L., Magni, L. R., Giovannini, C., Panetta, V., Zacchi, V., Rossi, G., & Placentino, A. (2009). Burnout in nonhospital psychiatric residential facilities. *Psychiatric Services, 60*(11), 1547–1551. doi:60/11/1547 [pii]

Pelech, W., Stalker, C. A., Regehr, C., & Jacobs, M. (1999). Making the grade: The quest for validity in admissions decisions. *Journal of Social Work Education, 35*(2), 215–226.

Perkonigg, A., Pfister, H., Stein, M. B., Höfler, M., Lieb, R., Maercker, A., & Wittchen, H.-U. (2005). Longitudinal course of posttraumatic stress disorder and posttraumatic stress disorder symptoms in a community sample of adolescents and young adults. *American Journal of Psychiatry, 162*(7), 1320–1327.

Pfouts, J. H., & Henley, H. C., Jr. (1977). Admissions roulette: Predictive factors for success in practice. *Journal of Education for Social Work, 13*(3), 56–62.

Pham, J. C., Girard, T., & Pronovost, P. J. (2013). What to do with healthcare incident reporting systems. *Journal of Public Health Research, 2*(3), 154–159.

Pines, A., & Maslach, C. (1978). Characteristics of staff burnout in mental health settings. *Psychiatric Services, 29*(4), 233–237.

Pole, N. (2007). The psychophysiology of posttraumatic stress disorder: A meta-analysis. *Psychological Bulletin, 133*(5), 725–746.

Porta, M. (2004). Is there life after evidence-based medicine? *Journal of Evaluation in Clinical Practice, 10*(2), 147–152.

Posner, K., Brown, G. K., Stanley, B., Brent, D. A., Yershova, K. V., Oquendo, M. A., . . . Shen, S. (2011). The Columbia–Suicide Severity Rating Scale: Initial validity and internal consistency findings from three multisite studies with adolescents and adults. *American Journal of Psychiatry, 168*(12), 1266–1277.

Poulin, J., & Walter, C. (1993). Social worker burnout: A longitudinal study. *Social Work Research and Abstracts 29*(4), 5–11.

Pugliesi, K. (1999). The consequences of emotional labor: Effects on work stress, job satisfaction, and well-being. *Motivation and Emotion, 23*(2), 125–154.

Purvanova, R. K., & Muros, J. P. (2010). Gender differences in burnout: A meta-analysis. *Journal of Vocational Behavior, 77*(2), 168–185.

Quill, T., & Williamson, P. (1990). Healthy approaches to physician stress. *Archives of Internal Medicine, 150*(9), 1857–1861.

Quinlivan, L., Cooper, J., Davies, L., Hawton, K., Gunnell, D., & Kapur, N. (2016). Which are the most useful scales for predicting repeat self-harm? A systematic review evaluating risk scales using measures of diagnostic accuracy. *BMJ Open, 6*(2), e009297.

Quinlivan, L., Cooper, J., Steeg, S., Davies, L., Hawton, K., Gunnell, D., & Kapur, N. (2014). Scales for predicting risk following self-harm: An observational study in 32 hospitals in England. *BMJ Open, 4*(5), e004732.

Quinsey, V. L., Harris, G., Rice, M., & Cormier, C. (1998). *Violent offenders: Appraising and managing risk.* Washington, DC: American Psychological Association.

Quinsey, V. L., Khanna, A., & Malcolm, P. B. (1998). A retrospective evaluation of the Regional Treatment Centre sex offender treatment program. *Journal of Interpersonal Violence, 13*(5), 621–644.

R. v. Heikamp and Martin. 1999. Ontario Court of Justice.

Rank, M. G., & Hutchison, W. S. (2000). An analysis of leadership within the social work profession. *Journal of Social Work Education, 36*(3), 487–502.

Raphael, B. (1986). *When disaster strikes: How individuals and communities cope with catastrophe.* New York, NY: Basic Books

Regehr, C. (1996). *Do not go gentle into that good night: Strengths in sexually assaulted women* (Unpublished doctoral dissertation). University of Toronto.

——. (2001). Crisis debriefing groups for emergency responders: Reviewing the evidence. *Brief Treatment and Crisis Intervention, 1*(2), 87–100.

——. (2005). Bringing the trauma home: Spouses of paramedics. *Journal of Loss and Trauma, 10*(2), 97–114.

——. (2009). Social support as a mediator of psychological distress in firefighters. *Irish Journal of Psychology, 30*(1), 85–96.

Regehr, C., & Antle, B. (1997). Coercive influences: Informed consent in court mandated social work practice. *Social Work, 42*(3), 300–306.

Regehr, C., & Bober, T. (2005). *In the line of fire: Trauma in the emergency services.* New York, NY: Oxford University Press.

Regehr, C., Bogo, M., Donovan, K., Lim, A., & Regehr, G. (2012). Evaluating a scale to measure student competencies in macro social work practice. *Journal of Social Service Research, 38*(1), 100–109.

Regehr, C., Bogo, M., LeBlanc, V. R., Baird, S., Paterson, J., & Birze, A. (2016). Suicide risk assessment: Clinicians' confidence in their professional judgment. *Journal of Loss and Trauma, 21*(1), 30–46.

Regehr, C., Bogo, M., & Regehr, G. (2011). Development of an online practice-based evaluation tool for social work. *Research on Social Work Practice, 21*(4), 469–475.

Regehr, C., Bogo, M., Shlonsky, A., & LeBlanc, V. (2010). Confidence and professional judgment in assessing children's risk of abuse. *Research on Social Work Practice, 20*(6), 621–628.

Regehr, C., & Cadell, S. (1999). Secondary Trauma in Sexual Assault Crisis Work: Implications for Therapists and Therapy. *Canadian Social Work, 1*(1), 56–63.

Regehr, C., Cadell, S., & Jansen, K. (1999). Perceptions of control and long-term recovery from rape. *American Journal of Orthopsychiatry, 69*(1), 110–115.

Regehr, C., Chau, S., Leslie, B., & Howe, P. (2002a). An exploration of supervisor's and manager's responses to child welfare reform. *Administration in Social Work, 26*(3), 17–36.

——. (2002b). Inquiries into deaths of children in care: The impact on child welfare workers and their organization. *Children and Youth Services Review, 24*(12), 885–902.

Regehr, C., Dimitropoulos, G., Bright, E., George, S., & Henderson, J. (2005). Behind the brotherhood: Rewards and challenges for wives of firefighters. *Family Relations, 54*(3), 423–435.

Regehr, C., & Glancy, G. (2014). *Mental Health Social Work Practice in Canada* (2nd ed.). Toronto, Ontario, Canada: Oxford University Press.

Regehr, C., Glancy, D., & Pitts, A. (2013). Interventions to reduce stress in university students. *Journal of Affective Disorders, 148*, 1–11.

Regehr, C., Glancy, D., Pitts, A., & LeBlanc, V. R. (2014). Interventions to reduce the consequences of stress in physicians: A review and meta-analysis. *Journal of Nervous and Mental Disease, 202*(5), 353–359.

Regehr, C., Goldberg, G., Glancy, G., & Knott, T. (2002). Posttraumatic symptoms and disability in paramedics. *Canadian Journal of Psychiatry, 47*(10), 953–958.

Regehr, C., Goldberg, G., & Hughes, J. (2002). Exposure to human tragedy, empathy, and trauma in ambulance paramedics. *American Journal of Orthopsychiatry, 72*(4), 505–513.

Regehr, C., Hemsworth, D., & Hill, J. (2001). Individual predictors of posttraumatic distress: A structural equation model. *Canadian Journal of Psychiatry, 46*(2), 156–161.

Regehr, C., Hemsworth, D., Leslie, B., Howe, P., & Chau, S. (2004). Predictors of posttraumatic distress in child welfare workers: A linear structural equation model. *Children and Youth Services Review, 26*(4), 331–346.

Regehr, C., & Hill, J. (2001). Evaluating the efficacy of crisis debriefing groups. *Social Work with Groups, 23*(3), 69–79.

Regehr, C., Hill, J., & Glancy, G. (2000). Individual predictors of traumatic reactions in firefighters. *Journal of Nervous and Mental Disease, 188*(6), 333–339.

Regehr, C., Hill, J., Goldberg, G., & Hughes, J. (2003). Postmortem inquiries and trauma responses in paramedics and firefighters. *Journal of Interpersonal Violence, 18*(6), 607–622.

Regehr, C., Johanis, D., Dimitropoulos, G., Bartram, C., & Hope, G. (2003). The police officer and the public inquiry: A qualitative inquiry into the aftermath of workplace trauma. *Brief Treatment and Crisis Intervention, 3*(4), 383–396.

Regehr, C., Kanani, K., McFadden, J., & Saini, M. (2015). *Essential law for social work practice in Canada* (3rd ed.). Toronto, Ontario, Canada: Oxford University Press.

Regehr, C., Kjerulf, M., Popova, S., & Baker, A. (2004). Trauma and tribulation: The experiences and attitudes of operating room nurses working with organ donors. *Journal of Clinical Nursing, 13*(4), 430–437.

Regehr, C., & LeBlanc, V. R. (2017). PTSD, acute stress, performance and decision-making in emergency service workers. *Journal of the American Academy of Psychiatry and the Law, 45*(2), 184–192.

Regehr, C., LeBlanc, V., Barath, I., Balch, J. & Birze, A. (2013). Predictors of physiological stress and psychological distress in police communicators. *Police Practice and Research, 14*(6), 451–463.

Regehr, C., LeBlanc, V., Bogo, M., Paterson, J., & Birze, A. (2015). Suicide risk assessments: Examining influences on clinicians' professional judgment. *American Journal of Orthopsychiatry, 85*(4), 295–301.

Regehr, C., LeBlanc, V., Jelley, B., & Barath, I. (2008). Acute Stress and Performance in Police Recruits. *Stress and Health, 24*(3), 295–303.

Regehr, C., LeBlanc, V., Jelley, B., Barath, I., & Daciuk, J. (2007). Previous trauma as a predictor of subjective and biological response to high stress situations in policing. *Canadian Journal of Psychiatry, 10*, 63–71.

Regehr, C., LeBlanc, V., Shlonsky, A., & Bogo, M. (2010). The influence of clinicians' previous trauma exposure on their assessment of child abuse risk. *Journal of Nervous and Mental Disease, 198*(9), 614–618.

Regehr, C., Leslie, B., Howe, P., & Chau, S. (2005). Stress, trauma and support in child welfare workers. *SPSAC Advisor Journal, 17*(2), 12–18.

Regehr, C., & Marziali, E. (1999). Response to sexual assault: A relational perspective. *Journal of Nervous and Mental Disease, 187*(10), 618–623.

Regehr, C., & Millar, D. (2007). Situation critical: High demand, low control, and low support in paramedic organizations. *Traumatology, 13*(1), 49–58.

Regehr, C., Regehr, G., Leeson, J., & Fusco, L. (2002). Setting priorities for learning in the field practicum: A comparative study of students and field instructors. *Journal of Social Work Education, 38*(1), 55–64.

Regehr, C., Stalker, C. A., Jacobs, M., & Pelech, W. (2001). The gatekeeper and the wounded healer. *Clinical Supervisor, 20*(1), 127–143.

Regehr, C., Stern, S., & Shlonsky, A. (2007). Operationalizing evidence based practice: The development of a research institute in evidence based social work. *Research on Social Work Practice, 17*, 408–416.

Regehr, G. (1994). Chickens and children do not an expert make. *Academic Medicine, 69*(12), 970–971.

Regehr, G., Hodges, B., Tiberius, R., & Lofchy, J. (1996). Measuring self-assessment skills: An innovative relative ranking model. *Academic Medicine, 71*(10), S52–S54.

Regehr, K., & Regehr, C. (2012). Let them satisfy their lust on thee: Titus Andronicus as a window into societal understanding of PTSD. *Traumatology, 18*(2), 27–34.

Renden, P. G., Landman, A., Geerts, S. F., Jansen, S. E., Faber, G. S., Savelsbergh, G. J., & Oudejans, R. R. (2014). Effects of anxiety on the execution of police arrest and self-defense skills. *Anxiety, Stress and Coping, 27*(1), 100–112.

Renzi, C., Tabolli, S., Ianni, A., Di Pietro, C., & Puddu, P. (2005). Burnout and job satisfaction comparing healthcare staff of a dermatological hospital and a general hospital. *Journal of the European Academy of Dermatology and Venereology, 19*(2), 153–157.

Resnick, H., Kilpatrick, D., Best, C., & Kramer, T. (1992). Vulnerability-stress factors in development of posttraumatic stress disorder. *Journal of Nervous and Mental Disease, 180*(7), 424–430.

Rey, L. (1996). What social workers need to know about client violence. *Families in Society, 77*(1), 33–39.

Ribeiro, V. F., Ferreira Filho, C., Valenti, V. E., Ferreira, M., de Abreu, L. C., de Carvalho, T. D., . . . Leão, E. R. (2014). Prevalence of burnout syndrome in clinical nurses at a hospital of excellence. *International Archives of Medicine, 7*(1), 22–37.

Richards, A., French, C. C., Calder, A. J., Webb, B., Fox, R., & Young, A. W. (2002). Anxiety-related bias in the classification of emotionally ambiguous facial expressions. *Emotion, 2*(3), 273–287.

Rizzolatti, G. (2005). The mirror neuron system and its function in humans. *Anatomy and embryology, 210*(5), 419–421.

Rogers, C. (1957). The necessary and sufficient conditions of therapeutic personality change. *Journal of Consulting Psychology, 21,* 95–103.

Rogers, R. (2000). The uncritical acceptance of risk assessment in forensic practice. *Law and Human Behavior, 24*(5), 595–605.

Rose, S. C., Bisson, J., Churchill, R., & Wessely, S. (2002). Psychological debriefing for preventing post traumatic stress disorder (PTSD). *Cochrane Library.* Retrieved from http://www.cochrane.org/CD000560/DEPRESSN_psychological-debriefing -for-preventing-post-traumatic-stress-disorder-ptsd

Rosenfeld, J. A. (2004). The view of evidence-based medicine from the trenches: Liberating or authoritarian? *Journal of Evaluation in Clinical Practice, 10*(2), 153–155.

Rothbaum, B. O., Foa, E. B., Riggs, D. S., Murdock, T., & Walsh, W. (1992). A prospective examination of post-traumatic stress disorder in rape victims. *Journal of Traumatic Stress, 5*(3), 455–475.

Rothschild, B. (2006). *Help for the helper: The psychophysiology of compassion fatigue and vicarious trauma.* New York, NY: W. W. Norton.

Rotter, J. (1975). Some problems and misconceptions related to the construct of internal versus external control of reinforcement. *Journal of Consulting and Clinical Psychology, 43,* 56–67.

Rutledge, T., Stucky, E., Dollarhide, A., Shively, M., Jain, S., Wolfson, T., . . . Dresselhaus, T. (2009). A real-time assessment of work stress in physicians and nurses. *Health Psychology, 28*(2), 194–200.

Rutter, M. (1985). Resilience in the face of adversity: Protective factors and resistance to psychiatric disorder. *British Journal of Psychiatry, 147*(6), 598–611.

Saarni, S. I., & Gylling, H. A. (2004). Evidence based medicine guidelines: A solution to rationing or politics disguised as science? *Journal of Medical Ethics, 30*(2), 171–175.

Salas, E., Rosen, M. A., & DiazGranados, D. (2009). Expertise-based intuition and decision making in organizations. *Journal of Management, 36*(4), 941–973.

Salovey, P., & Mayer, J. D. (1990). Emotional intelligence. *Imagination, Cognition and Personality, 9*(3), 185–211.

Salston, M., & Figley, C. R. (2003). Secondary traumatic stress effects of working with survivors of criminal victimization. *Journal of Traumatic Stress, 16*(2), 167–174.

Saltiel, D. (2016). Observing front line decision making in child protection. *British Journal of Social Work, 46*(7), 2104–2119.

Salyers, M. P., & Bond, G. R. (2001). An exploratory analysis of racial factors in staff burnout among assertive community treatment workers. *Community Mental Health Journal, 37*(5), 393–404.

Salzer, M. (2012). A comparative study of campus experiences of college students with mental illnesses versus a general college sample. *Journal of American College Health, 60*(1), 1–7.

Sanchez-Martin, J. R., Cardas, J., Ahedo, L., Fano, E., Echebarria, A., & Azpiroz, A. (2001). Social behavior, cortisol, and sIgA levels in preschool children. *Journal of Psychosomatic Research, 50*(4), 221–227.

Sanders, R., Colton, M., & Roberts, S. (1999). Child abuse fatalities and cases of extreme concern: Lessons from reviews. *Child Abuse & Neglect, 23*(3), 257–268.

Sanders, S., Jacobson, J., & Ting, L. (2008). Preparing for the inevitable: Training social workers to cope with client suicide. *Journal of Teaching in Social Work, 28*(1–2), 1–18.

Saunders, T., Driskell, J., Johnston, J., & Salas, E. (1996). The effect of stress inoculation training on anxiety and performance. *Journal of Occupational Health Psychology, 1*(2), 170–186.

Scardamalia, M., & Bereiter, C. (1991). Literate expertise. In A. Ericsson and J. Smith (Eds.), *Toward a general theory of expertise: Prospects and limits* (pp. 172–194). New York, NY; Cambridge University Press.

Schaefer, J. A., & Moos, R. H. (1998). The context for posttraumatic growth: Life crises, individual and social resources, and coping. In R. Tedeschi, C. Park & L. Calhoun (Eds.), *Posttraumatic growth: Positive changes in the aftermath of crisis* (pp. 99–125). Mahwah, NJ; Lawrence Erlbaum and Associates.

Schauben, L., & Frazier, P. (1995). Vicarious trauma: The effects on female counselors of working with sexual violence survivors. *Psychology of Women Quarterly, 19*, 49–54.

Schmidt, H. G., & Boshuizen, H. P. (1993). On acquiring expertise in medicine. *Educational Psychology Review, 5*(3), 205–221.

Schon, D. (1987). *Educating the reflective practitioner.* San Francisco, CA: Jossey-Bass.

Schuerman, J., Rossi, P. H., & Budde, S. (1999). Decisions on placement and family preservation: Agreement and targeting. *Evaluation Review, 23*(6), 599–618.

Scott, J. C., Matt, G. E., Wrocklage, K. M., Crnich, C., Jordan, J., Southwick, S. M., ... Schweinsburg, B. C. (2015). A quantitative meta-analysis of neurocognitive functioning in posttraumatic stress disorder. *Psychological Bulletin, 141*(1), 105–140.

Segal, Z., Teasdale, J., & Williams, M. (2002). *Mindfulness-based cognitive therapy for depression.* New York, NY: Guilford Press.

Seys, D., Wu, A. W., Gerven, E. V., Vleugels, A., Euwema, M., Panella, M., ... Vanhaecht, K. (2013). Health care professionals as second victims after adverse events: A systematic review. *Evaluation and the Health Professions, 36*(2), 135–162.

Shalev, A. (2002). Acute stress reactions in adults. *Biological Psychiatry, 51*(7), 532–543.

Shamay-Tsoory, S. G. (2011). The neural bases for empathy. *The Neuroscientist, 17*(1), 18–24.

Shamay-Tsoory, S. G., Aharon-Peretz, J., & Perry, D. (2009). Two systems for empathy: A double dissociation between emotional and cognitive empathy in inferior frontal gyrus versus ventromedial prefrontal lesions. *Brain, 132*(3), 617–627.

Shapiro, S., Brown, K., Thoresen, C., & Plante, T. (2011). The moderation of mindfulness-based stress reduction effects by trait mindfulness: Results from a randomized controlled trial. *Journal of Clinical Psychology, 67*(3), 267–277.

Shapiro, S., Schwartz, G., & Bonner, G. (1998). Effects of mindfulness-based stress reduction on medical and premedical students. *Journal of Behavioral Medicine, 21*(6), 581–599.

Shaw, I., Morris, K., & Edwards, A. (2009). Technology, social services and organizational innovation or how great expectations in London and Cardiff are dashed in Lowestoft and Cymtyrch. *Journal of Social Work Practice, 23*(4), 383–400.

Shaw, M., & Hannah-Moffat, K. (2000). Gender, diversity and risk assessment in Canadian corrections. *Probation Journal, 47*(3), 163–172.

Shay, J. (1994). *Achilles in Vietnam: Combat trauma and the undoing of character.* New York, NY: Scribner.

Shea, A., Walsh, C., MacMillan, H., & Steiner, M. (2004). Child maltreatment and HPA axis dysregulation: Relationship to major depressive disorder and post traumatic stress disorder in females. *Psychoneuroendocrinology, 30*(2), 162–178.

Sheehy, R., & Horan, J. (2004). The effects of stress-inoculation training for first year law students. *International Journal of Stress Management, 11*, 41–55.

Sherin, J. E., & Nemeroff, C. B. (2011). Post-traumatic stress disorder: The neurobiological impact of psychological trauma. *Dialogues in Clinical Neuroscience, 13*(3), 263–278.

Shields, R., & Milks, R. W. (1994). The role of organizational leadership in the rapid change environment. *Journal of Child and Youth Care, 9*(3) 1–9.

Shin, H., Park, Y. M., Ying, J. Y., Kim, B., Noh, H., & Lee, S. M. (2014). Relationships between coping strategies and burnout symptoms: A meta-analytic approach. *Professional Psychology: Research and Practice, 45*(1), 44–56.

Shirtcliff, E. A., Vitacco, M. J., Graf, A. R., Gostisha, A. J., Merz, J. L., & Zahn-Waxler, C. (2009). Neurobiology of empathy and callousness: Implications for the development of antisocial behavior. *Behavioral Sciences and the Law, 27*(2), 137–171.

Sijbrandij, M., Kleiboer, A., Bisson, J. I., Barbui, C., & Cuijpers, P. (2015). Pharmacological prevention of post-traumatic stress disorder and acute stress disorder: A systematic review and meta-analysis. *Lancet Psychiatry, 2*(5), 413–421.

Singh, J. P., Bjørkly, S., & Fazel, S. (2016). *International perspectives on violence risk assessment.* New York, NY: Oxford University Press.

Singh, J. P., Grann, M., & Fazel, S. (2011). A comparative study of violence risk assessment tools: A systematic review and metaregression analysis of 68 studies involving 25,980 participants. *Clinical Psychology Review, 31*(3), 499–513.

Slovic, P. (1999). Trust, emotion, sex, politics, and science: Surveying the risk-assessment battlefield. *Risk analysis, 19*(4), 689–701.

Slovic, P., Finucane, M. L., Peters, E., & MacGregor, D. G. (2004). Risk as analysis and risk as feelings: Some thoughts about affect, reason, risk, and rationality. *Risk analysis, 24*(2), 311–322.

Slovic, P., Monahan, J., & MacGregor, D. G. (2000). Violence risk assessment and risk communication: The effects of using actual cases, providing instruction, and employing probability versus frequency formats. *Law and Human Behavior, 24*(3), 271–296.

Smith, A. (2016, November 22). The miracle on the Hudson: How it happened. *Telegraph.* Retrieved from http://www.telegraph.co.uk/films/sully/miracle-on-the -hudson-how-it-happened

Smith, J. D., & Dumont, F. (2002). Confidence in psychodiagnosis: What makes us so sure? *Clinical Psychology and Psychotherapy, 9*(4), 292–298.

Spencer, P. C., & Munch, S. (2003). Client violence toward social workers: The role of management in community mental health programs. *Social Work, 48*(4), 532–544.

Spielberger, C. (1983). *Manual for the State-Trait Anxiety Inventory.* Palo Alto, CA: Consulting Psychologists Press.

Sreenivasan, S., Kirkish, P., Garrick, T., Weinberger, L. E., & Phenix, A. (2000). Actuarial risk assessment models: A review of critical issues related to violence and sex-offender recidivism assessments. *Journal of the American Academy of Psychiatry and the Law, 28*(4), 438–448.

Stanford, S. (2009). "Speaking back" to fear: Responding to the moral dilemmas of risk in social work practice. *British Journal of Social Work, 40*(4), 1065–1080.

Starcke, K., & Brand, M. (2012). Decision making under stress: A selective review. *Neuroscience and Biobehavioral Reviews, 36*(4), 1228–1248.

Steel, Z., Chey, T., Silove, D., Marnane, C., Bryant, R. A., & Van Ommeren, M. (2009). Association of torture and other potentially traumatic events with mental health outcomes among populations exposed to mass conflict and displacement: A systematic review and meta-analysis. *JAMA, 302*(5), 537–549.

Steele, C. M. (2011). *Whistling Vivaldi: And other clues to how stereotypes affect us (issues of our time).* New York, NY: W. W. Norton.

Steele, C. M., & Aronson, J. (1995). Stereotype threat and the intellectual test performance of African Americans. *Journal of Personality and Social Psychology, 69*(5), 797–811.

Stein, M. B., Jang, K. L., Taylor, S., Vernon, P. A., & Livesley, W. J. (2002). Genetic and environmental influences on trauma exposure and posttraumatic stress disorder symptoms: A twin study. *American Journal of Psychiatry, 159*(10), 1675–1681.

Storrie, K., Ahern, K., & Tuckett, A. (2010). A systematic review: Students with mental health problems: A growing problem. *International Journal of Nursing Practice, 16*(1), 1–6.

Stroop, J. R. (1935). Studies of interference in serial verbal reactions. *Journal of Experimental Psychology, 18*(6), 643–652.

Swider, B., & Zimmerman, R. (2010). Born to burnout: A meta-analytic path model of personality, job burnout, and work outcomes. *Journal of Vocational Behavior, 76*(3), 487–506.

Tedeschi, R. G., & Calhoun, L. G. (2004). "Posttraumatic growth: Conceptual foundations and empirical evidence." *Psychological Inquiry, 15*(1), 1–18.

Tedeschi, R. G., Park, C., & Calhoun, L. (1998). *Post-traumatic growth: Positive changes in the aftermath of crisis.* Mahwah, NJ: Erlbaum.

Thaler, R. H. (2015). *Misbehaving: The making of behavioral economics.* New York, NY: W. W. Norton.

——. (2016). Behavioral economics: Past, present, and future. *American Economic Review, 106*(7), 1577–1600.

Thoits, P. (1995). Stress, coping, and social support processes: Where are we? What next? *Journal of Health and Social Behavior, 35,* 53–79.

Thomas, E., Saumier, D., & Brunet, A. (2012). Peritraumatic distress and the course of posttraumatic stress disorder symptoms: A meta-analysis. *Canadian Journal of Psychiatry, 57*(2), 122–129.

Thomas, N. (2004). Resident burnout. *JAMA, 292*(23), 2880–2889.

Thorndike, E. (1920). Intelligence and its uses. *Harper's, 140,* 227–235.

Thorndike, R. L., & Stein, S. (1937). An evaluation of the attempts to measure social intelligence. *Psychological Bulletin, 34*(5), 275.

Ting, L., Jacobson, J., & Sanders, S. (2008). Available supports and coping behaviours of mental health social workers following fatal and nonfatal client suicidal behaviour. *Social Work, 53*(3), 210–221.

Tomaka, J., Blascovich, J., Kibler, J., & Ernst, J. M. (1997). Cognitive and physiological antecedents of threat and challenge appraisal. *Journal of Personality and Social Psychology, 73*(1), 63–72.

Travis, D. J., Lizano, E. L., & Barak, M. E. M. (2015). "I'm so stressed!": A longitudinal model of stress, burnout and engagement among social workers in child welfare settings. *British Journal of Social Work, 46*(4), 1076–1095.

Trickey, D., Siddaway, A., Meiser-Stedman, R., Serpell, L., & Field, A. P. (2012). A meta-analysis of risk factors for post-traumatic stress disorder in children and adolescents. *Clinical Psychology Review, 32,* 122–138.

Trope, Y., & Liberman, N. (2003). Temporal construal. *Psychological Review, 110*(3), 403–421.

True, W. R., Rice, J., Eisen, S. A., Heath, A. C., Goldberg, J., Lyons, M. J., & Nowak, J. (1993). A twin study of genetic and environmental contributions to liability for posttraumatic stress symptoms. *Archives of General Psychiatry, 50*(4), 257–264.

Tubbs, S. L., & Schulz, E. (2006). Exploring a taxonomy of global leadership competencies and meta-competencies. *Journal of American Academy of Business, 8*(2), 29–34.

Tversky, A., & Kahneman, D. (1973). Availability: A heuristic for judging frequency and probability. *Cognitive Psychology, 5*(2), 207–232.

——. (1974). Judgment under uncertainty: Heuristics and biases. *Science, 185*(4157), 1124–1131.

——. (1981). The framing of decisions and the psychology of choice. *Science, 211*(4481), 453–458.

Twamley, E., Hami, S., & Stein, M. (2004). Neuropsychological function in college students with and without posttraumatic stress disorder. *Psychiatry Research, 126,* 265–274.

Tzafrir, S. S., Enosh, G., & Gur, A. (2013). Client aggression and the disenchantment process among Israeli social workers: Realizing the gap. *Qualitative Social Work, 14*(1), 65–85.

Ulrich, C., O'Donnell, P., Taylor, C., Farrar, A., Danis, M., & Grady, C. (2007). Ethical climate, ethics stress, and the job satisfaction of nurses and social workers in the United States. *Social Science and Medicine, 65*(8), 1708–1719.

Um, M., & Harrison, D. (1998). Role stressors, burnout, mediators and job satisfaction: A stress-strain-outcome model and empirical test. *Social Work Research, 22*(2), 100–115.

Underman, K., & Hirshfield, L. E. (2016). Detached concern? Emotional socialization in twenty-first century medical education. *Social Science and Medicine, 160,* 94–101.

U.S. Department of State. (2013). *PTSD workers' comp claims.* Retrieved from http://www.state.gov/m/med/dsmp/c44957.htm

Vaiva, G., Ducrocq, F., Jezequel, K., Averland, B., Lestaval, P., Brunet, A., & Marmar, C. (2003). Immediate treatment with propranolol decreases posttraumatic stress disorder two months after trauma. *Biological Psychiatry, 54,* 947–949.

Van Ameringen, M., Mancini, C., Patterson, B., & Boyle, M. H. (2008). Post-traumatic stress disorder in Canada. *CNS Neuroscience and Therapeutics, 14*(3), 171–181.

Van Cauter, E., & Turek, F. (1995). Endocrine and other biological rhythms. In L. De Groot (Ed.), *Endocrinology* (pp. 2487–2548). Philadelphia, PA: Saunders.

Van de Luitgaarden, G. M. (2009). Evidence-based practice in social work: Lessons from judgment and decision-making theory. *British Journal of Social Work, 39*(2), 243–260. doi:10.1093/bjsw/bcm117

Van der Doef, M., & Maes, S. (1998). The job demand-control (-support) model and physical health outcomes: A review of the strain and buffer hypotheses. *Psychology and Health, 13*(5), 909–936.

van der Kolk, B. (1996). The complexity of adaptation to trauma: Self-regulation, stimulus discrimination, and characterological development. In B. van der Kolk, A. McFarlane, & L. Weisaeth (Eds.), *Traumatic stress: The effects of overwhelming experience on mind, body and society* (pp. 182–213). New York, NY: Guilford Press.

——. (1997). The psychobiology of posttraumatic stress disorder. *Journal of Clinical Psychiatry, 58*(Suppl. 9), 16–24.

van der Kolk, B., Hostetler, A., Herron, N., & Fisler, R. E. (1994). Trauma and the development of borderline personality disorder. *Psychiatric Clinics of North America 17*(4), 715–730.

Van Emmerik, A. A., Kamphuis, J. H., Hulsbosch, A. M., & Emmelkamp, P. M. (2002). Single session debriefing after psychological trauma: A meta-analysis. *Lancet, 360*(9335), 766–771.

Van Pelt, F. (2008). Peer support: Healthcare professionals supporting each other after adverse medical events. *Quality and Safety in Health Care, 17*(4), 249–252.

Vartanian, O., & Mandel, D. R. (2012). Neural bases of judgment and decision making. In M. K. Dhami, A. Schlottmann, & M. Waldmann (Eds.), *Judgment and Decision Making as a Skill: Learning, Development, and Evolution* (pp. 29–52). Cambridge, England: Cambridge University Press.

Vévodová, Š., Vévoda, J., Vetešníková, M., Kisvetrová, H., & Chrastina, J. (2016). The relationship between burnout syndrome and empathy among nurses in emergency medical services. *Kontakt, 18*(1), e17–e21.

Viehl, C., & Dispenza, F. (2015). Burnout and coping: An exploratory comparative study of heterosexual and sexual minority mental health practitioners. *Journal of LGBT Issues in Counseling, 9*(4), 311–328.

Vinokur-Kaplan, D. (1991). Job satisfaction among social workers in public and voluntary child welfare agencies. *Child Welfare, 70*(1), 81–91.

Virkki, T. (2007). Gender, care, and the normalization of violence: Similarities between occupational violence and intimate partner violence in Finland. *NORA— Nordic Journal of Women's Studies, 15*(4), 220–232.

——. (2008). Habitual trust in encountering violence at work: Attitudes towards client violence among Finnish social workers and nurses. *Journal of Social Work, 8*(3), 247–267.

Von Neumann, J., & Morgenstern, O. (1947). Theory of games and economic behavior (2nd ed.). Princeton, NJ: Princeton University Press.

von Thiele, U., Lindfors, P., & Lundberg, U. (2006). Self-rated recovery from work stress and allostatic load in women. *Journal of Psychosomatic Research, 61*(2), 237–242. doi:10.1016/j.jpsychores.2006.01.015

Wall, J. (2001). Trauma and the clinician: Therapeutic implications of clinical work with clients. *Clinical Social Work Journal, 29*(2), 133–145.

Walters, H. (2016). An introduction to use of self in field placement. *New Social Worker.* Retrieved from http://www.socialworker.com/feature-articles/field-placement/An_Introduction_to_Use_of_Self_in_Field_Placement/

Warnecke, E., Quinn, S., Ogden, K., Towle, N., & Nelson, M. (2011). A randomised controlled trial of the effects of mindfulness practice on medical student stress levels. *Medical Education, 45*(4), 381–388.

Warner, J. (2013). "Heads must roll"? Emotional politics, the press and the death of Baby P. *British Journal of Social Work, 44*(6), 1637–1653.

Wastell, C. A. (2002). Exposure to trauma: The long-term effects of suppressing emotional reactions. *Journal of Nervous and Mental Disease, 190*(12), 839–845. doi:10.1097/01.NMD.0000042454.90472.4F

Webster, C. D., Haque, Q., & Hucker, S. J. (2013). *Violence risk-assessment and management: Advances through structured professional judgement and sequential redirections.* Chichester, England: John Wiley.

Webster, C. D., Nicholls, T. L., Martin, M. L., Desmarais, S. L., & Brink, J. (2006). Short-Term Assessment of Risk and Treatability (START): The case for a new structured professional judgment scheme. *Behavioral Sciences and the Law, 24*(6), 747–766.

Wedding, D., & Faust, D. (1989). Clinical judgment and decision making in neuro-psychology. *Archives of Clinical Neuropsychology, 4*(3), 233–265.

Weingart, S. N., Callanan, L. D., Ship, A. N., & Aronson, M. D. (2001). A physician-based voluntary reporting system for adverse events and medical errors. *Journal of General Internal Medicine, 16*(12), 809–814.

Weiss, D., & Marmar, C. (1997). The impact of Event Scale-Revised. In J. W. T. Keane (Ed.), *Assessing psychological trauma and PTSD*. New York, NY: Guilford Press.

Weiss, D., Marmar, C., Metzler, T., & Ronfeldt, H. (1995). Predicting symptomatic distress in emergency services personnel. *Journal of Consulting and Clinical Psychology, 63*, 361–368.

Wharton, A. S. (1993). The affective consequences of service work: Managing emotions on the job. *Work and Occupations, 20*(2), 205–232.

——. (1999). The psychosocial consequences of emotional labor. *Annals of the American Academy of Political and Social Science, 561*(1), 158–176.

Wilson, J. P., & Thomas, R. B. (2004). *Empathy in the treatment of trauma and PTSD*. New York, NY: Routledge.

Wilson, M. C., Hayward, R. S., Tunis, S. R., Bass, E. B., Guyatt, G., Cook, D., . . . Moyer, V. (1995). Users' guides to the medical literature: VIII. How to use clinical practice guidelines. B. What are the recommendations and will they help you in caring for your patients? *JAMA, 274*(20), 1630–1632.

Winstanley, S., & Hales, L. (2008). Prevalence of aggression towards residential social workers: Do qualifications and experience make a difference? *Child & Youth Care Forum, 37*(2), 103–110.

Workers Compensation Board of Manitoba. (2017). *Frequently asked questions: PTSD presumption*. Retrieved from https://www.wcb.mb.ca/sites/default/files/resources/2990%20WCB%20PTSD%20Folder%20Inserts_Frequently%20Asked%20Questions-PTSD%20Presumption.pdf

Yehuda, R. (1999). Biological factors associated with susceptibility to posttraumatic stress disorder. *Canadian Journal of Psychiatry, 44*(1), 34–39.

——. (2002). Clinical relevance of biologic findings in PTSD. *Psychiatric Quarterly, 73*(2), 123–133.

Yehuda, R., Colier, J., Tischler, L., Stavitsky, K., & Harvey, P. (1995). Learning and memory in aging combat veterans with PTSD. *Journal of Clinical and Experimental Neuropsychology, 27*, 505–515.

Yehuda, R., Koenen, K., Galea, S., & Flory, J. (2011). The role of genes in defining a molecular biology of PTSD. *Disease Markers, 30*, 67–76.

Yehuda, R., McFarlane, A., & Shalev, A. (1998). Predicting the development of post-traumatic stress disorder from the acute response to a traumatic event. *Biological Psychiatry, 44*(12), 1305–1313.

Yorke, J., Grant, S., & Csiernik, R. (2016). Horses and baseball: Social work's cultivation of one's "third eye." *Social Work Education, 35*(7), 845–855.

Yuen, K. S., & Lee, T. M. (2003). Could mood state affect risk-taking decisions? *Journal of Affective Disorders, 75*(1), 11–18.

Zilberg, N., Weiss, D., & Horowitz, M. (1982). Impact of event scale: A cross validation study and some empirical evidence supporting a conceptual model of stress response syndromes. *Journal of Consulting and Clinical Psychology, 50*, 407–414.

Zilbert, N. R., Murnaghan, M. L., Gallinger, S., Regehr, G., & Moulton, C.-A. (2015). Taking a chance or playing it safe: Reframing risk assessment within the surgeon's comfort zone. *Annals of Surgery, 262*(2), 253–259.

Zuardi, A., Ishara, S., & Bandeira, M. (2011). Burden and stress among psychiatry residents and psychiatric health care providers. *Academic Psychiatry, 35*, 404–406.

Index

Page references in italics indicate figures.

Coping Strategies Inventory, 216–217

coping styles, 18, 114; avoidant-oriented, 103; development of, 7; emotion-oriented, 103, 114; exhaustion of, 104, 105; in integrated model for stress response, *113*; and job satisfaction, 104, 105; managing, 16; and stable personality traits, 97; stress response, 98, 102–103; task-oriented, 103; use of term, 97

coronary care decisions, 151

coroner's inquests, 208

cortisol: biological measure of, 99; peak measurement of, 101, *102*; salivary, 99

cortisol levels: measurement of salivary, 189–190; and memory, 185; in paramedics, 194; in perception of threat, 183; in PTSD, 82; and traumatic exposure, 61

Council on Social Work Education, 226

courage, demonstrating, 224–226

court appearances, 9; simulation training for, 212

court cases, brought against social workers, 108

court-mandated practice, role-conflict in, 105

Cowburn, J., 95

Creamer, M., 195

criminal charges, 211–212

criminal justice process, 243

crisis theory, 50, 70

Crisis Theory, Caplan's, 50

Critical Incident History Questionnaire (CIHQ), 189, 191

critical incident stress debriefing, 210

Croskerry, P., 251

Csiernik, R., 141, 208, 249

cultural bias, 246

DaCosta, J., 31

Dagan, K., 69–70

Damasio, A., 89

Dane, E., 140

dangerousness: assessment of future, 243d; cross-cultural assessments of, 158–159; prediction of, 211

Dawes, R., 246

death, child, 30; impact of inquiries into, 79–80; media attention to, 78–79, 214; in Ontario, 41, 110; public inquiries into, 40, 78–79, 81, *81*, 240; under supervision of child welfare services, 153; and supervisors' role, 208

death, impact on workers of, 30–31

Deber, R., 169

debriefing sessions, 210

decisional control, enhancing, 229, 230. *See also* control, sense of

decision analysis, 142

decision-making: affective elements in, 240; authoritarian model of, 109; automatic, nonanalytic, 249; charting responses for, *245*; cognitive aspects of, 236–240; by commercial airline pilot, 3–4; effects of stress and trauma on, 198–201; and emotion, 13, 177–178, *178*; toward empathic action, 93; and experiential thinking, 179; and exposure to trauma, 8; factors influencing, 239–240; heuristics in, 148–153, *152*, *153*; high-risk professional, 163; impact of PTSD on, 202; impact of stress and trauma on, 13–14; implications of consequences for, 251; improving, 20, 238, 255–256; incremental successes in models of, 216; intuitive, 115–116; judgment, 19; large-scale solutions for, 252–253;

measures, 166; social work, 226–228. *See also* students

Elias, N., 79

emergency medicine residents, stress appraisal of, 186

emergency responders: critical incident stress debriefing for, 210; PTSD in, 55; research with, 92; STS in, 35. *See also* paramedics; police communicators

emergency room, decision-making in, 249, 250

emergency service workers, 74; in postmortem reviews, 75; and posttraumatic stress, 187; traumatic stress experienced by, 189

emotional contagion, concept of, 87

emotional intelligence, 136, 141, 227

emotional labor, 18, 114, 223; and gender disparities, 97; increased, 95; in integrated model for stress response, *113*; managing, 94–95; strategies of, 94; and systemic issues, 96; workers at ease with, 95

emotional numbing, 38

emotions: and decision-making, 13, 177–178, *178*, 231, 241; effective management of, 96; inauthentic displays of, 96; in intuitive judgments, 140; and making judgments, 181, 230; positive, 241; and problem-solving, 141

empathic strain, consequences of, 89

empathy, 16, 18, 140; clinician, 221–222; cognitive, 89, 90, 140, 222–223; defined, 88, 89; elements of, 87, *91*; emotional, 140, 222; emotional *vs.* cognitive, 89, 90; expression of, 91; moderating, 221–224; objective in studies of, 90; as social work tool,

86; as two distinct processes, 90; types of, 222

Employer's Liability Act (1969), of UK, 32

endocrine system, and allostatic load, 47, *47*

England: mental health nurses in, 95; social workers in, 205–206; suicide risk assessment in, 157. *See also* United Kingdom

Enosh, G., 27

environment. *See* workplace environment

epinephrine, 48; in perception of threat, 183; under stress, 99

Eraut, M., 129

Ericsson, K., 117, 118, 120

ethics, social work, 233

ethnicity, and actuarial risk assessment tools, 158–159

evaluations, yearly performance, 235

Evans, S., 45

Evans, T., 226

evidence-based practice, 142; principles of, 251

Ewert vs. Canada, 159

exhaustion: in burnout, 43; coping style of, 104, 105; and role conflict, 106

expected utility model, 144

experience: and conceptual understanding, 123; and confidence in risk assessment, 172, 175; and expertise, 118–119; and overconfidence, 232; preexisting, 6; processes of, 5; work at boundaries of, 249

expert: art and skill of, 236; decision making of, 4; defined, 115; intuition of, 4–5

expertise: acquired in high-stress work environments, 139; acquisition of,

Gigerenzer, G., 148, 150
Gladwell, M., 120, 121
Glancy, G., 56, 153, 212
Glaser, R., 128
Goel, V., 181
Goldbloom, David, 126–127
Goroshit, M., 227
Grant, L., 227
Grant, S., 141, 249
Green, L., 151
grief, for mental health social workers, 31
grit, 5, 121
group identity, 122
Guidelines for Social Work Safety, of NASW, 206
guilt: by association, 80; and decision-making, 180; public, 79
Gunaratnam, Y., 96
guns, in worker violence, 27
Gur, A., 27
"gut feeling," 4–5, 88, 148, 176, 242–243; triggering of, 243

Hamilton Rating Scale for Depression (HRS-D), 167, 168, 196
Hammonds, C., 92, 222
hardiness: defined, 49; individual differences in, 186
Hardré, P., 127
hardship, positive outcomes related to, 51
Hart, S., 159–160, 246, 247
Hartford Geriatric Social Work Competency Scale, 235
Hayes, S., 218
health care: professionals in, 186; reporting and reviewing of adverse events in, 252
Healthy Minds Survey (2007), 217

heart rate, 99; and coping style, 103; measurement of, 99, 101, *102*; in PTSD, 82
heart rate monitor, Polar, 99
Heikamp, Jordan, 78
Hen, M., 227
heuristics, 148–153, *152, 153*; as cognitive processing, 14; decision trees in, 150; defined, 148; fast and frugal, 11; limitations of, 150; risks of bias with, 150; simplified but unarticulated, 152; unconscious, 148–149
Hill, J., 210
hippocampus, 48. *See also* brain
Hochschild, A., 94, 96–97
Hogan, M., 78
Hojat, M., 86
Holmstrom, L., 35
homeostasis: Cannon's 1932 theory of, 9; defined, 46
home visits, and safety concerns, 207
Horner, M., 188
Hospital Social Work Self-Efficacy Scale, 235
hydrocortisone, and development of PTSD, 62
hypervigilance, as trauma reaction, 8
hypothalmic-pituitary-adrenal (HPA) axis, 48, 99; measurement of activation of, 189–190; in perception of threat, 183

"illness scripts," 119, 126, 236
imagery: exposure to violent, 89; the third-eye, 141
immune suppression, 9
Impact of Event Scale (IES), 29, 36, 192
Impact of Event Scale—Revised (IES-R), 189, 191

litigation, decision making in, 240
loneliness, 92

Macgregor, D., 146
managed care, and mental health social
    work, 105
management: in integrated model for
    stress response, *113*; support from,
    20, 72, 111–112; and violence toward
    social workers, 206
managers: PSTs for, 211; social support
    from, 72
Mann, S., 95
Marshall, J., 161
Maslach, C., 42, 43
Maslach's Burnout Inventory, 196, 198
Mayer, J., 136
McCann, L., 37, 38, 67–68, 140
McEwen, B., 46, 47
media, 74, 213; focus of, 213; public
    opinions expressed in, 74
media attention, 9, 11, 18, 74, 79,
    212–213, 214; addressing, 214–215; in
    child welfare, *40*, 40–41; cognitive
    appraisal of risk in, 182; critical
    nature of, 111; "extensive," 79;
    high-profile, 214; negative, 9, 18;
    occurrence of, 212–213; in public
    inquiries, 76; result of, 213
Mehr, D., 151
Meichenbaum, D., 219
memory: and acute stress responses,
    202; consolidation, 185; digit span,
    188; impact of acute stress on, 185;
    and information retrieval, 185;
    PTSD associated with impairments
    in, 188; in sleep deprivation, 185; and
    suppression of negative emotions,
    95; working, 185
memory loss, as trauma reaction, 8

mental health practice: and managed
    care, 105; START in, 161–162
mental health practice, START in,
    161–162
mental health professionals, "detached
    concern" of, 93
mental health social workers, 30;
    burnout in, 45; detached concern of,
    218; emotional exhaustion in, 45; on
    IES-R, 36; in PTSD study, 196–198,
    198, 200
mental health stress leave, for
    paramedics, 109
mental status exam, standard, 126
meta-analysis, of fMRI studies, 177
meta-cognition, 127, 140, 249, 251
meta-competencies, 6, 133, 139, 233,
    234; in management literature, 135,
    135; self-appraisal of, 137; in social
    work practitioners, 135
Michael, K., 45
military trainees, under high stress,
    185–186
Miller, Danielle, 109
mimicking, 88
mimicry, in empathic engagement, 87–88
mindfulness-based interventions, 219,
    220
mindfulness-based stress reduction
    (MBSR), 219–220, 228
mirroring: in empathic engagement,
    87–88; role of brain in, 90
"mirror neurons," 87–88, 92
Mohr, P., 177
Monahan, J., 146
Moos, R., 50
"moral algebra," 145
moral distress, of social workers, 106,
    107
morale, and chronic stress, 43

attention on, 78; long-term effects for, 109–110, *110*; in postmortem reviews, 75; in PTSD study, 187, 193–194, 198, 199, 200, 201, 202; and safety issues, 205–206; social support for, 64; and stress exposure, 186; traumatic stress responses in, 91–92

Parton, N., 74

Patient Health Questionnaire (PHQ-9), 217

patient outcomes, and clinician empathy, 86

patients, standardized, 164, 192; in empathy studies, 90; interviewed by child protection workers, 243–244; student assessment of, 235

Pearlman, Laurie Anne, 37, 38, 67–68

peer consultation, 216

peer support, 16, 20, 208–209

peer support teams (PSTs), 209–210; critical incident stress debriefing for, 210; for supervisors and managers, 211

Perceived Stress Scale, 241

performance: and acute stress, 14; and chronic stress, 43; effects of PTSD on, 188, 202

peritraumatic distress, 60, 61, 62

perseverance, 121

personality: and competency, 133; and expertise, 117, 120–121; and posttraumatic growth, 84; and PTSD symptoms, 83; and resilience, 7, 49; traits, 60

physical assault, of social workers, 23, 24

physicians: burnout in, 43; emotional responses in, 93; interventions to reduce stress in, 220–221, *221*; primary care, 86; stressors for, 220

pilots, training programs for, 3

pocket probability calculator, 151

Polar heart rate monitor, 99

police communicators, 187; coping styles of, 102–103; in PTSD study, 194–195, 199, 200, 201, 202; role of, 194; stress in, 100

police officers: decision-making in acute stress of, 183–184; experiencing anxiety, 184–185; facing public inquiry, 75–76; impact of anxiety on, 185; impact of media attention on, 78; PTSD in, 92; in public inquiries, 76, *77*; traumatic exposure for, 32

police recruits: coping styles of, 102–103; in PTSD study, 190–191, 198, 199, 200, 201

police shooting, trauma symptoms following, 187

politics, and decision making, 11

postmortem review, 75; media coverage of, 75; subject officers in, 76; traumatic responses as result of, 75

posttraumatic growth, 8; concept of, 50; elements of, 50; in high-stress work environments, 139; and posttraumatic stress, 223; vicarious, 51

posttraumatic stress disorder (PTSD), 32, 35, 55; in child protection workers, 192; diagnosis of, 8, 14–15, 32, 35, 36, 60, 103; and environmental factors, 15, 82–83; genetic factors in, 60; legislative approach to, 187–188; neurocognitive effects associated with, 188; and perceived social support, 65; and personality, 83; predictors of, 60; prevalence of, 55, 56; on professional decision-making, 189–201; among social workers, 81–82 practice. *See* social work practice

Practice-Based Education Tool, 236

practice guidelines, media attention to, 213

practice settings, 25; and safety concerns, 206; violence reported in, 24. *See also* workplace environment

Pratt, M., 140

Priestly, J., 144–145

privacy, issues of, and safety education, 226

problem-solving: emotional responses to, 10–11; heuristic approaches to, 10; intuitive, 115–116; and resilience, 63; rule-bound models of professional, 140–141

Professional Capabilities Framework, of British Association of Social Workers, 17, 227

professional judgment tools, 17, 175; for professional decision-making, 175. *See also specific tools*

prospective cohort-based approach, 158

prospect theory, 146

psychiatric disorders, comorbid, 188

psychological appraisal, of posttraumatic distress, 62

psychological response: of individual to stress, 15; physiological arousal linked to, 82

psychologists, burnout in, 45

psychotherapy, and clinician empathy, 86

public accountability, 74, 225–226

public attention, and child welfare services, *40*, 40–41. *See also* media attention

public inquiries: cognitive appraisal of risk in, 182; organizational response to, 77

public opinion: critical nature of, 111; and media attention on child deaths, 80–81. *See also* media attention

Purvanova, R., 46

questionnaires: CIHQ, 189, 191; Compassion Fatigue Questionnaire, 36–37; General Health Questionnaire (GHQ-12), 45; Patient Health Questionnaire (PHQ-9), 217; in stress measurement study, 98

racial abuse, 23, 24, 26; of social workers, 7, 23, 24

racism, systemic, 96

racist verbal abuse, by clients, 7

Rakow, T., 151

rape victims, 35

rational choice theory, 10, 144–148; and behavioral economics, 145–146; factors influencing, 175; at policy level, 214

receiver operating characteristic (ROC) analysis, 156

reflecting in action, in developing expertise, 126

reflective process: in decision-making, 180; development of expertise through, 126, 140; four-stage, 27, *28*

Regehr, G., 122, 123

relational capacity, 139–140; and distress, 71; and trauma-induced pathology, 64–65

relational skills, of students, 133, 134

relative ranking model, 236, *237–238*

resilience: addressed by schools of social work, 17; building, 49; and commitment, 7–8; defined, 49; enhancing, *229*, 230; and

environmental factors, 15, 82–83; in
high-stress work environments, 139;
and personal characteristics, 118;
and posttraumatic growth, 48–53,
51, 52; prediction of, 83–84; qualities
enhancing, 118; and trauma
exposure, 59–60, 82; understanding
of, 62–63

resources: and coping styles, 97; and
media attention, 213; and moral
distress, 107

reviews, 79, 80

Richards, A., 180

riding with a drunk driver (RDD),
146–147

risk, 10; application of decision making
in, 17; caring for others despite, 212;
and clinician behavior, 146; and
coping styles, 97; of coronary
disease, 151; decision-making in, 10,
17, 19; decision making in, 19;
decision-making in, 242; decision-
making in situations of, 242; and
decision-making theory, 10; defined,
143; determination of overall, 11;
and emotions, 13, 19; and emotions
and decision making, 13; false hope
of eliminating, 214; and false hope
of eliminating, 214; forensic
psychiatrist's assessment of, 243;
impact of emotions on decisions in,
19; improving decision making in,
17; and managing liability, 211;
perceptions of, 140; and positive *vs.*
negative emotions, 180

risk appraisal: high confidence in,
171–173; judgment influenced by,
184; low confidence in, 173–174;
and physiological feedback loop,
183, *184*

risk assessment: in child welfare,
163–164; clinical example of, 179;
past feelings in, 179; and PTSD, 14;
SPJ approach, 12

risk assessment measures: actuarial,
153–160; for child protective
services, 41; child welfare agencies,
164; in child welfare practice, 155,
164; OFRA, 164–165; ORAM, 164,
165–166, 192; OSA, 164, 165, 192;
pocket probability calculator in, 151;
vs. professional judgment, 247;
qualitative comments on, 166–167

risk assessment tools: actuarial,
153–160; in child welfare practice,
155; pocket probability calculator in,
151

risk outcomes: with actuarial risk
assessment tools, 154; predicting, 11

Rizzolatti, G., 87–88

Rogers, C., 86, 89

role ambiguity, 105–107, 112; differences
in effects of, 106; in integrated
model for stress response, *113*

role conflict, 105, 112, 224; differences
in effects of, 106; in integrated
model for stress response, *113*; moral
distress in, 106–107

role stress autonomy, in predicting
burnout, 106

safety: addressed by schools of social
work, 17; attending to, 205–207; and
culture of support, 207–211; and
locus of control, 68; and trauma,
38–39; and trauma recovery, 39t;
and traumatic growth, 50

safety training, 206, 226

Sakheim, D., 38, 140

Salas, E., 141